MODERN TIMES

Modern Times is the third volume of the series, *The Canadian Novel*. Volume I, *Here and Now*, is a study of contemporary Canadian novels and their authors; Volume II, *Beginnings*, considers the major early works in the Canadian tradition. A fourth volume, a study of recent and avant garde Canadian fiction to be called ''Present Tense,'' is in preparation and another volume, on the novel in French Canada, is being planned.

The Canada Council
Conseil des Arts du Canada
1957-1982

THE CANADIAN NOVEL
VOLUME III

MODERN TIMES

A Critical Anthology
Edited with an Introductory Essay by

JOHN MOSS

NC Press Limited
Toronto

Cover illustration: Charles Comfort, *Young Canadians,* 1932 By permission of Hart House, University of Toronto

Canadian Cataloguing in Publication Data
    Main entry under title:
    The Canadian Novel

    Contents: v.3 Modern Times
    ISBN 0-919601-88-X (bound v.3)   ISBN 0-919601090-1 (pbk v.3)

    1. Canadian fiction (English) – 20th century – History and
       criticism – Addresses, essays, lectures. I. Moss, John, 1940 –

    PS8187.C36   C813'.5'09   C78-1385-9
    PR9192.5.C36

We would like to thank the Ontario Arts Council and the Canada Council for their assistance in the production of this book.

New Canada Publications, a division of NC Press Limited, Box 4010, Station A, Toronto, Ontario, M5W 1H8, (416) 593-6284

CONTENTS

INTRODUCTION

Modern Times is the third book in a series on the Canadian novel. The second contains essays on fiction that is important to our literary heritage. From a Canadian perspective, the works discussed are classics. Their lasting value is as much for their contribution to our cultural history, however, as for their intrinsic literary worth. Some of them, such as *The History of Emily Montague* (1769), *Wacousta* (1832) and *The Imperialist* (1904), are remarkably readable today, depending on taste, but clearly they are beginnings, they belong to the past. The first book in this series offers essays on the contemporary achievement of the Canadian tradition, its culmination here and now. The novels considered, by such writers as Alice Munro, Margaret Laurence and Mordecai Richler, are fine works in their own right, without deference to a particular context. They may have special meaning for Canadians, but this has little bearing on their merit as art. Between these two phases, when the literature's significance is primarily because it was Canadian and when its Canadian origin is incidental to its achievement (though we may take pride in its quality, and assurance from its source in the community we share), there is a transitional phase which vigourously resists coherent definition. This phase is the concern of the present volume.

The transition between the past that is clearly past and the unequivocally contemporary does not correspond to an exact historical period. The National Gallery of Canada recently mounted an exhibition on "Modernism in Quebec Art, 1916-1946". No such ready perimeters can be applied to the Canadian novel. It is generally easy to distinguish "early" Canadian writing, and the contemporary virtually identifies itself. Leacock belongs to the past; Laurence to the present. Of contemporary writers, only Robertson Davies is apparently out of step with his times, and that may be because he is ahead of them, rather than behind.

But what of those writers, some of them still writing, who provide a link between past and present, whose works are modern but not contemporary, whose works are immediate, dynamic, relevant, but redolent of times that have slipped away? To what period in our literary development do we assign the novels of

Morley Callaghan, whose canon extends through seven decades? What of Hugh MacLennan, whose most recent novel, *Voices in Time* (1981), expresses the world view of another era, in form and content very much of the present? What of W. O. Mitchell, whose work, the older he gets, seems ever more irrepressibly young?

Such writers are modern, by any definition of the term. Yet their fiction has more in common with the self-conscious modernism of Frederick Philip Grove and Martha Ostenso than with the aggressive contemporaneity of Robert Kroetsch or the casual authority of Mavis Gallant. They are writers upon whose work the Canadian tradition is built, and while they have continued to publish new fiction in the 1980s, their importance has been established for a generation and more.

And what of *The Double Hook* (1959) by Sheila Watson, and Elizabeth Smart's *By Grand Central Station I Sat Down and Wept* (1945)? Both novels are more avant-garde, even now, than anything by Margaret Atwood or Rudy Wiebe. In their lyricism, their narrative unconventionality, their rhetorical inventiveness, they are on the leading edge of modernism. Yet they are part of our heritage, and speak to us from the past. They have more in common with *As For Me and My House* (1941), *The Mountain and the Valley* (1952) and *Swamp Angel* (1954) than with *Surfacing* (1972) or *The Temptations of Big Bear* (1973). They speak with voices that are immediate but not contemporary, and they see from perspectives that are impossible in the present, except in fiction.

This book is an attempt to provide a common field for the consideration of work that falls between and yet overlaps two clearly defined phases in our cultural development. The challenge has been to bring together novels written as much as half a century apart, by people of widely dissimilar temperament and experience, in styles ranging from stolid to evanescent, forms from lumbering to ethereal, without intruding on their integrity as separate works of art, and without relying on inevitably misleading generalizations about their cultural and historical relevance. The concept implied by the title *Modern Times* seems appropriate in this regard. In terms of Canadian history, modern times probably originate in the trenches of World War I and extend into the present era of constitutional sovereignty. Culturally, the burgeoning West, the Depression, the Canadian Broadcasting Corporation, Mackenzie King, World War II, the National Film Board, are at the very centre of modern times in Canada, a centre from which we are inexorably drifting away. The word "times" represents an era, but also a sequence of separate events, all in the past, or passing.

"Modern" is a more elusive term, and conveniently more elastic. Modern thought may be said to originate with the Renaissance, and the modern sensibility with the Enlightenment; or modern thought with Darwin, Marx and Freud, and the modern sensibility with the holocausts of world war and genocide, very much within the living memory of many among us. Modern architecture, poetry and painting are determinedly of the present century, yet seem curiously dated now; arbitrary, solipsistic, ironically encumbered with preoccupations of the nineteenth century. The modern novel is equally a thing of the past; to describe a new work as modern is to indicate its limitations, its inappropriateness to our present experience of the world. The modern novel in English may be said to begin with Defoe, or a century later with Austen, or a century after that with Joyce, depending on perspective, and modern novels are still being written and will always be read, but we are no longer speaking of a tradition that culminates in the present. It was possible to say of Faulkner's *The Sound and the Fury* (1929), "this is what the novel has been building to." But with the best fiction of the 1970s and 1980s one would more likely say, "this is where the novel is now," and leave it at that. Its achievement is no less than in the past, but it is going in new directions not yet understood. The novel today speaks for the postmodernity of our experience, in a world of rampant television, the ubiquitous computer, and imminent universal annihilation, whether it participates in literary postmodernism or not.

Modernism in literature is characterized by a particular set of illusions which many of us came to accept as truths: these are the precepts of objectivity, impersonality, realism, rationalism and linguistic neutrality. The writer does not exist in his fiction; the reader certainly does not exist, except as a consumer. What is described is what is; the created world is more real, more coherent, lucid and meaningful than our own. Events and personalities within the fiction are logically formulated and subject to reasonable inquiry. The world and consciousness of the world are interdependent, yet consciousness has no control over the world, though the world does over consciousness (this unbalanced equation, in my opinion, provides the best possible definition of literary naturalism, a deterministic variant of realism). Words and syntax, style, remain under the writer's control, even when he no longer exists, and have no significant meaning but what the context intends; in other words, writing does not make literature, the writer does.

Modernism in the novel has become virtually synonymous with realism. But realism, ironically, has come to mean romance — in which the moral, social or psychological predispositions of the author are exercised, but the illusions of objectivity, autonomy and rationalism are sustained. In Canadian fiction, romantic-realism begins with the novels of Frederick Philip Grove and remains the dominant mode to the present day. There have been a few outstanding exceptions, but not until the super-realism of Munro, the psycho-romance of Davies, the expository confessionals of Laurence, the documentary visions of Wiebe, the confessional satire of Richler, did the modernist conventions in Canada begin to crumble.

Certainly the conventions of modernism are devoutly upheld by the fictions of Callaghan, MacLennan and Wilson, and in the major works of Buckler and Ross. Grove's *Settlers of the Marsh* and Ostenso's *Wild Geese*, both published in the mid twenties, blend romance with realism as early examples of Canadian modernist fiction; and Mitchell's novels, the most recent of which was published only last year, conforms in content and style if not always in form to the tenets of modernism. Perhaps the masterworks of Watson and Smart defy such conventions, but both are thoroughly modern, philosophically (and possibly postmodern as well). These writers and their works dominate the modernist movement in Canadian fiction. It is their writing we regard from a self-consciously Canadian perspective, in coming to terms with our developing tradition, during the transition from outpost of Empire to nation-state, as, by degrees, we lay claim to a sovereign Canadian imagination. These writers and their novels occupy the interval, not historical but aesthetic and ontological, between Leacock and Laurence. They and their work are the subject of this volume, which is intended to provide an appropriate context for their consideration.

Altogether, the work of ten Canadian novelists is represented on the following pages in essays by fifteen different critics. Most of the essays were written especially for this book. Several have been previously published and are reprinted here because it seemed important to make or keep them accessible. A number of writers or works are the subject of two essays. This is less a measure of their special merit than of the need I felt as editor to redress their neglect. Five of the writers are known for a number of works. Grove published nine novels, and Callaghan, MacLennan, Wilson and Mitchell are similarly celebrated for the variety of their achievement. The reputation of the other five rests primarily on the critical acclaim given a single work by each. In addition to *The Double Hook*, Sheila Watson has published only a few short stories, but Martha Ostenso, Sinclair Ross, Elizabeth Smart and Ernest Buckler have written other novels, some of which were very well received. Nevertheless, their contribution to the Canadian tradition centres on the singular works of outstanding merit which are discussed. The critics represent fifteen different perspectives on literature, fifteen different critical approaches. The fact that such diversity can be coherently gathered into a single volume is a tribute to the rich heritage of modern literature in Canada.

Grove's *Settlers of the Marsh*, originally published in 1925, marks a great leap forward for Canadian fiction into a morally and psychologically complex modern world, a turning away from the idyllic and gothic distortions of the past. Grove was not alone: others, like Ostenso, Douglas Durkin and Robert Stead, all writing from the West, participated in the modernist revolution. For Grove, however, this was just the beginning and what followed is a remarkably varied body of work extending over three decades. Grove may now seem to hover above the modern era like a great mechanical bird; but the intriguing thing is, he is still there. In this book, two critics consider the machinery that keeps him aloft.

Both Lee Thompson and Henry Makow write about *Settlers of the Marsh*, which many regard as Grove's most accomplished novel. Thompson illuminates the deliberate design of a work determined to be art — Grove's aspirations were never to anything less. Makow goes back to the drawing board, as it were, to compare the author's intent for his novel with his misleading responses to its less-than-enthusiastic reception. For Makow the text is important primarily as document; for Thompson, as structure. They work in ways utterly distinct from one another that are, nonetheless, complementary. Together they reveal much of what makes this Grove's best work, and something of its limitations.

Ostenso's *Wild Geese* appeared in the same year as *Settlers* and met with Grove's contempt, possibly for its financial and critical success. There is really no accounting for the subsequent neglect of Ostenso by critics. Stanley Atherton's essay in this volume is a fresh and eclectic attempt to offset the slight. Atherton, in effect, starts from the beginning; he relates *Wild Geese*, Ostenso's best known work, to her personal experience and to actual places and events, but he also offers revealing insights into the novel itself.

No one novel by Callaghan offers a similar focal centre for an assessment or appreciation of his work. Callaghan's principal metier has been the short story. His novels, when taken together, however, are of major significance. Even if one does not stand out, as a group they embody an austere moral and aesthetic determination unparalleled in our literature. A Callaghan novel does not suffer analysis gladly: any attempt to see what makes it work either reduces it to parable or inflates it into myth. Wilf Cude's unusual perspective fortunately reveals the author's achievement without dismantling or distorting it for critical convenience.

Sinclair Ross is also celebrated for his short stories. It is the novel *As For Me and My House*, however, that assures his paramount place in the Canadian tradition. Much has been written about this novel, including a number of fine essays by critics represented in this book. Nothing I have read, though, seemed to get inside the enigma of the novel, rather than explain it away. Since I had a definite idea of what was needed, rather than subject someone else to editorial imposition, I undertook the job myself. An essay with emphasis on the text of *As For Me and My House* and its impact on the reader is the result.

MacLennan offers an unusual problem for the critical anthologist. Since a number of his novels are arguably of comparable stature, which, if any, is to be taken as representative? *Each Man's Son* (1951) contains some of MacLennan's most sensitive writing and the powerful themes of *Two Solitudes* (1945) seem ever more relevant. *The Watch that Ends the Night* (1959), however, holds within it the greatest depths of experience, and *Barometer Rising* (1941) remains the most popularly appealing. Elspeth Cameron's approach to *The Watch* provides fascinating insight into both the novel and the author as she draws extensively on researched materials to explicate MacLennan's method and intent. David Arnason adeptly relates the form of *Barometer Rising* to its historical context, illuminating a primary source of the novel's power and lasting appeal.

The most satisfying thing about criticism of good writing is that it can take such varied forms with equal effectiveness. Arnason and Cameron display entirely different relationships to author and text, yet each shows splendid originality. Lorraine McMullen in her fine treatment of Elizabeth Smart's unusual poetic novel, *By Grand Central Station I Sat Down and Wept*, proves equally imaginative, and necessarily so. She responds to the generic ambiguity of the author's art and to its neglect by critics with an agile analysis that combines a broad overview with specific inquiry, much as if it were a lyric poem. A very different but complementary approach to Smart is John Goddard's personal essay on her life and work, reprinted for its disconcerting insight into both from a popular periodical. Together the journalist and the scholar go a great way towards penetrating the shroud of obscurity that has surrounded Smart's Canadian reputation until now.

In her discussion of Ethel Wilson's *Swamp Angel*, Donna Smyth concentrates on its feminist aspects, bringing into focus the subtle power of the novel and the sources of its profound and lasting impact. In contrast to Smyth's singular approach, George Woodcock takes in the whole of Wilson's remarkable canon with a critical sweep of great perception and wit. As usual Woodcock is the equal of his subject and the reader is treated to what amounts to a critical dialogue between peers — Wilson through her fiction and he, through the art of his essay.

With an obvious affection for the combination of research and speculative thought (which he shares with Henry Makow), Alan R. Young leads the reader through an exhaustive and exhilarating quest for the creative origins of Buckler's *The Mountain and the Valley*. George Bowering, in an idiosyncratic essay that reveals a great deal about the postmodern aesthetic of Bowering's own work, draws everything that has been written about *The Double Hook* into summation and offers a fresh new beginning for our appreciation of Watson's genius.

The two final essays in this book are devoted to works by W. O. Mitchell. Mitchell is underrated or ignored by many critics because of his populist style and apparently simplistic themes, yet as Ken Mitchell and Catherine McLay show, there is depth, breadth and subtlety to his work, if you know where to look, and how. Both *Who Has Seen the Wind* (1947), long rather solemnly regarded as a classic without being taken seriously as art, and *The Vanishing Point*, the most recent novel (1973) considered in this book, receive comprehensive introductory analyses by Mitchell and McLay, the kind of thorough and thoughtful treatment that lesser works could not sustain.

W. O. Mitchell is popular, although MacLennan remains our most celebrated novelist and Callaghan our most enduring. Perhaps the least known of our major writers is Elizabeth Smart. Yet for those who open to her complex and allusive poetic prose, hers is a moving achievement. Smart is just coming into her own, although her novel was published nearly forty years ago. Oddly enough, our most analyzed novel is also highly poetic. However, Sheila Watson draws image, form and style not from her own private anguish and ecstasy, as Smart does, but from mythology and literature. *The Double Hook* remains so haunting in the reader's mind because it is a violent fusion of the familiar; *By Grand Central Station*, because it renders the familiar alien and bizarre.

Perhaps the most accessible of all our novelists is Ethel Wilson. Her prose is pellucid; her narratives immediate, direct, subtle and without ambiguity. She writes humane stories; treats her characters with compassion, even those she despises; treats the world warily but with affection. Her greatest gift, though, is in the scope she allows for the reader's imagination, the finesse she demands of it. She does not lay everything before the reader the way, for instance, Mitchell does; she draws on the reader's own experience of the world and himself. One reacts to Mitchell's writing; one becomes, reading Wilson.

There are many other writers and other works which might have been included under the rubric "modern times". Adele Wiseman's powerful novel, *The Sacrifice* (1956), is a major Canadian work, as disturbing to read now as when it appeared over a quarter of a century ago. Critically, A. M. Klein's brilliant and eccentric novel, *The Second Scroll* (1951), belongs with those included, as does *Tay John* (1939), by Howard O'Hagan. Some would argue that Gwethalyn Graham's *Earth and High Heaven* (1944) should have been considered, though I would strongly disagree — personally, I would have included Patricia Blondal's fine flawed novel, *A Candle to Light the Sun* (1960), and Charles Bruce's evocative regional novel, *The Channel Shore* (1954), and Thomas Raddall's *The Nymph and the Lamp* (1950), a mature and moving story of love in a lonely place. However, personal preference gave way to editorial discretion. As editor, I had to make decisions based on my perception of the Canadian literary tradition. Those novels represented, those novelists discussed, seemed to me the most central to an understanding of the novel in modern times in a Canadian context. There are other works which might have been considered, and were not; but none I hope which were, and should not have been.

John Moss
Bellrock, 1982

FREDERICK PHILIP GROVE

IN SEARCH OF ORDER: THE STRUCTURE OF GROVE'S *SETTLERS OF THE MARSH*

Lee Briscoe Thompson

In his pseudo-autobiographical *In Search of Myself* (1946), Frederick Philip Grove pilloried "that terrible, three volume novel which I called *Pioneers*" and was no less sparing of its abbreviated form, "a garbled extract" which was published "in 1925, under the title of one of its parts, *Settlers of the Marsh.*"[1] He decried the process of condensation as a "ruthless cutting-down" in which he claimed he was forced by the publishers to go "to work slashing the book [*Pioneers*] to *Settlers* as "some of my best work" and followed it with a straightfaced comparison of that novel with Flaubert's *Madame Bovary*, terming each "a serious work of art."[3]

Grove's vacillation is shared by many who subject *Settlers* to close scrutiny. His characterizations are not quite felt upon the pulse; dialogue is frequently stilted; plot developments occasionally seem incredible to readers unaccustomed to the extremes that prairie environment may encourage. Yet the novel as a whole works for the majority of readers, and indeed is often so engrossing as to mask the complexity and subtlety of its structure. Nor is it merely an exercise in craft; Grove is as concerned with idea as order. Interwoven upon a primary framework of themes considered by Grove to be of cosmic significance are intricate subordinate themes, symbols, and images, producing a tight fabric deserving of the name art.

There are four major themes; four structural pillars of the novel, to which the symbols, images and sub-themes direct themselves and lend support. These "themes" cannot easily be wedged into tidy pigeonholes, any more than human experience can be rigidly compartmentalized. But certain designations will conveniently indicate the various patterns revealed by close analysis. Speaking in simplified and sweeping terms, one may say that Grove has built his story of Niels upon:

    i.   Visions and dreams;
    ii.   Fatedness and freedom;
   iii.   Passion and its frequent associate, sin;
   iv.   Isolation.

Examination of the text will show how structurally dominant these "pillars" are.

I

The most arresting theme of the novel is "Visions", with Niels' recurring and subtly altering dream constantly modulated by the visions of others. The first mention of such imaginings comes early in the novel, when, in the midst of a prairie snowstorm, a modest "vision of some small room, hot with the glow and flicker of an open fire" seizes Niels.[5] Mrs. Lund more ambitiously hopes for "everything as it should be. A large, good house; a hot-bed for the garden; real, up-to-date stables; and ... everything .... We want Bobby to go to college ..." (p. 33). Left at this, the revelation of her dream would seem unrelated and meaningless, but the author continues:

> ... suddenly he understood far more than the mere words. He understood that this woman knew she was at the end of her life and that life had not kept faith with her. Her voice was only half that with which we tell of a marvelous dream; half of it was a passionate protest against the squalor surrounding her; it reared a triumphant vision above the ruins of reality. It was the cry of despair which says, It shall not be so! (p. 33)

We now have a dramatic indication of the futilities and set-backs that are inherent in any vision, Niels' no exception. It is also Grove's first suggestion of the Promethean nobility of the struggle in which, he avows, each person must engage.

Olga Lund, like Niels, is said at this point to nurture a "dream of the future ... capable of fulfillment, not fraught with pathos as her mother's ... " (p. 34). Then, in corroboration of the damage that unrealized dreams can deal to human dignity, the elder Lunds proceed to strip each other of harmless little illusions they have cherished, reduced by frustration to spite (p. 35).

Despite these ominous incidents, Niels' dream continues to blossom and flourish undaunted, and the author's articulation of it binds Niels' individual longings to those of the human race. "Suddenly, ... a vision took hold of Niels: of himself and a woman, sitting of a mid-winter night by the light of a lamp and in front of a fire, with the pitter-patter of children's feet sounding down from above: the eternal vision that has moved the world and that was to direct his fate" (p. 36). The mechanics of human dreaming increase in complexity when Grove reveals that the vision of land, house, and wife is rooted in a negative vision of the past: "that vision of himself as a child, as a poor child, [which] had haunted him when he grew up till fierce and impotent hatreds devastated his heart" and planted the seeds of his New World vision in the ash heap of aspirations impossible in Sweden (p. 39).

If we are not disturbed by the unpromising derivation of Niels' dream, we are certainly alarmed by his reaction to the very first suggestion of its attainability. Women, he muses, have thus far been only a symbol in his dreams; he sees no specific face in the visions. "Now that he was in the country of his dreams and gaining a foothold, it seemed as if individual women were bent on replacing the vague, schematic figures he had had in his mind. He found this *intrusion* strangely disquieting" (p. 40, italics supplied). Is there, then, something within him that will resist or impede the realization of the very goals he seeks?

The vision theme becomes all the more intricate when closely interwoven with a subordinate theme concerning mothers. Part of the reason that Niels' vision has had no clearly defined woman and that the possibility of a real wife disturbs him is that he has subconsciously filled the position: "Niels was hushed with a sense of longing for his own old home, for his mother..." (p. 42). That Ellen does not mother him is the source of "a trace of resentment" against her "unyielding aloofness" (p. 44). For both Niels and Ellen, part of the struggle of life is presented in the process of resolving distortions of the mother-child relationship.

The land and Ellen make their impressions on the young Swede, who finds himself more and more dominated by his vision. The woman in the image becomes Ellen, and Niels finds himself impatient to progress and succeed. Now, "in the first flush of reality; now, when all that was needed seemed to be a retracing in fact of what had already been traced in vision: now that vision became an obsession" (pp. 48-9). In these days of exalted agony, Clara Vogel re-enters the picture. Fleeing her company is, for Niels, like "waking up from a terrible dream" (p. 53). In spite of, perhaps because of, his innocence, he can sense the threat to his dream that she represents. The dream, in a life spent with Mrs. Vogel, will indeed be a nightmare.

Naturally, in retreating from Clara, he aches for security. Again he longs "to be with his mother, to feel her gnarled, calloused

fingers rumpling his hair, and to hear her crooning voice dron-
ing some old tune ..." (pp. 55-6). The vision taking shape before
his eyes undergoes a peculiar series of transformations. Niels is
at his mother's knee. We suddenly become aware that the maternal eyes gazing pityingly at him are the "sky-blue eyes" of Ellen.
But the transposition is not yet complete. The vision clarifies and
the young Swede is crouching in a childless home before the third
female competitor for his soul, Clara. In this single sequence,
Grove has granted a glimpse at the close and complex interrela-
tionships of the three women and has given a definite indication
of the imprecision of perception that will prove Niels' downfall:
the confusion of sexual allure with mother love.

Random encounters with Ellen reaffirm her place in Niels' vision. As the moment for Ellen's revelation of her abhorrence of
sex nears, Niels' sense of vision loses its former clarity. In the
presence of half-mad Sigurdsen he comes to participate in "wild
visions", "as if he could have got up and howled and whistled,
vying with the wind ..." (p. 84). Instinct warns him of
"Something dreadful ... coming, coming ..." (p. 85). A confrontation in the field after the summer storm is postponed by Ellen,
but Niels walks in the subsequent silence "as through a vacant
dream devoid of feeling." Then just before Ellen begins the story
of her mother, Niels finds that "His vision [is] a blank" (p. 104).

The profound effects that their mothers have had on the couple's formative years is revealed. The crisis comes and goes, a
mere moment in the interminable life cycle of men. Nature fills
part of the void created by Ellen's rejection with the passage of
time and incessant work. The change wrought in Niels by the
"gradual negation of his old dream" has become common talk:

> ... it gave him such an air of superiority over his en-
> vironment that the few words which he still had to
> speak were listened to almost with deference. They
> seemed to come out of vast hidden caverns of meaning.
> His face, scored and lined so that it sometimes seemed
> outright ugly, held all in awe, some in terror ....
>
> The truth was, lightning flashes of pain sometimes
> went through his look, giving him the appearance of
> one insane; or of one who communed with different
> worlds ....
>
> A new dream rose: a longing to leave and to go to

the very margin of civilisation, there to clear a new
place; and when it was cleared and people began to set-
tle about it, to move on once more, again to the very
edge of pioneerdom, and to start it all over anew ....
That way his enormous strength would still have a
meaning. Woman would have no place in his life ....

He looked upon himself as belonging to a special race
— a race not comprised in any limited nation, but one
that cross-sectioned all nations: a race doomed to
everlasting extinction and yet recruited out of the
wastage of all other nations ....

But, of course, it was only the dream of the slave who
dreams of freedom .... (p. 119)

This final remark refers to Grove's reintroduction, on the very
next page, of the widow Vogel, "a dismal dream, almost forgotten." Niels' new vision is as imperilled as was his old. The subsequent marriage immediately confirms this impression. The house,
so much a part of Niels' initial dream, becomes "much changed" (p. 127). The sweetish scents and luxurious, even decadent,
atmosphere Clara injects are beyond the understanding of his fatal
innocence. Children, an important part of the initial dream, are
another victim of mismating, for he decides that they "would be
a perpetuation of the sin of a moment ..." (p. 138).

Clara too appears to have thwarted dreams. As the marriage
disintegrates, her eyes more and more frequently hold "a new
expression ... a dreamy quality," "as if she [wishes] to erase reality" (p. 141). Her husband is aware that she, "a city woman, with
the tastes and inclinations of such a one," is "banished to the
farm .... [He realizes] the dreariness, the utter emptiness of her
life" (p. 139). Finally, as Clara prepares to leave the farm permanently, "the remnant of a happy dream" that has lain in her
eyes dies completely (p. 151). She falls into the nightmare confrontation with Niels, and upon awaking from that, proceeds to
create a nightmare for a Niels totally unaware of the furies he
has unleashed.

Maternal influences resurface as Clara ruthlessly anatomizes
their marriage. She says, "I thought you were a man" (p. 155);
but Niels is, as discussed before, essentially passive, with a child's
lack of insight into the emotional demands of adulthood. He
wants a mother; she does not want a child. We are left with the

reality of this "mother fixation" until after the murder and Niels' eventual release from jail. Restored to his farm, he experiences a vision which provides the final resolution of that identity problem: superimposed very gradually upon "the homely face of his mother" are "the features of his old man, of Sigurdsen, his neighbour whom he had loved" (p. 210). Herein lies recognition at last of Niels' relationship with Sigurdsen; this knowledge frees him from the need for further dependent relationships. He has embarked upon the self-sufficiency of adulthood.

A third dream of the future develops when Niels and Ellen are reunited: "the dream of the restful perpetuation of this state of dusk, of mutual wordless comprehension, of dispassionate friendship, brotherly love ..." (p. 213). And it is perhaps artistically necessary that Niels come to this level of sincerely platonic thought before the old dream, the dream of "the summer [rather than the autumn] of life" (p. 213), may reassert itself in all its creative vitality. The cycle of vision completes itself as Niels finds himself once more beginning to develop a "strange, new hope." He felt as if he must hold still so as not to frighten away what was building within him: "a new health, a new strength, a new hope, a new life ..." (p. 214).

In a final, triumphant confrontation, Ellen too resolves the distorted mother-child relationship under which she has struggled. She shows herself both willing and needing to assume her own role as a mother. With the deliberate caution of those who have suffered, the couple permit their dreams to reassert themselves and a mutual vision comes into view. It is a dream whose success is not to be perfect, is not guaranteed, for sin and ignorance have precluded that, but it is the hope which always follows on tragic suffering.

II

Settlers of the Marsh has as a second structural pillar, Grove's paradoxical views on man's Fatedness and man's Freedom. Many of Grove's personal pronouncements tend toward a view of man beset by the blind whims of an indifferent universe, "defending himself on all fronts against a cosmic attack."[6] A more specific and poignant statement of the frustrating, impersonal nature of these attacks is presented in Grove's unpublished poem, "The Gods". We are not even flies for wanton gods to kill in sport.

They, as we, are blind

And cannot see where leads their unled dance.
Above them, dangling, hangs the spider Chance,
And spins No-meaning, balm to soul or mind.[7]

Yet Grove also harbours the belief that the human spirit has a responsibility to pit its strength against "the gods", and he often sees the forces of fate operating from within the individual. This brings us into the realm of human responsibility, an issue important both here and in later discussion of the passion-sin theme.

The transplanted Swede has every reason to feel that he is master of his own destiny in the exciting New World atmosphere of opportunity and success. "In Sweden it had seemed to him as if his and everybody's fate had been fixed for all eternity. He could not win out because he had to overcome not only his own poverty but that of all his ancestors to boot ..." (p. 39). In comparison, the prairie setting, unconfined by finite spaces, open and honestly challenging, seemed to offer freedom and the control of one's destiny (p. 27). But the land counters the atmosphere of freedom with a strong sense of both the immense inevitability of timeless natural forces and the tremendous impersonal ruthlessness of the forces which would move against him. "To Niels his doings seemed inconsequential and irrelevant; such was the influence of the boundless landscape which stretched away in the dim light of the moon ... life had him in its grip and played with him; the vastness of the spaces looked calmly on" (p. 34).

A multitude of details throughout the novel contribute to the aura of fate, of external controls, molding the patterns of a man's life. The countless calamities besetting the Lunds give rise to the thought, "Success and failure! It seemed to depend on who you were, an Amundsen or a Lund ..." (p. 36). Frequently, the snares set for the unwary are embodied in one's acquaintances as in Niels' "terrible destiny" in the form of Clara (p. 51). Still, it is evident that however predetermined events may appear, there is room for rebellion. Olga was able to escape; could not Niels? He fled physically, but the horrible new knowledge had taken hold that "he was a leaf borne along by the wind, a prey to things beyond his control, a fragment swept away by torrents" (p. 55). Niels' immediate response to this insight is the one to which he would turn again and again when confronted with the unendurable or the incomprehensible: he would "cling to the landscape as something abiding, something to steady him" (p. 55).

Often it seems to Niels that stern fate has less to say in matters than sheer blind chance. "If he had remained in Sweden ... he would have accepted what is as immutable and pre-arranged." Instead, the uprooting and emigration "had awakened powers of vision and sympathy in him which were far beyond his education and upbringing. If one single thing had been different, everything might have run a different course ...." "How chance played into life," he mused, "with considerable fearfulness" (p. 60).

Crucially, however, Niels realizes "that the torrent which swept him away, the wind that bore him whither it listed came from his inner-most self. If, for what had happened to him anybody was to blame at all, it was he ...." (p. 56). Without this participation of self in the process, the drama would not achieve tragic dimensions.

Grove tends to play fate, chance, and freedom against one another throughout his narrative. Niels notes that the townspeople are bound to ennui and dissatisfaction by their own lack of imagination (p. 86). But it is the whims of fortune which persist in throwing Niels and Mrs. Vogel together. And outright necessity, "a tragic necessity no longer to be evaded," appears to control his relationship with Ellen. "The moment was coming. It was rushing along the lane of time where neither he nor she could escape it. Yes, it was already here. It stood in front of them; and its face was not smiling; it was grimly tragical ...." (pp. 94-5).

"Make your own life, Ellen, and let nobody make it for you!" (p. 112). So speaks a woman with whom, as with Mrs. Lund, life had not kept faith. But with these words, Mrs. Amundsen both frees and binds her daughter who has had to distort and suppress her natural needs for home, love and children to obey. It is in acquiescence to her female destiny that she paradoxically finds final freedom.

The images of slavery begin to make a cumulative impression. Niels, "the slave who dreams of freedom" (p. 119), meets Mrs. Vogel by "a blind chance happening" (p. 119). Like a beast under a yoke, tightly reined, the wedded Niels finds "no way of turning" (p. 126). Ellen asks in anguish, "Niels, how could you! ...." (p. 126), but the more relevant question seems to be, "How could you not?" Niels is cornered and haunted by "the feeling of disaster, of a shameful bondage that was inescapable. His doom had overtaken him irrevocably, irremediably: he was bond-slave to a moment in his life, to a moment in the past, for all future times ...." (p. 138). Then there is Niels peonage to the land. Time and again we are reminded that "The farm was a law unto itself ...." (p. 149). Finally, there is the bondage of the ultimate force grinding his fate, Niels own nature. Repeatedly the solution to a situation lies in following the dictates of intuition or impulse.

> But it was a peculiarity of his nature that, having
> thought out and laid down a plan, he must go on along
> the demarcated line and carry out that plan even
> though circumstances might have arisen which made it
> absurd. Thus he had broken his land, thus built his
> house, thus made himself the servant of the soil .... It
> was his peasant nature going on by inertia .... (p. 152)

As the action moves towards the murder, the references to forms of slavery, a fitting preface to rebellion and self-assertion, pile up. The paradox of Clara's view of freedom is revealed in the impassioned kitchen scene. An artificial, possessive woman, she desires a similar love. To feel loved, she needs her freedom curtailed. Indeed, her three tests of Niels' love all centre on freedom, and he fails in declining to restrict her (p. 155). Once convinced that he does not love her, Clara changes her tune. "I cannot stay here, a prisoner, condemned to a life-sentence. I won't" (p. 158). The restriction she seeks in love has become vile imprisonment in hatred.

In probing the raw nerves of the marriage which his wife has exposed, Niels comes to understand the inevitability of his past course of action as well as the unaltered blame he bears for it. "He could not help himself; he was he; he could not act or speak except according to laws inherent in him. What must happen would happen. He had sinned. He saw no atonement. None, nowhere" (p. 161). These insights foster a new sympathy and understanding towards others fallen, now men of his own kind. But the composition of Niels' soul and mind fail to extend in the really crucial direction: toward his wife. "Had he made a single motion ... had he said a single word, even though it had been a word of forgiveness instead of desire, perhaps the worst might still have been averted; fate might have been stayed ..." (p. 165). This possibility of averting fate is, of course, illusory, for "fate" derives from the self and Niels' nature determines his "destiny".

In the process of investigating fully his own bondage, Niels unwittingly reduces his once-beloved Percheron team to slavery. "Horses know as well as dogs whether their masters feel friendly towards them or not. Unlike dogs, they do not cling to or fawn upon him who does not deserve their love. They cannot but do the work demanded of them; but they are henceforth mere slaves" (p. 165). The important point here is the qualitative difference in the types of slavery man and beast endure. Jock enslaved can assume at best only a dramatically stoic stature; Niels enslaved can utilize the human spirit and human reason to challenge his cosmic masters in Promethean, tragic terms. That these masters may issue primarily from within only accentuates the titanic scope of the inner struggle.

In dealing with Niels as he embarks upon the murder of his wife, Grove chooses a curious image, one of springs and clockwork. The impetus to murder appears totally mechanical: "There was not a spark of consciousness in Niels. He acted entirely under the compulsion of the spring" (p. 186). Does the author absolve Niels of responsibility through this device? It would seem more likely that Grove chose this technique simply to dramatize the power that forces, internal and external, working upon an individual, may exert. Niels becomes a sort of puppet, a tool, but controlled by what or whom? Surely a clue lies in the kitchen confrontation with Clara. At that time, "when his wife's revelations had hit him like so many hammer-blows, he had been stunned. Then, in life's first reaction against injury and death, he had been subject to fits of rage, sudden wellings-up in him of primeval impulses, of the desire to kill, to crush ..." (p. 159). The impetus is then a primeval instinct. Niels is both guilty and guiltless, in control and possessed, a murderer and victim of a nature he did not choose.

Grove is consistent regarding the fatedness of things. Chance no longer operates: Niels and Ellen, betrayed once by their own and others' natures, move together as inevitably and consciously as they once parted (p. 214). The now older couple are both free and destined. They deliberately reunite, but the forces which make their union acceptable and promising derive from sources more in the realm of the uncontrolled, the elemental — in a sense, fated. Niels has resolved the maternal dependency and blind morality which bound him and has expiated the sin those produced. Ellen has also freed herself from a legacy of fear and denial, and the indomitable procreative need of all living species has triumphed. In each instance, the integrity of the human spirit has been sustained throughout.

III

The themes of Passion and Sin, inextricable from a discussion of fate and freedom, are so thoroughly developed a structural support of *Settlers* as to warrant separate consideration.

Niels is a character completely "pure" in the ways of sex, "chaste to the very core of his being" (p. 40). For such a man, no mate could be more ill-chosen than "a being that was almost sexless," Ellen Amundsen (p. 38). Her rejection of natural processes, although based on traumatic experiences in childhood, was nevertheless a violation of nature for which she has paid in pain and loneliness. In the rarefied atmosphere of two such unnaturally virgin souls, sensations of passion and sensitivity to sin and guilt must play an accentuated role. Thus, early in the novel, Niels undergoes the stirrings of guilt-feelings without knowing why; "... whenever he had been dreaming of her [Mrs. Vogel] and his thoughts then reverted to Ellen, he felt guilty; he felt defiled, as if he had given in to sin" (p. 46).

Niels experiences "the ultimate, supreme, physical desire" (p. 49) for Ellen that he would have regarded with shame if directed toward the cloyingly intimate widow. Thus we find the word "glowing" used in his response to both women; but in the case of Ellen, the tone is ecstatic and reverent, while Mrs. Vogel's environment is one of fear (pp. 48, 51). "His chastity felt attacked" (p. 52). It does not seem accidental that "in order to save himself, he slipped out of the door and crossed the yard to where the children were playing ..." (p. 53). As, in times of trial, he longs for his mother, and seeks to be mothered by Clara, so, upon the instinct of flight and fear of sin, he tries to return to the state of innocence, to become one with childhood again.

The agony of Niels' situation and the mechanics of tragedy depend to a large degree on the Swede's unnatural innocence or ignorance. Gazing at Mrs. Vogel, he puts the nature of sin in the category of the ineffable. "She was incomprehensible." She "looked like sin" (p. 54). Therefore, sin is incomprehensible. The syllogism may be reversed, but the significance is the same: by neglecting this and other opportunities to increase his understanding of sin and passion, he exposes himself to inevitable disaster.

"His world, his workaday world of toil and worry, seemed suddenly so sane as compared with his own world of passion, desire, and longing" (p. 54). It is natural, then, that he would throw himself into work to release pent-up passions and soothe his spirit. In this novel Grove departs from his usual depiction of the land as a nearly personified force with which to fight for survival. The stark prairie, for all the hardships it represents, tends to ally itself with Niels in providing an external outlet for the true battle waged within.

Ellen's revelation of her mother's marital ordeals is a soliloquy on lust and its results. The sexual relationship is reduced to terms of power, and it is almost a foregone conclusion to hear Ellen say, "I vowed to myself: No man, whether I liked him or loathed him, was ever to have power over me!" (p. 112). In thus wanting only the spiritual, she drives Niels to the purely physical.

As Niels proceeds toward his downfall, his feelings of guilt intensify. Playing against this is his stolid and incredible innocence, revealed in the conversation with Hahn. An incomplete sentence harboured the information that might have averted tragedy. "There's one like that Hefter woman in every district ....There's one in yours ..." (p. 118). Ironically, it is unselfish concern for Bobby's moral welfare that diverts Niels' attention at that critical moment from the gossip that might have prevented his marriage and preserved his own moral integrity.

Lindstedt's complex reactions to his first sexual experience encompass all the fragmentary passion and guilt feelings he has previously undergone: the blood aflame, hatred of the seductress, desire for oblivion and death-in-life, fear and impulses to flight (p. 121). In literal and figurative darkness, he yields to sin. The wages of sin are soon apparent: "Already this marriage seemed to him almost an indecency" (p. 125). A new awareness of lust as "the defiling of an instinct of nature" arises (p. 138); but, amazingly, Niels' innate innocence and, probably, aversion to such a truth, prevent his grasping the logical deduction of his wife's calling. And, his vitality drained away, he "could no longer respond with any great passion" (p. 125). Yet he has to meet the demand of "her strange, ardent, erratic desires" (p. 126).

The unnatural type of "love" the couple bear for each other in their earliest married days gradually turns to hate and Niels "felt as if he must purge himself of an infection, of things unimaginable, horrors unspeakable — the more horrible as they were vague, vague ..." (p. 149). It is convenient for Niels to speak

of an infection, since the image shifts the blame for their situation from his shoulders to something external, mostly to Clara.
But his wife does not permit him to maintain this fiction, charg-
ing Niels with having

> "...prostituted me if you know what that means ....
> After having made a convenience of me, when you
> married me, you committed a crime!" ...That woman
> was right! That was why he had married her! Not she,
> he stood indicted. (p. 154)

Wanderings in the labyrinths of guilt produce in Niels a sensitivity to similar failings in others. The pioneer Dahlbeck is now
a "slave of passion" ruled by an evil genius of a woman (p. 161).
Niels feels himself kin to that man, and realizes at last that he
could never again judge others as he had in the innocent arrogance of his youth. Yet, refraining from judging, never does
he go the step further to forgiveness that might have proved his
salvation.

The extremity of Clara's new passion, hatred, made revenge
her entire *raison d'être*. The marriage brings to her the death-in-
life that Niels experiences through the shame of lust. It also brings
on her madness. Nor is Niels untouched: "the decay in Niels con-
sisted ... in a gradual disintegration of will and purpose" (p. 175).
His "care for the farm was almost passionate. But it was the last
flicker of a dying flame" (p. 172). Lust and its effects, however,
are not yet finished with the Lindstedts. Clara, as part of her
revenge, chooses to flaunt her lovers before Niels, prompting his
eventual murderous anger. The Dahlbeck woman, whose lust,
when thwarted, turns to vindictiveness and to cruel revelation,
hisses at Niels, "You hypocrite .... You can't play the innocent
with me! You married the district whore ..." (p. 177).

Two provocative facets of the nature of sin emerge after the
murder. One is the tendency to involvement that a crime effects.
Just as each man loses by another's death, so crime is not an exclusive thing, but spreads like ripples in a pond. Bobby,
presumably uninvolved, becomes entangled in the guilt and the
tragedy and the implications. "If it had not been for him, Bobby,
there would have been no fire-arms on the place .... He had been
happy, constitutionally happy. He would never be quite so happy again; but he would be more thoughtful .... Bobby, young as
he was, came to know the bitterness of regret and repentance"

(pp. 188-9).

The other interesting aspect of the murder's aftermath is the pattern of ritual redemption and renewal. Niels falls into a profound and death-like sleep that initiates a dormant period for his soul. Although he wakes physically, his spirit comes "from another world" and his "voice, too, sounded as from an infinite distance" (p. 189). Niels then begins an elaborate cleansing ritual, "slowly, painstakingly, splashing and splashing for fully five minutes" (p. 189). By the time he leaves prison, he has achieved inward balance, "the peace of resignation" (p. 208).

One sin's weight lingers in his conscience. He "had done a great wrong; he had left alone a human being that had been in need of him" (p. 208). Niels' final peace of mind depends on Ellen's forgiveness. He still regards her through "mists of passion" (p. 209), but would suppress these entirely for the sake of brotherhood with her. The situation acquires delicacy and balance when Ellen meets Niels with, "I have been to blame towards you .... Can you forgive? ..." (p. 213). They are reunited by the sorrows of the past, the needs of the present, and the hopes of the future. "Life has involved them in guilt; regret and repentance have led them together; they know that never again must they part. It is not passion that will unite them: what will unite them is love ..." (p. 216).

IV

The fourth major structural pillar is "Isolation", a designation which serves to include both physical or natural separateness and the alienation of mind or soul. It is a theme which informs the novel from the first glimpse of the vast, depersonalized, bleak prairie setting. By nature a loner, Niels echoes the isolation of the prairie reaches and proves a vehicle as fit as the landscape for Grove's artistic response, tragic, and exulting, to geography unlocking cosmic significances.[8]

The general isolation Niels feels at Nelson's wedding becomes particularized as he realizes the effect marriage would have on their friendship. "Nelson had stepped aside; he was going to live in a world from which Niels was excluded. Niels was left alone" (p. 54). The desire to evade the world becomes "a desire to evade life's issues ...," to return to the dependent, one-to-one relationship he has had with his mother (p. 55). One cannot really fault his wish to cut the world out, when one is aware of the almost sinister picture he has gained of human relationships. Mrs. Vogel confuses and frightens him; Ellen is cold and inscrutable; Olga marries to escape; the Lunds and the Amundsens present appalling views of married life.

The association between Niels and Ellen vacillates. For a while "an abyss seemed to yawn [between them] which nothing could bridge" (p. 68). Later there comes to be "no barrier between them: they looked at each other, as it were, stripped of all conventions, all disguises ..." (p. 95). But it is a candour which could be washed away by a summer storm: "... already something [had] stepped in between them: ... a great, infinite remoteness not to be bridged .... As he [sat] there and [looked], it [was] as if her face were receding and fading from view" (p. 99). The schism drives him again from society, "wishing it were winter and he were out, fighting the old, savage fight against the elements ..." (p. 100), a battle for which he is so much more suited.

It is significant that the same image of "the abyss" is used for the pain Ellen encounters in hearing her father force himself on her mother and for all the various moments of alienation that Niels experiences throughout the novel. This device neatly weaves individual incidents into the universal, tragic pattern of human alienation. The sense of isolation controls much of the force of Grove's tragic vision, for it is one thing to be engaged in heroic combat with actively interested and participating superhuman agents (e.g. gods, Nature), but quite another thing to swing blindly and frantically at random, yet inevitable, disinterested cosmic forces (e.g. fate, Nature).

The separation of Ellen and Niels finds its objective correlative in the actual road-chasm where the two inadvertently meet after Niels' marriage. It serves also to presage the social and personal isolation that his new wife has brought: "... not a congratulation, not an invitation for neighbourly intercourse: nothing. ... Niels could not but be aware of enveloping reticences; he felt as if he were surrounded by a huge vacuum in which the air was too thin for human relationships to flourish ..." (p. 129). More painful is Niels' grim picture of his life with Clara, existing side by side: "without common memories in the past, without common interests in the present, without common aims in the future. ... decades upon decades of exactly the same thing ahead, ... facing eternity alone! ..." (p. 137). The emotional separation of the couple becomes concrete in physical separation, with each move away from one another compounded by misunderstandings, absences and reticences into a "demoralization of all human relationships" (p. 141). Finally, faced with Clara's accusations, Niels finds himself "walking along an abyss, blindfolded" (p. 157). Their relationship has hit a depth from which there seems no return. The "blindfolded" Niels fails to interpret his wife's penetrating analysis in any other terms than that "She had given her body" (p. 157), and he misses the last opportunity for reconciliation in ignoring her proud displays of herself to him "as no woman could show herself to any man but her husband ..." (p. 164).

As the impact of Clara's mad revenge takes hold of Niels, he begins to show signs of instability himself. He clings to Bobby as "the last link that connected him with the world of living men: the last barrier between him and insanity ..." (p. 167). Yet he contradicts this in deliberately hiding from Bobby to avoid the judgement that he is mad (p. 166). In shaving and barbering Niels' wild unkemptness, Bobby finally serves as Niels' usher back to some bond with life and with people. It is significantly this shaved, "civilized" Niels who decides to destroy the active force in his life for isolation and nonliving, his wife.

The final sin which Niels and Ellen have to resolve involves, in both instances, violations of love which had produced alienation and loneliness. She has rejected Niels pledge of life, love, and secure intimacy, then lets him go away without a hint of change to sustain his hopes. He in turn does not return, but leaves Ellen alone to suffer. Through mutual contrition and forgiveness, they expiate their transgressions and bridge the crevasses which have too long held them captive and alien. "There is no barrier between them which would need to be bridged by words. They are not looking at each other; they are one" (p. 215). It is appropriate that the last word of the novel be "both", to stress that they have overcome isolation, achieved unity, and are united through love's power. The past is no barrier, but a bond.

V

Textual analysis reveals the domination of four themes — vision, fate, sinful passion, and isolation — in the structure of *Settlers of the Marsh*. These emerge as the strongest elements of the work, the elements about which all characters, incidents, and insights weave themselves. There are, in addition, a number of sub-themes which strengthen and enrich both the major themes and the work of art as a whole. It has been demonstrated, for example, how fully a major theme like "visions" may be informed by a secondary concern like the mother-child relationship. In the same way, motifs of life-death, success, and even the recurrence of the colour white substantially reward investigation. Nature, social issues, and the threads provided by individual characterizations, while comparatively minor structurally, also contribute to the organic quality of the fiction.

Probably the single feature of *Settlers* most troubling to critics' sense of a unified and tightly-knit novel has been the ending. Does it destroy or upset the cohesion and symmetry of the novel's structure? Is it not a shallow acquiescence to the popular demand for a "happy ending", the very phenomenon Grove repudiates in an essay by that name? Thomas Saunders feels that it "is not enough to blind us to the high quality of the narrative up to that point."[9] One might pose an even more loyal defense of Grove's artistic sensibilities by examining the original ending of *Settlers*, in which Niels and Ellen are portrayed in sugary domestic bliss, snug by the fire, with the howl of winter wind outside and "the pitter-patter of little feet" upstairs.[10] Realizing the artistic objections that would be raised to such a patently "happy" and convenient ending, Grove removed it from the novel. It was a decision totally in harmony with his view of tragedy.

> What, then is tragic?
> To have greatly tried and to have failed, to have greatly longed for purity and to be sullied; to have greatly craved for life and to receive death: all that is the common lot of greatness upon earth .... [In] acceptance or acquiescence lies true tragic greatness: it mirrors the indomitable spirit of mankind. All great endeavour, great ambition, great love, great pride, great thought disturb the placid order of the flow of events. That order is restored when failure is accepted and when it is seen and acknowledged that life proceeds by compromises only.[11]

The couple are now proceeding toward a vision as unguaranteed as their previous broken dreams. But they have tried and failed and have been exalted by the final acceptance of compromise. In Grovian terms, catharsis has been achieved. It becomes apparent how appropriate, consistent, and realistic the conclusion of *Settlers* actually is; indeed, how artificial, melodramatic, and clicheed the predictable "tragic" ending would have been.

Settlers of the Marsh, like all of Frederic Philip Grove's work, exhibits a constant awareness of the demands of the form-content relationship, a particular sensitivity to structure and motif. One might, with considerable support, claim that Grove meets these demands more fully in this novel than anywhere else. Each of the structural themes that the author employs has the status of a chain link: secondary and contributory but absolutely vital to the unity of the chain. The "parts" examined are naturally only parts, but they comprise an artistic totality greater than their sum. In coming to know the parts, then, we approach comprehension of the whole.

Grove's was an ordered mind in search of itself and its world, attempting to work out an ordered view of both. From first glance at the table of contents, wherein may be discerned complicated cycles and parallels of human destiny, one senses this artistic impulse to structure and unity. Time and again, in his "autobiographies" and through his characters, Grove went beyond the "givens" of a situation, attempting to establish patterns for a coherent reality. If the coherence went no further than the pattern itself, no matter. With tacit acceptance of the value of design in itself as a key to or manifestation of the cosmic mysteries, Grove assumes a legitimate place among form-content-reality theorists.

Notes

[1] Frederick Philip Grove, *In Search of Myself* (Toronto: Macmillan of Canada, Ltd., 1946), p. 352.

[2] *Ibid*, p. 379.

[3] *Ibid*, pp. 370, 381.

[4] Frederick Philip Grove, from "The Palinode, Part I" (University of Manitoba, the Grove Collection, Part III, no. 5, Box 15, Envelope No. 3).

[5] Frederick Philip Grove, *Settlers of the Marsh* (New York: Doran, 1925; rpt. Toronto: McClelland and Stewart, 1966, introduction by Thomas Saunders), p. 17. Further references are to the 1966 edition.

[6] *In Search of Myself*, p. 163.

[7] Grove, from "The Gods" (University of Manitoba, the Grove Collection, Part III, no. 5, Box 15, Envelope No. 3).

[8] For an account of the tremendous response of the author (imaginatively if not factually) to such stark, dramatic landscapes as the desert and Siberia, see *In Search of Myself*, pp. 149-50, 153-4, and 162. That the

author found Canada a parallel sort of experience is evidenced by remarks to that effect in his pseudo-autobiography and by a letter from Grove to Carleton Stanley, dated Simcoe, 14 May 1946: "Yes, apart from the Canadian, Siberia was my deepest experience [sic]." (Grove Collection, Box 5).

9   Thomas Saunders, introduction to *Settlers of the Marsh*, p. xiii.
10 Grove, The Grove Papers, Pt. II (Box No. 9, p. 196, dated 1917ì924).
11 Frederick Philip Grove, *It Needs to be Said* (Toronto: Macmillan of Canada, Ltd., 1929), p. 87.

GROVE'S "GARBLED EXTRACT": THE BIBLIOGRAPHICAL ORIGINS OF *SETTLERS OF THE MARSH*

Henry Makow

Settlers of the Marsh is the most read of Grove's works and is widely regarded as one of his highest achievements.[1] Critics and students therefore are puzzled by Grove's repeated deprecation of the novel. In an oft-repeated passage from his autobiography, Grove writes that in 1920 he rewrote "that terrible, three-volume novel which I called 'Pioneers' ... of which a garbled extract was to appear in 1925, under the title of one of its parts, *Settlers of the Marsh*."[2] Elsewhere Grove fosters the impression that his publisher forced him to cut "Pioneers" ruthlessly, and that the dots which appear on almost every page of *Settlers of the Marsh* represent deletions. Grove writes to Desmond Pacey in 1943: "It was by the way, *Settlers* which was so ruthlessly cut down, from three long volumes to one short one. Hence the dots."[3] Grove's statements greatly influenced Pacey's assessment of the novel and subsequently that of many other critics.

On the basis of contemporary correspondence and a comparison of the "Pioneers" typescript with *Settlers of the Marsh*, Grove's statements can now be discounted. *Settlers of the Marsh* is not a "garbled extract"; the dots do not refer to deletions. The evidence indicates that Grove expected the novel to bring him international recognition. He was extremely disappointed with the uncomprehending reviews and miserable sales. The stories he invented were his way of "retracting" the novel, of rationalizing its failure. The published work accurately represents Grove's intentions. The manuscript was readily accepted by Ryerson Press in April, 1925, and published without significant changes. The previous year Grove had decided to condense the two completed volumes of the "Pioneers" trilogy into a shorter work. A comparison of "Pioneers" with the final version will show that nothing of importance was lost in the process. Finally, the evidence will suggest that Grove did not write a third volume of "Pioneers", although in his original conception of the trilogy he had intended to tell the story of Niels' and Ellen's marriage.

The first clue that *Settlers of the Marsh* faithfully represents Grove's intent is the affection the author felt for the work throughout his life. Despite his repeated disclaimers, he held the novel to be one of his most important achievements. In his autobiography, Grove writes of *Settlers of the Marsh*:

... I thought it a great book; ... I loved it as a beautiful thing; but .... To this day I am not quite sure that it conveys to others what it conveys to me. If it does, nobody had ever said so.[4]

In 1941, Grove wrote to Desmond Pacey that he considered *Settlers of the Marsh* "the most important of my prairie novels."[5] In his unpublished lectures, Grove refers nostalgically to the writing of *Settlers of the Marsh* as the novel in which most often the "miracle" took place, "that miracle by means of which words transcend themselves and shadow forth realities beyond the power of conscious intention."[6]

Grove had high expectations for *Settlers of the Marsh*, expectations encouraged by Arthur Phelps, an English professor at Wesley College in Winnipeg. Phelps read "Pioneers" in progress and communicated his enthusiasm in his letters to Grove. "I am sure it is a big thing, a very big thing. Somehow I know this. I have walked about in excitement over it."[7] Shortly after publication, Phelps predicted that *Settlers of the Marsh* would make Grove's name internationally known.[8]

Lorne Pierce, the editor of Ryerson Press, who published the novel, was equally sanguine about the prospects in store for the novel and its author. "Please take good care of yourself," he wrote Grove. "We are anxious to have more novels from you and you may yet find yourself sitting down enjoying an opulent old age."[9] Again, he wrote: "Should this prove a success — and we have no doubt that it will — we are hoping to create a Grove vogue before long."[10]

Any man would find these predictions tantalizing. A man such as Grove would find them particularly exciting. According to D. O. Spettigue's account, Felix Paul Grove was intent on making his mark on the world. He craved recognition and acclaim. "The trouble was, he was always on the margins and he wanted to be at the centre ...."[11]

After failing to gain recognition in the literary circles of Europe, Grove came to America in 1909. According to his autobiographical novel, *A Search for America*, he spent three years as an itinerant before becoming a high school teacher in Manitoba. There, under

a new name, Grove unabashedly set about his aim which was
to create literary works with the permanence of the pyramids.[12]
With *Settlers of the Marsh* his first published "Canadian" novel,
Grove no doubt hoped to achieve part of his ambition, and some
of the recognition that had so far eluded him.

Grove was greatly disappointed. Despite a vigourous promotion campaign by Ryerson, the novel, published in October 1925,
sold poorly. In the two years after publication, the novel sold only
1758 copies in Canada and the U.S.[13] Orders for the book had
been so bad that in November Pierce suggested that Grove can-
vas his local drug store in Rapid City for an order.[14] In March,
1926, Pierce wrote Grove: "As we stand to lose a great deal on
Settlers of the Marsh, I do not think you have any fault to find with
the way it was handled in Canada. I think few novels have had
more active promotion than this."[15]

The meagre royalties which Grove received were depleted by
charges for corrections which he ordered at his own expense.
(Despite his "exceeding care" in correcting proofs, he complained that the book "swarmed with misprints."[16] In Sept. 1926,
Grove angrily returned to Ryerson a royalty cheque for ninety
cents. The cheque had included a deduction of $27.81 charged
for corrections by the New York printers.[17] In January, 1928,
Grove learned to his surprise that a new, cheaper edition of the
novel issued in New York had sold 1927 copies in the Christmas
trade.[18] But these belated sales did not assuage Grove's initial
humiliation and disappointment.

The public reaction to the novel contributed to Grove's disappointment. A controversy arose over Ellen's uninhibited account
in *Settlers of the Marsh* of her mother's marital history. In his
autobiography, Grove writes that the publication of *Settlers of the
Marsh* became a "public scandal".

> Libraries barred it — London, Ontario, forming an
> honourable exception; reviewers called it "filthy" — W.
> T. Allison over the radio; Lorne Pierce nearly lost his
> job over it; people who had been ready to lionize me
> cut me dead in the street.
>
> As a trade proposition the book never had a chance;
> what sale it had was surreptitious. I resented this; it
> was the old story of Flaubert's *Madame Bovary* over
> again. A serious work of art was classed as porno-

graphy; but with this difference that the error in Flaubert's case, increased the sales; he lived in France. In my case, and in Canada, it killed them.[19]

M.R. Stobie quotes a letter by the Winnipeg librarian of the day which indicates that no books were banned by the library.[20] The false impression was created by a press report that some aldermen had called for a cutback on purchases of "trashy" and "prurient" novels. Nevertheless, by Stobie's own account, the controversy was real enough. Many people believed the novel had been banned. Phelps wrote Grove: "The library has banned the *Settlers* and Eatons sells it but quietly!" W.A. Deacon, the book editor of *The Globe and Mail* waxed indignant, and *The Ottawa Journal* took up the cudgel.

In 1962, Lorne Pierce recalled the controversy:

> The publishing house was invaded by angry mail, and by delegates of various sorts condemning us unsparingly. Dr. Fallis, the head of the house was enraged by it all and I believed my time also had come. Then one day he walked into the office and laid a letter before me having the Canadian coat of arms embossed on it. It read roughly as follows: "I congratulate you on having the literary insight to recognize a work of art when you see it, and on having the courage to publish it. Yours truly, Arthur Meighen, Prime Minister." The war was over.[21]

Grove's novel shared the brunt of the criticism with Martha Ostenso's *Wild Geese*, but this only contributed to Grove's frustration. Grove considered *Wild Geese* "deplorably, even unusually immature." He was piqued that *Wild Geese*, also a first novel, had won its 25-year-old author the $13,500 Dodd Mead prize as well as critical accolades. A month after his own novel was published, Grove took time to upbraid a critic who had praised *Wild Geese* at a meeting of the Canadian Authors' Association. Many passages in *Wild Geese* "make a mature person smile," Grove wrote to the critic. "In fact, how could a young girl know anything of the fierce antagonisms that discharge themselves in sex? Nobody will accuse me of prudishness. What I object to is the incompetence, psychologic and artistic, in dealing with these things ...." And he concluded: "It's an old story: only trash wins a prize."[22]

Grove was also disappointed with the critical treatment of *Settlers of the Marsh*. The most obtuse reviews were from closest to home. In a *Winnipeg Free Press* review, November 2, 1925, the critic contended that the women of the settlement would not socialize with a well-known courtesan: "They will not condone immorality. That is simply not done, and in making his womenfolk do it, Mr. Grove, not for the first time in his story, forces the characters ruthlessly to follow his story instead of making the story flow naturally from them."

In a *Winnipeg Tribune* review, November 21, 1925, W. T. Allison, a professor at the University of Manitoba, says that Grove "should have had enough consideration for the majority of his readers to omit two nauseating passages. The introduction of the immoral widow into his novel is in itself enough to cause many people to refuse to allow his book on the family shelf."

However, the other reviews, while cursory, were generally positive. The influential *Montreal Star* reviewer, S. Morgan-Powell, wrote on October 31, 1925: "It is essentially a big thing to have done and I regard it as an important contribution to the contemporary fiction of the English speaking world." In general, however, Grove was not satisfied with the reviews. He wrote Ryerson advertising manager E. J. Moore on November 30, 1925:

> I wish to add that what I have seen of reviews, with the exception of Morgan-Powell's, is singularly unintelligent. And without any exception, they seem to me to miss the point.[23]

Grove felt that his novel was not understood by reviewers and the public. He tried to attribute blame for this to the dust jacket which boldly heralds the novel as a "North Country Romance." He wrote Moore on December 21, 1925:

> The jacket killed it. I know for a fact that the 3 leading reviews of what may be called "literature" ignored the book for the sake of the jacket (Danby, Sherman, Mencken). The buyer of North Country Romance, not getting what he wanted, returned the book to the booksellers. So it fell between two stools. I doubt whether even a few hundred copies were sold.[24]

In his reply, the Ryerson advertising manager defended Doran, the New York firm who published the novel and designed the jacket. He also deprived Grove of his rationalization: "Mencken and those other chaps you mention are rather too conversant with marketing methods to let the matter of a jacket influence them either pro or con if they were at all interested in the book itself."[25]

In late March, 1926, Pierce wrote to commiserate with Grove for the poor sales and reviews, the public outcry and other problems attending publication:

> I am sorry that *Settlers of the Marsh* has been such an unhappy undertaking for you throughout. From the time the Ms. was accepted until the present it seems to have brought you little pleasure.[26]

Even Grove's cordial relations with Pierce, however, were not to survive the debacle. In an attempt to relieve the gloom, Pierce made some flippant but insensitive remarks to Grove with reference to a review of *Settlers of the Marsh* by their mutual friend, Arthur Phelps.[27] Referring to Phelps' praise of Grove's "three dimensional characters," Pierce remarked that even a moron has three dimensions. He also assured Grove that by the time his next book is published, the "milieu created by the *Settlers*" will be "of only Paleozoic interest." Grove mistook both remarks and addressed the editor in recriminating tones. Pierce sought in vain to redress the injury. His reference to the milieu created by the novel was to the public outcry, not to the pioneer district depicted therein. He assured Grove that he had no intention of being "outright unkind," and that he was the staunchest supporter of the novel and its author. The slighted author, however, was not to be placated, and the relationship between the two men lapsed for more than a decade, and never regained its former warmth. Grove was not exaggerating very much when he wrote in his autobiography: "In the spring of 1926, the publication of *Settlers of the Marsh* had proved an unmitigated disaster...."[28]

Grove regarded his first Canadian novel as "a beautiful thing." It was the most important of his prairie works. Because the world did not share his opinion, he felt he had failed to communicate. Grove wrote Pierce explaining that when he feels he has failed to communicate, he becomes so nervous that he wishes he had not published.[29] Grove sought excuses, rationalizing his failure in terms of the obscenity controversy and the dust jacket. Later, he made Pierce his emotional scapegoat. Finally, the story of the "garbled extract" and the dots became Grove's lasting explanation for the novel's failure.

The correspondence shows that Grove recognized almost immediately that the reception of his novel would not meet his high expectations. The first suggestion that *Settlers of the Marsh* was not a bonafide expression of the author's intent is found in a review by Arthur Phelps in the *Winnipeg Free Press* of December 7, 1925. Phelps was replying to the negative review which the newspaper had run a month earlier:

> This last published book and first novel, *Settlers of the Marsh*, was originally planned as a work of 900,000 words in three volumes. As actually written it contained about 400,000 words. It was cut to 85,000 words to meet the publisher's demand in connection with a first novel. Hence the dots, which represent the loss to the reader of a rich quantity of supporting interpretive and descriptive material in the writing of which Mr. Grove's pen can be most satisfying. Hence the nervousness of the book and the seemingly rather sudden ending.

Most likely Phelps adopted the story of the publisher's demand and the dots after discussion with Grove. It was Grove who perpetuated the story. In lectures such as one he wrote in 1935, Grove said *Settlers of the Marsh* appeared in "a mutilated form."[30] He wrote Henry Miller of Graphic Publishers in November 1926: "Once before, in the case of the *Settlers*, I have spoiled a good book by cutting it to the bone."[30] Grove told Pacey in 1943 that "ruthless" cutting resulted in the dots and Pacey gave the story greater currency. In his book, *Frederick Philip Grove*, published in 1945, Pacey says *Settlers of the Marsh* has certain structural defects:

> Of these, perhaps the most obvious is a result of the ruthless process of abridgement to which the novel was subjected. Especially in the first half of the book, which was presumably reduced most severely, there is a plethora of scenes and sentences which trail off into a row of dots: [Pacey gives examples]. The dots, one assumes, indicate passages which were excised; but the critic must judge the work as it stands, and from this point of view these unfinished scenes and sentences are are a constant irritation .... They lend an air of the loose and episodic, the diffuse and scrappy, to the first half of

the novel. A few such passages, to indicate the passage of time, would have been acceptable; but there are too many of them.[32]

Watson Kirkconnell, a colleague of Phelps' at Wesley College and a friend of Grove's, expanded on Grove's rationalization in 1962:

> The novels also suffer because we do not get them in printed form as they were planned. *Settlers of the Marsh* for instance was just hewn out of a vast work on the pioneers that Art Phelps and I saw in Rapid City in the early 1920's. It was simply hacked out of his larger work in order to have something of such a limited length that a publisher would take at all. He is structually the best in novels like *Our Daily Bread* which were not formed by amputation from a larger work, but were planned entire.[33]

Grove's rationalization gets its widest currency in Thomas Saunders' *Introduction* to the New Canadian Library edition of *Settlers of the Marsh*, first issued in 1965. Saunders quotes Grove's statement that *Settlers* is no more than a "garbled extract" of the original version. Although he does not question Grove's statement, Saunders makes a germane point when he questions Pacey's contention that the dots are a defect. "One wonders, indeed, if he [Pacey] had had no knowledge of the abridgement, if he would have complained ...."[34]

Ronald Sutherland and D. O. Spettigue perpetuate Grove's rationalization in their 1969 books, both entitled *Frederick Philip Grove*.[35] Only Margaret Stobie in her book by the same title refers to the dots for what they are, "a fashion Grove took up for a while."[36] But critics continue to accept Grove's word about the editing, and are influenced by it. In an article originally published in the *Journal of Canadian Fiction*, J. Lee Thompson refers to Grove's contradictory claims for *Settlers* as both a "work of art", and a "garbled extract." She concludes: "Grove's vacillation is shared by many who subject the novel to close scrutiny."[37]

Contrary to the general assumption, Grove revised "Pioneers" of his own volition. He records in his autobiography that Volume One of "Pioneers" was submitted to Macmillan and rejected. "A letter accompanying the rejection stated that no book of the kind stood a chance in Canada .... Whereupon I went to work slashing the book to pieces and reducing it to its present one-volume form."[38] Macmillan's letter is in the Grove Collection. The letter is dated February 25, 1924, almost a full year before Grove submitted *Settlers of the Marsh* to Ryerson, who published it. Macmillan did not say that "no book of the kind stood a chance in Canada." They complimented Grove for his truthful portrayal of pioneer conditions. They said that the material might have been "much more effectively presented in a novel of two thirds the space."

> It seems to us that condensation is greatly to be desired and yet we feel that with your avowed purpose of a trilogy in mind, such a suggestion perhaps would not be particularly welcome to you.[39]

A month earlier, McClelland and Stewart also rejected the novel saying the Canadian market was not large enough for a commercial success. They recommended a New York literary agency and expressed interest in taking a Canadian edition.[40]

Volume One of "Pioneers", rejected by Macmillan, and McClelland and Stewart, consists of 203 pages of single-space type and covers Niels' story only until his marriage with Clara, and Ellen's exclamation: "Niels, how could you!" After hearing from the publishers, Grove decided to amalgamate this volume with the second one. Volume Two of "Pioneers", of similar length, continues Niels' story through the marriage, the murder, and ends with Niels' decision to turn himself in. For reasons that I will discuss later, I believe that the projected third volume of "Pioneers" was never written. Grove concluded his shortened novel with a new chapter entitled "Ellen Again" which describes Niel's trial and jail term, his return to the farm and his reconciliation with Ellen. A letter from Phelps to Grove dated January 20, 1925 indicates the novel was complete three weeks before it was submitted to Lorne Pierce in early February. Phelps refers to "the whole last part dealing with Ellen and Niels' ultimate coming together ...." Although prompted by publishers' rejections of Volume One, Grove decided of his own volition to recast his unfinished trilogy in one book.

Lorne Pierce was present February 9, 1925, when Grove gave a reading of his work to the Winnipeg branch of the Canadian Author's Association. In his autobiography Grove records that after the meeting, Pierce asked for the manuscript of *Settlers of the Marsh* and invited him to breakfast at his hotel the following morning.[41] At that time Grove gave an enthusiastic Pierce permission to take the manuscript back to Toronto with him. Here is Pierce's recollection of the breakfast meeting:

> I told Grove that I had been unable to lay down his manuscript and that I had read it on into the morning. I was so deeply impressed as a matter of fact that I assured him publication. He seemed pleased but not unduly elated especially when I told him that the great length of the manuscript would require drastic cutting. There was an episode in the story which did not seem essential, and I felt that those pages would cause more trouble than they were worth.[42]

Significantly, Pierce does not elaborate on the "drastic cutting" required but rather focuses on his objection to the episode dealing with Ellen's mother. He waived his objection when Grove, "white with anger," and "with surprising vehemence," staked his integrity on the inclusion of that episode. It is doubtful that any other cuts were requested. Pierce's account of the meeting, recorded in 1962, thirty-seven years after the event, was probably influenced by Grove's references to the novel as a "garbled extract."

There are compelling reasons for the conclusions that "drastic cutting" was not ordered. First, we have the evidence that Grove reduced "Pioneers" to its one-volume form after hearing from Macmillan the previous year. Second, Pierce likely would not have been kept awake reading a long manscript that required "drastic cutting." Third and most significantly, there was no time for major revisions. Grove's meeting with Pierce took place on February 10, 1925. On April 8, 1925, Pierce made an official offer to publish *Settlers of the Marsh*. Between early February and April there was no time for major revisions, let alone the transformation of an unfinished trilogy into one volume. Pierce's letter suggests that the editor took the finished manuscript to Toronto with him, as Grove says; and the intervening time was expended in consideration of the novel:

> My telegram expresses my great disappointment over the delay in getting word to you. It was impossible to move more rapidly. We are besieged with changes and committees of one sort or another which makes a meeting of the publication committee well nigh impossible.[43]

Pierce goes on to say he is "so impressed" with Grove's manuscript that he wants to arrange for simultaneous publication in New York and London. He says the novel will be set up during the summer and will be ready for late August. There is no mention of cuts in the letter or in any of the Grove-Pierce correspondence on the novel. Grove read the proofs in July and the novel was off the presses in the middle of October. The evidence suggests that the manscript which Grove submitted to Pierce in February 1925 was complete, and was published without significant changes.[44]

Extensive cutting and revision were a normal part of Grove's creative process. As *Settlers* was going to press, Grove wrote Pierce that *Our Daily Bread* must be cut to about 100,000 words: "The trouble with that book is the usual one with me — that it is far too long."[45] Grove tells us without complaint that he cut *A Search for America* by half from its original length of 600,000 words.[46] He claims to have cut *The Master of the Mill* from a first draft of 1300 pages to 400 pages.[47] He advised the young writer not to rest until he has cut his first draft to one quarter its length taking care that "nothing of what he omits actually disappears."[48]

A brief examination of how the "Pioneers" trilogy became *Settlers of the Marsh* is of value. "Latter Day Pioneers", the full title of the trilogy, was conceived in 1917 when Grove was teaching in the marsh country just west of the south tip of Lake Manitoba. In the conception of the trilogy, Grove appears to have had two distinct and ultimately incompatible aims. "Pioneers" was to be the story of Niels Lindstedt and his dream of Ellen as presented in *Settlers of the Marsh*. Grove wished imaginatively to express his vision of the tragic failure of man's highest aspirations. The abandoned white range line house which Grove passed on his journeys became the symbol of an unrealized ideal. The decrepit house became, in Grove's imagination, the magnificent mansion that Niels had built for Ellen but which she never occupied. The early drafts of "Pioneers" begin with a promise to tell the story of this house.

Grove's second aim in "Pioneers" was not related to the imagination. He wished to present a factual chronicle of life in a growing pioneer district. In a plan found at the beginning of the handwritten draft, Grove budgets for four national groups consisting of five characters, each of whom are typical of a pioneer district. The short epithets beside the names include: "middle aged, cattle in the bush the great idea: wife a slut, children lousy. But a dint of hard work makes success," "slow, incompetent as a farmer. Wife ambitious in a frivolous sense, sell to soldier, become store keepers. Lord car," "the man of hard luck, hail, fire," "the Poles, slovenly intelligent, but full of pride." These characters, some of whom never appear in "Pioneers" were probably based on real persons. Residents of the marsh country who were Grove's students say that the Lunds are based on a family Grove knew, the Brandons.[49] In his plan, the Lunds are described as "the typical failure." Fred Brandon was partially blind and borrowed money without repaying it. Bobby Brandon was an orphan who later looked after his mother. There was also a daughter named Olga. As well, there was a well-driller who answers Nelson's description and a giant who appears in the novel under his real name, "Hahn". In contrast to the "pioneer" figures, the three central characters of "Pioneers", Niels, Ellen and Clara were purely a product of Grove's imagination. There is no recollection of persons resembling them or of a young farmer who murdered his wife.

The reconciliation of his imaginative and chronicling impulses is one of Grove's perennial problems. In his book *Frederick Philip Grove*, Spettigue remarks: "To the end of his days Grove was to struggle to reconcile his interest in and awareness of the simple annals of the small town or farm family, with his desire for the fully charged stage, for tragedy wrought to its uttermost."[50]

In *Fruits of the Earth*, Grove opted for the chronicle over the imaginative aim. The first four drafts of the novel have a tragic ending. Rather than defer to authority, Spalding murders his daughter's seducer. Spalding says the man has flouted "every human and divine law," and his murder is intended as an example to future generations. Spalding is tracked down by a posse and spotter plane, and shot. However, Grove tells us in his autobiography that he intended the novel to serve a documentary function as the original title, "The Chronicle of Spalding District", suggests: "Abe Spalding's death, and what followed after, was necessary in order to round off his life before I could write it; but for the story of the district as I conceived it, it was irrelevant; and in the finished work it is never mentioned."[51]

With "Pioneers", a decade earlier, Grove made the opposite decision. He opted for the imaginative portrayal of the human tragedy over the chronicle account of the district. When he edited "Pioneers", Grove cut away an abundance of material which had been included for its documentary value only. *Settlers of the Marsh* therefore is not strictly speaking, a condensation of "Pioneers". The novel existed largely intact within the body of "Pioneers". Grove merely stripped away the documentary material, thereby throwing the story of Niels, Ellen and Clara into relief. With one minor exception, *every* scene in "Pioneers" in which Niels appears with Ellen or Clara has been reproduced in *Settlers of the Marsh* without significant change. This accounts for most of the novel and preserves the original pattern in which Niels' story unfolded.

The editing of "Pioneers" was nevertheless a painstaking process. Grove eliminated all details, characters and events which did not directly advance Niels' story. For example the stories, "The First Day of an Immigrant", "The Marsh Fire", "The Sale" and "Snow", which are found in *Tales from the Margin*, were all originally part of "Pioneers". Grove dropped discussions of subjects such as well-drilling and the virtues of barley as a crop. The progress of the neighbours — the topic of long sections in "Pioneers" — is suggested in a few paragraphs which also indicate the passage of time.

Superfluous anecdotes which only enforce our opinion of Amundson and Lund were dropped. Sigurdson's background, similar to that of the Sower in *The Turn of the Year* was left out. Long passages detailing Niels' introspection were carefully compressed. Details of Niels' progress — how he "proved up" or became a citizen — were dropped. Explicit statements of thematic importance were toned down or eliminated. Omissions were not indicated by dots or in any other manner. Grove placed dots in *Settlers of the Marsh* where no passages from "Pioneers" were omitted.[52]

On the other hand, all the "set pieces" in *Settlers of the Marsh* — among which Niels' moment of truth with Ellen and Clara are the most important — were reproduced without significant changes. It is not a great exaggeration to say that *Settlers of the Marsh* was lifted whole from its background in "Pioneers".

Finally, the question of whether Grove ever actually wrote the third volume of "Pioneers" is germane. As mentioned, the first two volumes takes Niels' story up to his decision to turn himself in for the murder of Clara. The third volume of "Pioneers", if it was ever written, is not extant. The final chapter of *Settlers of the Marsh* is not part of the "Pioneers" manuscript. The chapter, "Ellen Again", was found in 1964 in five examination booklets in Grove's handwriting almost as published. On the basis of a letter Phelps wrote to Grove on January 20, 1925, Stobie believes these booklets represent a condensation of the third volume.[53] Here is what Phelps said:

> My feeling at present ... is that (i) the jail description and (ii) the whole last part dealing with Ellen and Niels' ultimate coming together would bear some sort of compression; in the latter case it might not be compression I want. It may be something quite different; maybe I don't want anything. But on the first reading I wasn't "gathered up tight" by it as I was by some of the other "scenes" in the book.[54]

Stobie's view that the final chapter represents a condensation of the third volume of "Pioneers" is unlikely to be true for the following reasons. First, Phelps' advice was written on January 20, 1925, less than three weeks before Grove presented the finished manuscript to Lorne Pierce. It is unlikely that Grove, acting on Phelps' muddled advice, revised a whole volume in such short space. Second, we have Phelps' review in the *Winnipeg Free Press* of December 7, 1925, in which he says Grove completed only 400,000 of the contemplated 900,000 words of the trilogy. Third, according to Grove's plan, the third volume of "Pioneers" was tentatively entitled "Male and Female" and presumably would have dealt with the married life of Niels and Ellen, not just with their reunion. In the "Epilogue" which Grove deleted from the end of "Ellen Again", in the exam booklets, Niels' and Ellen's married life is "the subject of a different story." Finally, we have a seventeen-page fragment in Grove's handwriting which Spettigue calls "Ellen Lindstedt". The fragment appears to represent the beginning of the abortive third volume. "Ellen Lindstedt" begins with the marriage of Niels and Ellen, recapitulates their history and foreshadows possible areas of conflict before ending abruptly on an ominous note.

All the evidence suggests that Grove never completed the third volume of "Pioneers". Only two volumes were complete when, after hearing from Macmillan, Grove decided to shorten his novel. At that time he wrote the "Ellen Again" chapter to conclude the shortened work. "Ellen Lindstedt", which takes the marriage of Ellen and Niels as its starting point, was likely an attempt to write a sequel to *Settlers of the Marsh* based on Grove's earlier plans for a third volume entitled "Male and Female".

Critics may speculate on the nature of the projected sequel, but they need no longer guess about the authenticity of *Settlers of the Marsh* itself. Grove's repeated statements that *Settlers of the Marsh* is a "garbled extract" of the "Pioneers" trilogy, and that the frequent use of dots indicate omissions, may be discounted. Grove and his supporters had high expectations for his first Canadian novel which they all regarded as a great work. The novel's failure caused Grove to invent an elaborate rationalization which, valid for apologist and detractor alike, found widespread acceptance. Grove was reacting in part to the lack of perception displayed by the critics and public. Ironically his disavowal of the novel did his cause greater harm. It hampered future generations, who Grove said were his true public, from giving his novel the serious consideration which he desired. Grove's rationalizations now may be ignored and *Settlers of the Marsh* may be regarded as an accurate statement of Grove's artistic purpose.

Notes

[1]   As of June 30, 1975, *Settlers of the Marsh* had sold 29,832 copies in the NCL edition first published in 1965. *Fruits of the Earth*, published the same year, had sold 26,988. (McClelland and Stewart to Makow, July 14, 1975).
Ronald Sutherland and Wilfred Eggleston describe *Settlers of the Marsh* as Grove's finest achievement. W. E. Collins writes in 1946: "Le conflict tragique est souvent evoqué dans les livres de Grove mais nulle part avec autant de succès que dans *Settlers of the Marsh*, ou il atteint aux proportions d'une tragedie classique et represente une des plus grandes reussites artistiques de Grove."

[2]   F. P. Grove, *In Search of Myself*, introduction by D. O. Spettigue (Toronto: McClelland and Stewart, 1974), p. 352. (Hereafter referred to as *ISM*).

[3]   Grove to Pacey, June 1, 1943. Unless otherwise indicated, letters may be found in the Grove Collection at the University of Manitoba.

[4]   *ISM*, p. 379.

[5]   Grove to Pacey, April 2, 1941.

[6]   F. P. Grove, Unpublished Address: "Certain Phases of My Life", (1940), p. 11, Grove Collection. Grove also refers to this miracle in *ISM*, p. 409.

[7]   Phelps to Grove, July 12, 1923.

[8]   Phelps to Grove, November 15, 1925.

[9]   Pierce to Grove, June 15, 1925.

[10] Pierce to Grove, June 24, 1925.
[11] D. O. Spettigue, *FPG: The European Years* (Ottawa: Oberon, 1973), p. 68.
[12] F. P. Grove, "Apologia pro vita et opere sua", *Canadian Forum*, XI (August, 1931), p. 420.
[13] Grove to Kirkconnell, January 24, 1928.
[14] Pierce to Grove, November 10, 1925.
[15] Pierce to Grove, March 15, 1926.
[16] Grove to Moore, November 17, 1925. (Lorne Pierce Collection, Queen's University).
[17] Ryerson to Grove, October 4, 1926, January 29, 1927.
[18] Grove to Kirkconnell, January 24, 1928.
[19] *ISM*, p. 381.
[20] Margaret Stobie, *Frederick Philip Grove* (New York: Twayne, 1973), pp. 111-114.
[21] "The Search for Frederick Philip Grove" *CBC Wednesday Night* broadcast in December 1962. Tape transcript in Grove Collection. Part I, p. 17.
[22] Grove to A. M. Bothwell, November 18, 1925.
[23] Grove to Moore, November 30, 1925 (Queen's).
[24] Grove to Moore, December 21, 1925.
[25] Moore to Grove, December 30, 1925.
[26] Pierce to Grove, March 24, 1926.
[27] Pierce to Grove, April 21, 1926 and April 28, 1926.
[28] *ISM*, p. 387.
[29] Grove to Pierce, September 12, 1925 (Queen's).
[30] F. P. Grove, Unpublished Address: "Some Aspects of a Writer's Life", (1935), p. 13.
[31] Grove to Miller, November 14, 1926.
[32] Desmond Pacey, *Frederick Philip Grove* (Toronto: Ryerson, 1945), p. 45.
[33] "The Search for Frederick Philip Grove", CBC tape transcription, II, p. 37.
[34] Thomas Saunders, "Introduction", *Settlers of the Marsh*, (Toronto: McClelland and Stewart, 1965), pp. vii, xii.
[35] Professor Sutherland guesses correctly that the shorter version is "most likely a happy improvement over the original, ... for Grove had a tendency to overload his works with explanatory detail ...." But Sutherland goes on to state, incorrectly, that Grove indicates omissions "by the use of ellipses." *Frederick Philip Grove* (Toronto: McClelland and Stewart, 1969), p. 47. Professor Spettigue writes: "The number of dots in the printed *Settlers of the Marsh* testifies to the impatience of the editor with Grove's dogged perseverance." Spettigue goes on to cite a comment by Pierce that Grove had a slavish tendency to accumulate detail. *Frederick Philip Grove* (Toronto: Copp Clark, 1969), p. 90. Spettigue has told me that he would now retract the suggestions that Pierce edited Groves manuscript and inserted the dots.
[36] Stobie, p. 83.
[37] J. Lee Thompson, "In Search of Order: The Structure of Grove's *Settlers of the Marsh*", *Journal of Canadian Fiction*, III, 2, 1974, pp. 65-73. Reprinted in a somewhat altered form in the present volume.
[38] *ISM*, p. 379.
[39] Macmillan to Grove, February 25, 1924.
[40] McClelland and Stewart to Grove, January 30, 1924.
[41] *ISM*, p. 381. According to Pierce, he agreed to read the Ms. the

following day. If this is true, the breakfast meeting took place February 11, 1925.

42 "The Search for Frederick Philip Grove", CBC tape transcript, II, p. 16.

43 Pierce to Grove, April 8, 1925 (Queen's).

44 Although Stobie does not mention and refute Grove's statements, her brief account is consistent with these conclusions. *Frederick Philip Grove*, p. 78.

45 Grove to Pierce, September 12, 1925.

46 *ISM*, p. 351.

47 Grove to Carleton Stanley, November 3, 1945.

48 F. P. Grove, Unpublished Address: "The Novel", April 10, 1934, p. 16.

49 Interview with Mr. and Mrs. Otto Brown, Amaranth, Manitoba, May 1975.

50 Spettigue, *Frederick Philip Grove*, p. 91.

51 *ISM*, p. 384.

52 Professor Spettigue was kind enough to show me examples of Grove's German work where dots and other devices are used for effect.

53 Stobie, p. 77.

54 Phelps to Grove, January 20, 1926.

MARTHA OSTENSO

OSTENSO REVISITED

Stanley S. Atherton

In a sense, Martha Ostenso is not a Canadian writer at all. Like the wild geese of her best known novel, she came from and soon returned to the United States; her literary career flourished almost entirely south of the forty-ninth parallel. Born on September 17, 1900 in the Norwegian village of Haukeland, near Bergen, she was taken to the mid-western United States two years later when her parents emigrated. For the next thirteen years, she was to live in a string of "mean yet glorious little towns" in Minnesota and South Dakota, and dream of becoming a writer.[1] Precocious and talented, she was being paid for contributions to the Junior page of the *Minneapolis Journal* by the age of eleven. And soon after the family moved to Brandon, Manitoba at the beginning of the First World War, she had won a prize for poetry in a contest sponsored by the *Winnipeg Telegram*.[2]

As the title of a literary notebook she kept at the time suggests, even as a schoolgirl she enjoyed casting herself in the role of creative writer. "Runaway Rhymes: A Book of Spasmodic outbursts from the cranium of ye youthfull poet Laureate of ye Goldenn Schoole Days" contains entries dating from January, 1915, and includes the only manuscript section still existing of her first novel, *Wild Geese*.[3] On graduation from Brandon Collegiate Institute, she moved to Winnipeg, where she attended classes at the University of Manitoba, taught school and worked as a reporter until she left for New York in 1921.

In New York she found a position as social worker with the Brooklyn Bureau of Charities, and continued to write. She took a course in creative writing called Techniques of the Novel at Columbia University, worked on a novel entitled "The Passionate Flight" she had begun in Manitoba, and began to submit her poems and stories to the magazines. By the end of 1924 she had achieved a modest success, with work appearing in a number of periodicals including the *American Scandinavian Review*, *Literary Digest*, *Poetry* and the *Saturday Review of Literature*. And she had published her first book, a collection of poems entitled *A Far Land*.[4]

In 1925 she entered "The Passionate Flight" under the revised title of "Wild Geese" in a competition sponsored by *The Pictorial*

Review, the publishing firm of Dodd, Mead and Company and the Famous Players-Lasky Corporation to find the best first novel by an American author. It won the $13,500 first prize over 1,388 other entries. More than half a century later *Wild Geese* still validates the judges' decision, for it is on this remarkably good novel, more than any of the others which bear her name, that her reputation rests today.

Wild Geese grew out of Ostenso's personal experience. In one of her summer breaks from study in Winnipeg, probably in 1918, she taught in a one-room schoolhouse in the farming community of Hayland, near the Narrows of Lake Manitoba.[5] She boarded with a family named Hay, and modelled one of her characters in the novel, Judith, on the Hay's daughter Aggie.[6] Hayland was to provide her with far more than the setting and a model for one of her principal characters, however. Here in a frontier community, at what must have seemed the edge of civilization, she was able to observe for the first time that special combination of unrestrained human passion and elemental natural forces which could galvanize her peculiar creative imagination.

Clara Thomas has suggested that Martha Ostenso's imagination "did not move toward the heroic, but rather toward the grotesque."[7] Whatever the reasons for this imaginative cast of mind — it is intriguing to speculate, for example, on childhood enchantment with the darker aspects of Norse mythology — it is clearly at work in *Wild Geese* and, to a lesser extent, in *The Young May Moon*, the only other novel in which she used a Manitoba setting. The idea of the grotesque suggests the unnatural, the distorted and the absurd, and these elements are all present in her characterization of Caleb, one of the most memorable figures in Canadian fiction. Caleb Gare is at the centre of *Wild Geese*, a mad and monstrous being who terrorizes his wife and children, cheats and bullies his neighbours, and is seen as "a spiritual counterpart of the land, as harsh, as demanding, as tyrannical as the very soil from which he drew his existence."[8] The source of Caleb's malevolence is his lust for power, his insensate need to dominate; and it is exercised over his family through the unwilling help of his wife, Amelia, who will do anything to stop Caleb revealing the parentage of her illegitimate son, Mark Jordan. Inevitably the children of Caleb and Amelia become unnatural caricatures, subjugating their dreams and desires to Caleb's will, beaten into passive acceptance of their lot by his unquenchable appetite for power, wealth and land. Ellen, the elder daughter, "reasoned only as Caleb had taught her to reason, in terms of advantage to their land and to him" (p. 96); her twin brother Martin "worked with the bowed, unquestioning resignation of an old unfruitful man" (p. 36). Only one of them, seventeen year old Judith, finds strength to rebel against her father's oppression.

It is in the confrontation between Judith and Caleb that the important issues of *Wild Geese* are dramatized. Their struggle is a contest of individual wills; but it is also a collision between the life-denying forces embodied by Caleb and the life-embracing and affirming forces which Judith represents. The opposition is clearly apparent in their differing reactions to the land. For Caleb the land is something to be owned and dominated. It is above all else "*his* land", and whatever it produced is the "result of *his* industry" (p. 249). Although for him the time of growth in the fields is "a terrific, prolonged hour of passion," it is a passion perverted:

> While he was raptly considering the tender field of flax — now in blue flower — Amelia did not exist to him ... Caleb would stand for long moments outside the fence beside the flax. Then he would turn quickly to see that no one was looking. He would creep between the wires and run his hand across the flowering, gentle tops of the growth. A stealthy caress — more intimate than any he had ever given to woman. (p. 171).

"The land has become a substitute for Caleb's wife," as Laurence Ricou has pointed out, and like Amelia, the land must be bent to his will.[9] It remains an implacable adversary, however, offering him only the perennial challenge "to force from the soil all that it would withhold" (p. 250). Blinded to other considerations, Caleb comes to see the land (even his favoured field of flax) only in terms of profit, as a means to secure ever greater amounts of the wealth and power he obsessively craves. [10]

In sharp contrast, Judith's relationship with the natural world is one of passionate kinship. Early in the novel she lies naked on the warm spring earth, revelling in "the waxy feeling of new sunless vegetation under her," knowing intuitively that she had been "singled ... out from the rest of the Gares" to apprehend the mystery of life, "something forbiddenly beautiful, secret as one's own body" (p. 67). Judith embraces the natural world, literally and figuratively, in a scene that is powerfully reminiscent of D. H. Lawrence:

> ... at the spring ... she threw herself upon the moss
> under the birches, grasping the slender trunks of the
> trees in her hands and straining her body against the
> earth. She has taken off the heavy overalls and the
> coolness of the ground crept into her loose clothing.
> The light from the setting sun seemed to run down the
> smooth white bark of the birches like gilt. There was no
> movement, except the narrow trickle of the water from
> the spring, and the occasional flare of a bird above the
> brown depth of the pool. There was no sound save the
> tuning of the frogs in the marsh that seemed far away,
> and the infrequent call of a catbird on the wing. Here
> was clarity undreamed of, such clarity as the soul
> should have in desire and fulfillment. Judith held her
> breasts in ecstasy. (p. 216)

Judith's openness, her ability to accept and respond to the elemental rhythms of the natural world, stands in direct opposition to the perverted responses of Caleb, who must turn everything he touches to his own unnatural ends.

Physically as well as spiritually, Caleb and Judith are poles apart. Caleb is physically repulsive. His "tremendous and massive head" at first "gave him a towering appearance. [But] when attention was directed to the lower half of his body, he seemed visibly to dwindle" (p. 5). "Broad and bent over," he moves with a "dragging step", "his top-heavy body forming an arc toward the earth" (pp. 262, 269, 270). Other characters in the novel see him as a hypocrite, "too sly for honest people," an insane egoist, and a murderer (p. 286). In extra-human terms he is "demoniacal", "an old satyr", and "the devil himself" (pp. 8, 36, 104). Judith, on the other hand, is a sensual passionate beauty, "the embryonic ecstasy of all life" (p. 35). She is "like some dark young goddess," and sees herself as "an alien spirit ... in no way related to the life about her," unwilling to submit like her mother and siblings to a "meager and warped" life under her tyrannical father (pp. 97, 124, 332).

She defies him openly, denouncing his insatiable demands on members of the family, and clandestinely, in meetings with her lover Sven Sandbo, a young Norwegian "god" from the neighbouring farm (p. 216). When Caleb threatens to beat her into submission, after spying on her love-making with Sven, she flings an axe at him, narrowly missing his head. The scene is superbly drawn, and provides the novel with a memorable metaphor for the fundamental antagonism of the forces Judith and Caleb represent. The confrontation is not climactic: Caleb has yet to provoke the terrible defiance of Amelia. But, it does dramatically reinforce the patterns of conflict — repression and freedom, denial and affirmation — which are at the heart of *Wild Geese*. After the attempt to kill her father, Judith is virtually imprisoned on the farm and Caleb's tyranny seems unassailable. A resolution is achieved when Judith, who is bearing Sven's child, is helped to escape by Lind Archer, the school-teacher who boards at the Gares, and by Amelia, who is unwilling to let Caleb destroy her daughter's life as he had her own. Caleb's death, which swiftly follows Judith's flight into life, is both appalling and ironically appropriate.[11] Frantically trying to save his precious flax from fire, he is trapped in the muskeg that borders it and swallowed up in "the over-strong embrace of the earth" (p. 352).

It has been argued that the resolution of *Wild Geese* is too compressed, that "the suddenness with which the fire follows Amelia's critical defiance and Caleb's moment of 'shame and self-loathing' is inconsistent with the subtle development of the novel to this point."[12] Such a reading fails to take into account the enormity of Caleb's transgressions, which require a retributive devastation of his being that must be swift and complete to achieve the optimum dramatic effect. So it is appropriate that man and nature combine in a single powerfully-drawn sequence of events to annihilate him — spiritually through the knowledge of Judith's escape and the harrowing impact of Ameilia's defiance, physically by earth, air, fire and water. The resolution is artistically consistent with the rest of the novel: there is no place for subtlety here.

It would be foolish to claim that *Wild Geese* is technically flawless. It was, after all, a first novel. There are problems with point of view, as Carlyle King pointed out in his introduction to the New Canadian Library edition.[13] Although much of the story is revealed through the consciousness of Lind Archer, there are frequent forays into the minds of Judith, Amelia and Caleb. Dr. King found these shifts disconcerting, but they are unlikely to bother most readers, since they do provide consistent and credi-

ble motivation for the actions of the central characters. Ostenso's
unsure control of dialoque is more jarring. It is particularly
noticeable in the prissy speeches of Mark Jordan, though there
are times when the language of most of the main characters is
stilted and unconvincing. On the other hand, dialogue carries
much of the burden of characterization in the description of Sigri
Sandbo, Sven's mother, and it is splendidly effective:

> "It iss him, upon the vall. And a stinker he vass, too.
> Good Land, I say, t'ousand times a day, I em heppy he
> iss gone. Vhat he could drink, that von! Never vonce
> sober in six years!"

> "Was he not kind to you?" Lind asked gently.

"Kind? Him? Good land, I vass a dog under him. Now I live
good, not much money, but no dirt from him, t'ank God!" She
lifted her eyes up to the photograph, and Lind saw unmistakably
a look of wistfulness in them. (pp. 29-30)

There are minor irritants — the heavy-handed treatment of
Judith's "secret" pregnancy is an example — but these are rare.
More predictable is the pleasure to be derived from Ostenso's
mastery of mood, in particular from her ability to capture in a
few sure strokes the elements in the natural world which complement and highlight the emotional situation of her characters.
One of the finest examples of this is her description of Anton
Klovacz' final journey, as Mark Jordan and the farmer's eldest
son take his body to the Catholic mission for burial. The passage,
too long to quote here, is marked by a mood of great loneliness,
and in that sense it offers a paradigm of the entire novel.

For *Wild Geese* is a superb study of isolation: each of the central
characters (and many of the minor ones as well) is touched by
loneliness and forced in some way to explore its mystery. It is
a powerful vision, reinforced by Ostenso's skillful use of the
words "alone", "lonely", and "loneliness" in one scene after
another to create an effect that is almost incantatory. The reader,
caught up in the novelist's fascination with the "unmeasurable
Alone surrounding each soul," is left at the end with the indeli-
ble, haunting image of the wild geese, whose "cry smote upon
the heart like the loneliness of the universe ... a magnificent seeking through solitude — and endless quest" (pp. 57, 356).

Ostenso's second Manitoba novel, *The Young May Moon*, appeared four years after the publication of *Wild Geese*. It is, as Clara

Thomas has observed, "a novel whose seriousness of theme is more satisfyingly matched by its tightness of structure" than is the case in *Wild Geese*.[14] This achievement should not be attributed solely to an improvement in Ostenso's control of her material, however, for there is evidence to suggest it is the result of dual authorship.

It is highly probable that *The Young May Moon* was written in careful collaboration with Douglas Durkin, the Canadian academic and author who became Ostenso's mentor as early as 1919 and her husband in 1944.[15] Durkin's command of narrative technique may be seen in a number of ways: the development of events in this novel is more measured than in *Wild Geese*, the opposition of characters is more carefully balanced, their confrontations are more predictable and controlled, the opening and closing scenes are neatly parallel and echo one another, and so on. It is important to remember, however, that the darkly powerful imagination that informed *Wild Geese* is still at work in *The Young May Moon*, exploring and developing meaningful patterns of isolation and integration, denial and affirmation.

The Young May Moon, set in the fictional prairie town of Amaranth, is the story of Marcia Vorse, the young wife of Rolf Gunther.[16] After a winter of living in "the house of Dorcas Gunther," the dominating, repressive mother-in-law who has hung a sample above their bed with "Repent Ye!" "worked in red wool against a white background," Marcia is reduced to pleading with Rolf for physical love (p. 21). After a passionate argument she impulsively runs away, returning a few hours later to find her husband drowned, a probable suicide. She stays on with Dorcas, partly to atone for the guilt she feels over Rolf's death, and submits to a soul-destroying regimen of domestic and spiritual tyranny.

With the painful recognition that her life has become "dwarfed and twisted under the old woman's blighting intolerance," Marcia is finally able to confess her "responsibility" for Rolf's drowning to Dorcas, and to leave (p. 102). Her departure marks a turning point in the novel. In self-imposed isolation in a ruined house at the edge of town, she wrestles with her special demons, by turns exultant and terrified at what is happening to her. In the end, after a harrowing journey through self reproach, denial, doubt and fear, she comes to terms with herself and her obsession, helped in no small way by the young doctor Paul Brule, who has survived a similar crisis of his own.

The Young May Moon, unlike Wild Geese, was never made into a film, nor was it ever issued in a paperback edition, but it deserves to be better known. Indeed, it is arguable that the two novels should be read in tandem, for The Young May Moon offers an intriguing reversal of the pattern of characterization evident in Wild Geese. In both novels the central characters are obsessed by unacceptable variations of the most basic human events, a birth that is illegitimate and a death that is premature. In coming to terms with their obsessions, the protagonists move in opposite directions on a moral spectrum. Caleb Gare sees himself as a victim and turns into a vengeful, life-denying tyrant, while Marcia Vorse, at first an apologist for atonement, rids herself of "the recurrent obsession" and joyously reaffirms life: "all eternity was [for her now] but a single fierce stroke of rapture" (p. 298). The treatment of other characters in the novel reinforces this pattern.[17]

Ostenso's influence on other prairie writers has received little attention from contemporary critics, yet it offers a number of avenues for research. The connection with Margaret Laurence, for example, is rich in possibilities. Marcia Vorse would seem to prefigure Rachel Cameron in A Jest of God. Some of the external similarities between Ostenso's own life and that of Morag Gunn in The Diviners suggest that Laurence may have had her in mind when she created Morag. And the imagery of the geese in The Diviners finds an obvious parallel in Wild Geese. There is also an interesting parallel between Amaranth in The Young May Moon and Sinclair Ross's Horizon in As For Me And My House; and it may be that the character of Judith in that novel was suggested by Ostenso's Judith. On a lighter note, one might speculate where Aritha van Herk found the model for her pig farmer, the title character in Judith, bearing in mind that in Wild Geese it was Judith Gare who "fed the pigs" (p. 232).

It is demonstrably clear that the Manitoba novels of Martha Ostenso are worth serious critical evaluation. Although the author spent only a short time in Canada, her work represents a significant contribution to Canadian prairie fiction. Like the best work of her contemporaries, her novels "dramatize the difficulties of affirming life in a world constantly threatened by absurdity, suffering, and death."[18] It is time we paid her greater attention.

Notes

1   Grant Overton, *The Women Who Make Our Novels* (New York: Essay Index Reprint Series, 1967), p. 247.
2   Manuscript note dated January 12, 1915 beside poem entitled "The Price of War" in Martha Ostenso's notebook.
3   The section consists of eight pages from Chapter III, with minor variations from the published text. The notebook was made available to me through the kindness of Professor Stan Stanko, London, Ontario, Miss Ostenso's literary executor.
4   Martha Ostenso, *A Far Land* (New York: Thomas Seltzer, 1924).
5   Hayland became Oeland in *Wild Geese*. The pronunciation is similar in Norwegian and Icelandic.
6   This information was given to me by Professor Stanko, and has been corroborated elsewhere.
7   Clara Thomas, "Martha Ostenso's Trial of Strength", in Donald G. Stephens, ed., *Writers of the Prairies* (Vancouver: U.B.C. Press, 1973), p. 41. Hereafter cited as Thomas.
8   Martha Ostenso, *Wild Geese* (New York: Dodd, Mead & Co., 1925). All page references in citations are to this original edition.
9   Laurence Ricou, *Vertical Man Horizontal World*: Man and Landscape in Canadian Prairie Fiction (Vancouver: U.B.C. Press, 1973), p. 75. Hereafter cited as Ricou.
10 See *Wild Geese*, p. 311, final paragraph.
11 Judith's escape with Sven is the "passionate flight" which gave the novel its working title.
12 Ricou, p. 79.
13 Martha Ostenso, *Wild Geese* (New York: Dodd, Mead & Co., 1925; rpt. Toronto: McClelland and Stewart, 1961, introduction by Carlyle King.).
14 Thomas, p. 43.
15 This information was given to me by Professor Stanko, who has described published contracts in his possession which link the two writers.
16 Martha Ostenso, *The Young May Moon* (New York: Dodd, Mead & Co., 1929). All page references in citations are to this original edition. Ostenso may simply have used the name of Amaranth, a small town quite near the Narrows of Lake Manitoba, as a substitute for Brandon, whose general topography and possession of a college match the characteristics of the fictional Amaranth.
17 Foils for the protagonists offer an interesting extension of the pattern. Judith Gare's youth and openness oppose Caleb's age and habitual egoism in *Wild Geese*; in *The Young May Moon* Dorcas Gunther's age and puritanical nature oppose Marcia's youth and sensuality.
18 D. G. Jones, *Butterfly on Rock* (Toronto: University of Toronto Press, 1970), p. 8. The quoted passage did not originally refer to Ostenso, but offers a particularly apt description of her work.

MORLEY CALLAGHAN

MORLEY CALLAGHAN'S PRACTICAL MONSTERS: DOWNHILL FROM WHERE AND WHEN?

Wilf Cude

"I know why I like you," Carol Finley tells Ira Groome, her lover and the protagonist of Morley Callaghan's latest novel, *Close to the Sun Again*! "You're a monster .... I'll bet you don't throw a shadow when you're walking in the sunlight."[1] Ira Groome is, in truth, a monster — a moral monster, and Callaghan makes us see exactly how he got that way. An imposing figure at fifty-three, a much decorated veteran of the Battle of the Atlantic nicknamed "Ribbons," a dominating presence in corporate boardrooms after the war, Groome seems a most unlikely candidate for monstrosity.

But Carol, assessing him with her "crazy" blue eyes, knows well enough what he lacks. "You've no past," (CSA p. 29) she says simply, touching him on a raw psychological wound. For "Ribbons" Groome, "the Commander" to past and present associates alike, had ruthlessly amputated all memory of his innocent youth in response to one night of trauma during the war: and from that moment on, he forced his way through existence as a dispassionate, even cold calculating, man of reason, masking with a worldly persona the poor emotionally-truncated thing he had elected to become.

Alerted by his mistress to something he had "long ago forgotten," that "before the war he had been another kind of man," he is moved despite himself to muse over his metamorphosis into "this Commander who might never again be able to hear the voices of his own heart" (CSA p. 2). The death of his dipsomaniac wife, Julia; the estrangement from his hippy son Chris; the resignation from his position as Chairman of the Brazilian Power Corporation in Sao Paulo; and his return to Toronto as Police Commissioner; bringing Carol Finley almost casually into his bed: these events free him to confront his self-imposed isolation, to ask the question he has avoided for decades. "Downhill from where and when?" (CSA p. 32). It is a question that informs, not only this retrospective and summational book, but also the entire body of Callaghan's work.

Carol's words only trigger a reaction that had been building in Ira for a long time. His resignation from the Brazilian Power

Corporation came swiftly after he saw his colleagues in a different manner. "These weren't his people," he suddenly understood: "these careful men, these bookkeepers who knew only the tragedies of trivia, and nothing of a beauty born in excess."

Drifting loosely in a daydream, he visualized "lawless men and women, holed up somewhere, nursing passions that made life so real"; and he recoiled almost in pain from a touch to his wound, the unavoidable realization that one such as he could not "feel" anything of "their ruthless passions and their suffering." He was a monster of practicality, and he was hurt by his exclusion from a more vital, important and demanding state of being. "He felt fettered, pushed away, scorned, and doomed to stay where he was and as he was."

His agonized stream of questions "Yet why? What had he done? Where had he done it?" (CSA p. 5). Would it bring him, first to Carol and the restated question, "Downhill from where and when?" and then to the answers he seeks? The process is a complex one, involving the disinterment of memories long ago excised and laid away, memories of Gina Bixby and Jethroe Chone. "Wild ones, weren't they, sir?" (CSA p. 27) asks Horler anxiously, the former navy bosun turned faithful manservant, hesistantly acquiescing in the Commander's probing of a past long repressed and discarded. Wild, indeed. Wild and lawless and yet terribly, awesomely alive, matching in their own excesses even the excesses of the Second World War. They passed in an instant, an instant either to be nurtured or slashed away, for it underscored the dichotomy of Ira's own soul — a dichotomy Callaghan has probed ceaselessly, in one form or another, over the course of his lengthy career.

"Downhill from where and when," within the context of Ira Groome's life in *Close to the Sun Again*, is readily answered: from the moment Ira decided to repress his memories of a Carley float swirling across a frigid moonlit Atlantic, when Jethroe Chone and Gina Bixby vanished before his horrified eyes, eluding his numbed and bloody hands forever. We will return to that; but we should perhaps first determine, within the context of Callaghan's full range of writing, where this central question is anticipated with the greatest clarity and force.

My choice will no doubt surprise most Callaghan enthusiasts: within the pages of *Luke Baldwin's Vow*, the usually-neglected novel intended for young readers, the novel that appeared in shorter form in the *Saturday Evening Post* in 1947, reappeared in full length in 1948, and then — so far as literary analysis was concerned — vanished. Like Jethroe Chone and Gina Bixby, gone without a trace.

And that is something of a pity, since it is here, in the pages of a book written with particular attention to the dichotomy between reason and emotion that sunders each person's soul, that we can trace Callaghan's fascination with the evils of our workaday middle-class world. Or, to rephrase the matter somewhat, if we are ever tempted to wonder whatever became of Luke Baldwin when he grew up, we need only move from the centre of the Callaghan canon to the end. The chances are, I would argue, that little Luke might have turned out perilously akin to Ira Groome — practical monster.

Luke should be of interest, if for no other reason than that he constitutes Callaghan's most unqualified portrait of an innocent. Bereft of his mother when he was an infant and of his father when he was about to enter adolescence, Luke bravely faces, at the novel's opening, a new life with his Uncle Henry and Aunt Helen. He is a sensitive, perceptive and intelligent boy eager to learn from his practical uncle, just as he had promised his dying father he would try to do. Moreover, his uncle and aunt are kindly folk, intent upon making this bright young nephew feel at home.

All should go well, but everything goes wrong, simply because Uncle Henry's practicality renders him monstrously blind to any values other than the economic ones. "In the long run you pay for what you get,"[2] he tells Luke; and, from that pronouncement, Luke works out the essence of the philosophy he is expected to acquire. "A thing that was needed had to be obtained. A thing that was no longer needed had to be tossed aside" (LBV p. 40).

This is a philosophy he cannot accept, for he knows it threatens Dan, the old purebred collie that Uncle Henry intends to destroy. To Luke, Dan is an almost mystical presence, "more than a dog; the collie seemed to have come out of that good part of his life, the part he had shared with his own father" (LBV p. 132). To Uncle Henry, Dan can only be useful one last time, as an example to his too-imaginative nephew of how "you have to do the sensible thing" (LBV p. 148). Luke's desperate struggle to save the dog becomes an outward manifestation of the conflict between the polarities of his own young soul. "You'd wonder, wouldn't you, Dan," he confides to the dog, "that my father and Uncle

Henry could be so far apart on what was useful in the world?''
(LBV p. 109). His father, the quiet and dedicated doctor who read
''fairy stories by Hans Andersen'' to him when he ''was small''
(LBV p. 25), would never destroy a faithful old dog; but his uncle, the hearty and prosperous mill-owner who denounced the
''fairy book'' as ''lies'' (LBV p. 27), could not tolerate the irrita-
tion of an animal ''no good even as a watchdog'' (LBV p. 27).
Luke loved his father, but he admires his uncle; and, in shielding
the dog, he can remain faithful to the one only by opposing the
other — choosing emotion and intuition over practicality and
calculation. It is a choice Callaghan would have all his innocents
make, though the choice is rarely possible and never unequivocal
in the benighted money-grubbing world he depicts with such accuracy and distaste.

Even Luke, sustained by his youthful resilience and his
awareness of a ''world of strange wonders'' (LBV p. 52) cannot
hold aloof from the taint of practicality. Drawn with Dan to the
house of Willie Stanowski, a Polish mill-hand who is ''quick and
intelligent'' and who has ''eight children,'' he enjoys a taste of
life his practical relatives would keep from him. One of the
Stanowski children is Tillie, ''a pretty and friendly kid'' (LBV p.
87) of thirteen, a classmate of his; and another is Maria, the eldest
at twenty with ''the largest dark eyes'' and hair ''so black it gleam-
ed in the sun,'' the ''prettiest girl Luke had even seen'' (LBV p.
90). Luke and Dan cavort about the old home with the Stanowski
brood, until Maria brings the unrestrained romp to a close by playing the piano and singing ''*Alouette.*''

Luke's pleasure with this hearty approach to life, however, is
abruptly terminated when Aunt Helen forbids him to associate
further with people who ''can't do you any good'' (LBV p. 93).
Against his will, he avoids Tillie and stays away from the
Stanowski place, ''filled with discontent because all the wild hap-
piness contained in that house was never to be touched by him''
(LBV p. 94). He is tempted one moonlit night to approach the
Stanowski place again, listening to the music and the laughter;
but, despite Dan's blandishments, he dare not knock and enter.
He walks away, knowing that ''for years afterwards the
Stanowskis would live in his mind as a fabulous family, and that
whenever he heard a piano in the darkness he would remember''
(LBV p. 96).

The poignancy of his loss is driven home to him the very next day, in a wounding encounter with Maria. When she realizes he will not be back, she shrugs her shoulders "contemptuously," and says "I'll see that Tillie doesn't stay around here." She speaks in a soft voice, "as if she had forgotten Luke was there" (LBV p. 97). This is, in effect, banishment from a more passionate world; and Luke is left disconsolate, to reflect that "perhaps God hadn't intended him to be a shrewd and useful man" (LBV p. 98).

Callaghan renders Luke's spiritual failure more apparent by having the boy wander aimlessly in the woods with Dan, seeking in solitude some clue concerning what is happening to him. After eating some raspberries, he notices his hands "were stained as if with blood," and he concludes: "It's blood on my hands from some great wrong I've done" (LBV p. 108). The "wrong" is in fact his acceptance of his uncle's values, no matter how reluctantly and no matter with what justification.

This perception is designed to undermine the otherwise superficial, slick and happy ending, in which Luke saves Dan by making Uncle Henry "a practical proposition" (LBV p. 183). Acting on the advice of old Mr. Kemp, a sympathetic neighbour whose attitude reminds Luke of his father, the boy offers to pay for Dan's keep with the money he will earn by tending Mr. Kemp's cows. Confronted with the boy and dog, shaken by forces he only dimly apprehends, Uncle Henry accepts the arrangement: and Luke is left with his dog, to make in the last paragraph the vow of the novel's title.

> Putting his head on the dog's neck, he vowed to himself fervently that he would always have some money on hand, no matter what became of him, so that he would be able to protect all that was truly valuable from the practical people in the world. (LBV p. 182)

For Luke Baldwin, it could be downhill from there and then. To earn Uncle Henry's respect, he had to fashion himself into a junior version of Uncle Henry; and that, we have already seen from Maria's reaction, converts the triumph over Dan into a Pyrrhic victory at best. Spiritually speaking, Luke has won only by losing; he has moved, with all the commitment of his youthful innocence, further into the world of the practical man — the world that, in Callaghan's view, produces moral monsters.

The relevance of *Luke Baldwin's Vow* to *Close to the Sun Again* should be apparent from the details of the latest novel, since the progression of the young Ira Groome from innocence to monstrosity is more than slightly reminiscent of Luke's movement towards what Uncle Henry termed "the hard bright world" (LBV p. 28) of the practical man. Before the war, Ira was a junior archeologist working "on a dig in the Yucatan" (CSA p. 75), seeking in "a great mound covered with vegetation" some hint of "the life that had been lived there." But he could not shake the eerie sensation that "he was working in a boneyard, a graveyard, and the skulls they dug up, the ruins, the sacrificial stones, told nothing ...."

To ease the sensation, he turned to an ardent relationship with a local girl, an eighteen-year-old named Marina with "black hair" to "her waist," a "simple warmth" and "great dignity." He finds "a strange, terribly heightened feeling of enchantment" (CSA p. 80), one that leads him to taunt his superior with the statement: "You're dead, Dr. Ball." The senior professor, enraged at this insolence from a junior walking off the project, screams "come back here" (CSA p. 81): and the men fight, before Ira leaves. This story fascinates Gina Bixby, the sensual castaway Groome's corvette picks up from a drifting boat during the Battle of the Atlantic. Something of a mystery herself, accompanied even in shipwreck by a polished thug named Jethroe Chone, she is drawn to Ira's account of what he had learned from Marina: that the Mayan vision was "cruel and senseless, a nightmare" and "all we can do is make something beautiful out of the nightmare" (CSA p. 81).

Confiding to Ira her own philosophy, "if we do know in this world, then we should seize the time of knowing" (CSA p. 110), she tells her own wild, inchoate and barely believable tale. The fragile harmony building between them, menaced by the ominous presence of Chone, is shattered when the corvette takes a torpedo — spilling Gina, Chone, Ira and two sailors into a cold and moonlit sea, where they cling for very life to a Carley float. Ira had received a nasty splinter wound in his arm, and "in the dark he could feel the warm blood in his hand" (CSA p. 144).

Like Luke, the still-innocent Lieutenant Groome had encountered two attractive girls, one older and more sophisticated than the other, who introduced him into a world of passions. And, like Luke, the still-innocent Lieutenant Groome was to prove insufficient for that world: he would turn away from it, a sin against the self greater than any other, a sin marked by his own blood on his hands. For Jethroe Chone, only a day before the corvette went down, had challenged his claim to passionate life with words suggesting his own taunt to the professor in Yucatan: "You've got the cold hand, Mr. Groome .... Archeology, my ass. You're a gravedigger" (CSA p. 128).

Lurching across the frigid night sea, clinging to each other for warmth, and love, and life itself, the five in the float move towards the time when Ira will fail as a human being. Chone, hopelessly wounded, whispers "contemptuously" to Ira, "You were nothing" (CSA p. 155); and then, renouncing his own claim to life, slips back into the dark waters. Gina, watching, screams, "Jethroe, come back here ... come back, you bastard"; and then, as nobody else moves, she dives after him into those same dark waters. Ira is left, "bewildered by his stunned moment of indecision" (CSA p. 156), with numbness spreading up his arm and his own blood on his hands, gathering the thoughts that will later convince him "he had been betrayed" (CSA p. 164). His response to those thoughts, when he recollects them aboard the rescue packet that lifted the survivors out of the sea the next day, is to seal his soul off from all but the practical, immediate, tangible world:

> ... he lay down and shut his ears to the moaning wind, and shut his heart to his wonder about Chone, and to the voices in his own heart, and thought instead about tomorrow and about being dressed and out on the deck. He concentrated on seeing himself in his lieutenant's uniform .... (CSA p. 165)

Downhill from there and then. At that moment,"Ribbons" Groome was born, the man of prudence replacing the wide-eyed innocent questing after passion. But, as "Ribbons" himself comes to conclude decades later, "prudence in the heart makes cowards of us all" (CSA p. 48). The echo of Hamlet applies to him, to Luke, to all the other innocents who sell themselves into practicality in the Callaghan canon.

Nowhere in Callaghan's writing is this complex of themes entwined in a more accomplished manner than in the short story "Getting on in the World." Henry Forbes, piano player at the Clairmont Hotel on his last two weeks of work before an indefinite lay-off, is joined as he is playing one evening by the kid sister of a former friend. Jean Gorman is a beautiful and impressionable

eighteen-year-old, convinced by her brother Tommy's stories that
Harry must be "a pretty glamorous figure," a man of the world
who "knew everybody in town."[3] Harry is naive enough to be
convinced, in his turn, that this must indeed be so, since this lovely young girl takes it to be evident.

Over the next few days a romance blossoms between the two,
marred slightly for Henry by his feeling that "the pair of them
looked like a couple of kids on a merry-go-round." He would
have preferred a girl "like some of the smart blondes" with "that
lazy, half-mocking aloofness"; (GW p. 42) but he comes to see
Jean anew when Eddie Convey, "who just about ran the city hall
and was one of the hotel owners, too" (GW p. 40), asks him to
send Jean to a party as his place. Jean is reluctant to accept the
offer, until Harry persuades her to oblige by blurting out the truth:
"It looks like I'm through around here. Unless Convey or
somebody like that steps in I'm washed up" (GW p. 40). After
delivering Jean to Convey's apartment, he returns to his piano
and scrutinizes the audience:

> ... his heart began to ache, and he turned around and
> looked at all the well-fed men and their women and he
> heard their deep-toned voices and their lazy laughter
> and he suddenly felt corrupt. (GW pp. 44-5)

He returns to Convey's place, but cannot nerve himself to go in.
Instead, he waits until all the guests leave, and then he waits some
more. At four in the morning, Jean finally comes out, no longer
looking "worried," but rather "blooming, lazy and proud" (GW
p. 45). He accuses her of staying with Convey, "just like a tramp";
and she replies by slapping him, "appraising him contemptuously," and dismissing him with a sudden laugh. "Get back to your
piano," she orders. He mutters: "I'll show you ... I'll show
everybody"; and the story closes with him "watching her go
down the street with a slow, self-satisfied sway of her body" (GW
p. 46).

In my estimation, and making due allowance for the difficulties
of a comparison with a work in translation, the story is fairly rank-
ed as an achievement with Anton Chekhov's "At Sea — A Sailor's
Story." The Chekhov tale is narrated by a sailor, who tells how
he and his father won by lot the privilege of viewing the interior
of a passenger's cabin through two covert peep-holes cut by the
crewmen in the cabin walls. The cabin was usually occupied by

honeymooning couples, and the present occupants seemed especially promising, "a young pastor" and his bride, "a very beautiful, shapely young woman." What the voyeurs witnessed, however, was not the amorous coupling of two attractive people; instead, they watched in a revolted fascination as the pastor sold his bride's favours to a monied elderly tourist. The older sailor, "that drunken, debauched old man," pulled his son away and said: "Let's go away from here! You shouldn't see that. You're still a boy."[4]

The Chekhov tale, in its brevity and precision, constitutes a classic treatment of violated innocence; and the reader is left to ponder the question, with all its convolutions, of just who in the tale was the innocent. We encounter similarly classic elements, executed with a comparable economy and force, in the Callaghan story. Harry, the would-be sophisticate, materializes as a hopelessly naive young man crushed by his own callow ineptitude. And Jean, the archetypal ingenue, the stereotyped girl from the small town come wide-eyed to the city, metamorphoses in a few hours into the knowingly chic sort of woman a man like Harry will lust after in vain. Who, here, was really the innocent? And how could it be that any seeming innocent can fall so readily into the trap of "Getting on in the World?" Callaghan's work, in this story, is unmistakably of enduring value.

It would appear I have come to endorse Edmund Wilson's still controversial dictum that Callaghan is an author "whose work may be mentioned without absurdity in association with Chekhov's ...." Indeed, in the instance of "Getting on in the World," I take the assertion as valid; however, with respect to the entire body of Callaghan's writing, I am not so sure the generalization holds. The scope of this essay prevents me from pursuing the issue further, but this at least in fairness should be said: one work of demonstrable excellence is warrant enough to search for more.

Callaghan's themes are of continuing interest in a materialistic world; his execution of those themes across the full range of his writing should therefore be considered with care, in order to determine exactly to what extent he might be reckoned a figure of world literature. That this process has not already started, at the culmination of decades of recognized and often-praised artistry, is no reflection on Callaghan; it is, rather, yet another indication of the reluctance of Canadian critics to attempt the most fundamental of aesthetic functions — honest evaluation.

Notes

1   Morley Callaghan, *Close to the Sun Again* (Toronto: Macmillan, 1977), p. 29. All subsequent references to this work will be given in parentheses in the text.

2   Morley Callaghan, *Luke Baldwin's Vow* (Toronto: Macmillan, 1974), p. 39. All subsequent references to this work will be given in parentheses in the text.

3   Morley Callaghan, "Getting on in the World" in John Stevens, ed. *Modern Canadian Stories* (New York: Bantam, 1975), p. 40. All subsequent references to this work will be given in parentheses in the text.

4   Anton Chekhov, "At Sea — A Sailor's Story," *Anton Chekhov: Selected Stories*, trans. Ann Dunnigan (New York: Signet, 1960), pp. 33-6.

SINCLAIR ROSS

MRS. BENTLEY AND THE BICAMERAL MIND: A HERMENEUTICAL ENCOUNTER WITH *AS FOR ME AND MY HOUSE*.

John Moss

Virtually all the criticism that has been written about *As For Me and My House* holds in common the intent to explain, to interpret the narrative as if it were a portion of real life, somehow isolated by the author through an act of genius or grace. Critics have offered diverse readings of Sinclair Ross's novel, some of them intriguing, and yet the novel remains remarkably opaque. As much as I enjoy the commentaries by Wilf Cude, Lorraine McMullen, W. H. New, David Stouck, Sandra Djwa and others, I am no closer for reading them to comprehending the nature of Ross's achievement. They have told me about life, a bit about style and about voice, less about form, but (and I have been among them in writing towards meaning) they have not illuminated the novel itself. They have moved with their readers away from the text, towards explanation, rather than into it, towards understanding.

Mrs. Bentley's world is a contained reality generated by a text, manifest in the minds of its readers. Yet rare is the critic who resists offering a resolution to the novel as if it were a problem to be solved, or a map to be decoded in order to see where it will lead. Of critics I am familiar with, only Morton L. Ross in his essay, "The Canonization of *As For Me and My House*", avoids this textual fallacy, possibly because his concern is more with criticism of the novel than with the novel itself.

A more appropriate analogy for the text of *As For Me and My House* would be a labryrinth. There are two things to remember about labyrinths: you have to get in, and you have to get out again. To do so you need guides and markers. These cannot be drawn from the text, for the nature of a labyrinth is to mislead. They must come from outside the novel, specifically from other texts where they have already been summoned into coherence out of the chaos of abstract thought and actual experience. They need not be works which might have influenced the author. He had other guides and markers: you do not build a labyrinth and explore it in the same way.

The most useful work to me in this regard was the novel *Badlands* by Robert Kroetsch, published long after I first became familiar with *As For Me and My House*. In considering Kroetsch's novel, recently, I came to recognize the unusual possibilities of representing opposing concepts of reality in terms of male and female gender. Kroetsch does not develop a struggle between two factions within his narrative, but two narratives — the man's, a quest for meaning; the woman's, an escape from meaning. The novel as a whole describes a dichotomy based on current critical theories of structuralism and phenomenology. Kroetsch's chief male protagonist articulates a phenomenological world, and embodies precepts of contemporary existentialism. His female protagonists, both called Anna, occupy a structuralist reality and, then, at the novel's close, animate a deconstructionist vision which seems to inform Kroetsch's subsequent work.

In the arcane textual strategies of postmodern criticism, the reader and critic are set free to be, to exist. The text alone is incomplete, a script for a play to occur in theatres of the mind. The sources of my own limited knowledge of these strategies are of no particular interest to the present exploration. Critical thought associated with Claude Levi-Strauss and Martin Heidegger, whose works inform the extremes of structuralism and phenomenology, and the hermeneutical responses to literary texts modelled on the work of Frank Kermode, are for the most part as obscure as they are illuminating — like a luminescent fog. The freedom they allow within the text and beyond it, combined with their opacity makes them useful here, without them being considered further in themselves.

In postmodern novels like *Badlands* and, even more, in John Fowles's *The French Lieutenant's Woman*, the relations between text and reader are wilfully exploited. The author, as a trickster-god, intrudes, manipulates, lays himself and the machinery of his art exposed, all to free the imagination of the reader from the tyranny of the text as an alternative reality continuous with our own. It is all an illusion, insist both Kroetsch and Fowles: see, they say, this is how it's done. But, of course, such revelations are themselves illusion. That is the anomaly of postmodernism.

As For Me and My House is a modern novel, not postmodern. Ross is nowhere to be found in his text. His novel is of its time, and he is out of it. All that we receive as readers is the product of Mrs. Bentley's mind. Nor does she enact a drama devised by the author's will against a carefully extolled background of nature and society. Such is the mode of nineteenth-century realism.

Rather, in the best tradition of modernism from Joyce to the present, reality and consciousness share mutual boundaries. While the surrounding world and the mind alive within it are not equivalents, each reflects the condition of the other, each exists at the other's pleasure. The author is not to be seen; the proposition essential to the modernist is fostered that he does not exist.

In one sense, the reality of the novel is entirely subjective, originating as it does with Mrs. Bentley. In another sense, it is entirely objective, the created world of Sinclair Ross. But Ross defers to Mrs. Bentley. What we receive, in the final analysis, is neither subjective nor objective but a fusion of the two. To filter them, one from the other, in a critical quest for clarity, insults the structural integrity of the text and denies the author's prerogative to be absent from it. To consider Mrs. Bentley unreliable is an evasion. Mrs. Bentley observes and interprets the world and that same world she lives in, occupies, often revealing far more of it than she intends. Sometimes her observations are objective and reliable, her commentaries fair and perceptive, while the world revealed appears a sham. At other times, she is unreliable indeed, and the world appears a solid separate place.

The dualities, dichotomies, polarities that fibrillate throughout the text like random static charges can all be traced to the mind in which they seem to originate. There are not two realities in this novel, but a single world perceived from the same perspective, Mrs. Bentley's, in two distinctly different ways. It is as if the text articulates the interaction between two sides or, more accurately, two chambers in Mrs. Bentley's mind, roughly corresponding to the two hemispheres of the human brain, or two legislative bodies in a single parliament. I have no intention here of acceding to the extravagant arguments of Julian Jaynes in his book *The Origin of Consciousness in the Breakdown of the Bicameral Mind*, but its principal concept offers a revealing model for understanding the textual anomalies of *As For Me and My House*.

Mrs. Bentley's mind, as text, is bicameral. One side is dominated by words and meaning, by linearity, logic and progression. This is the side conventionally associated with the masculine, and its ascendancy, with existentialism and phenomenology. The other side is dominated by form and pattern, by intuition and discontinuous connections. This, by convention, is deemed the feminine side, and is associated with structuralism. Both exist, side by side, as parallel functions of the mind, sometimes competing, sometimes complementary. In Kroetsch's novel, gender determines the reality of the moment. Narrative reality in *As For Me and My House*, however, cannot be reduced to a simple arrangement of antitheses based either on gender stereotype or the ambivalence of gender in the mindtext itself.

Badlands offers a useful paradigm to work from, in considering the labyrinthine complexity of *As For Me and My House*. Kroetsch's novel quite clearly differentiates between masculine and feminine conceptions of reality. Kroetsch depicts male reality as an existential search for continuity and historical relevance. Dawe's journey down the Red Deer River in pursuit of dinosaur bones which will give him fame and redeem his name for a time from oblivion, is an archetypal quest for meaning through experience; a male quest. Anna Yellowbird watches from the riverbank, occasionally connecting in a random pattern with the different males, and withdraws to watch with Anna Dawe, some fifty-six years later, the Dawe account re-enacted as their common dream. The female presence in the narrative, both structurally and thematically, is spatial not temporal, embodying not progression but discontinuity and transformation. Between them, Anna Dawe and Anna Yellowbird represent escape from myth and language; freedom from meaning.

Kroetsch is doing more in *Badlands* than fleshing out an argument, but there is little question that the informing dialectic of his novel originates in the philosophical bases of current and opposing schools of critical thought. One conception of reality in his novel is existential; one is structuralist. The existential, following empirically unfounded convention, is associated with the male; the structuralist, with the female. Truth, with the success of his narrative as proof that truth is a possibility, lies in the shared configuration of the two within the text. The text is truth, but the way to truth is through the pact between author and reader to rise above the text, to agree that only by rejecting both conceptions of reality at work in the novel will the truth be revealed.

The artist in Kroetsch's fiction subsumes opposing philosophies to his purpose, and the method of his art elevates the receptive reader to share the heady sensation with its creator. Ross, as much of his own age as Kroetsch of his, remains concealed behind his fiction, but he allows the same antitheses to work within it. Ross, as the creative source of his novel, to all intents and purposes, ceases to exist in 1941 when it was published. Kroetsch, the postmodern, refuses to stay behind — through arrogance or humility (the two are inseparable) he remains within the text of *Badlands* in the present presence of his reader's mind.

Ross, as the source of his fiction, generates from his experience of the world and himself a text as labyrinth. Having given us the labyrinth, we are set free of Ross, by Ross, to make our own way. Critics to date have tried to lead us out by the shortest routes conceivable. But it might be more appropriate to a labyrinth to move inwards, away from meaning, towards the centre, towards an appreciation of the enigmatic and anomalous form we find ourselves within. Such a procedure will, at the very least, leave the labyrinth intact.

....

Mrs. Bentley needs desperately to see her husband as an existential hero; a man who turns inwards to himself alone, each time he enters his study; a man in search of consolation within, for the indignities of his personal history, for abandoning Christianity, for his failure to be "manly"; consolation through solitude, and most of all, through art. Yet he is a failed hero, because in her estimation he has not the sufficient requirements of his gender to sustain the existential role she imposes on him. She is the victim of her own sophistry. She needs to see him as an artist-hero in order to make sense of her own life, to make the mean conditions of their lives yield meaning. She must build a myth out of his past and personality which will in effect justify her continuing existence. But this myth depends on Philip's masculinity, his function as the heromale, and this function she repeatedly usurps. To build the myth, she must shape the man; and in shaping the man, she destroys the myth.

Only a few instances need be drawn from the text to affirm the point. As the novel opens, Mrs. Bentley allows, "today I let him be the man about the house."[1] A short time later she suggests that there are times "when I think he has never quite forgiven me for being a woman" (p. 24). And she surmises that his art "can only remind him of his failure, of the man he tried to be" (p. 23). She revells, that he "manfully" refuses convalescence for a cold (p. 34), and later that he displays "masculine aloofness" (p. 82), even though she is its object, but she repeatedly sneers that his "useless hands" cannot accomplish manly tasks as Paul's can, and that he lacks the set of mind of "other men". In a fit of pas-

sionate self-pity she derides Philip, the "sensitive, fine-grained
... genuine man" as "a poor contemptible coward" (p. 86). The
paradox momentarily becomes clear, to us at least, while they are
visiting Paul's family:

> ... perhaps ... years ago, trying to measure up intellec-
> tually to Philip, I read Carlyle too impressionably, his
> thunder that a great man is part of a universal plan,
> that he can't be pushed aside or lost .... Perhaps had he
> been stronger he might not have let me stop him. He
> might have shouldered me, gone on his own way too.
> But there was a hardness lacking. His grain was too
> fine. It doesn't follow that the sensitive qualities that
> make an artist are accompanied by the unflinching,
> stubborn ones that make a man of action and success.
> (p. 103)

Her winning his affection seems, ironically, the proof of Philip's
failure as both an artist and a man.

Mrs. Bentley's identification with her own gender is no more
stable than that which she allows her husband. This instability
in turn undermines her estimation of herself at the centre of what
amounts to a structuralist world, the complement in a bicamerally
conceived reality to the willed presence of her husband at the centre of an existential world. She watches herself with a mixture
of exultation and despair caught up in a mounting struggle to
seize control of the myth, born of Philip's childhood, or her
perception of it, which sees them together repeating endlessly
the mean achievements and petty failures of his past. She com-
forts herself against the squalid condition of their domestic life
by envisioning in the patterns of their shared experience the
possibility of a transformation, wherein they will remain
themselves, yet be changed. A move to the city, a new career,
a child to call their own, such changes will redeem their fallen
lot. The myth will be subsumed by history of Mrs. Bentley's
making.

She does not recognize that such a transformation is merely
the illusion of change. The very act of bringing it about as an expression of her will ensures the perpetuation of their same relationship: she will possess Philip, control his destiny, as it were,
in order to submerge herself within him, in order to be somebody,
to take possession of herself, to be free, to be. Such irony is not

a projection beyond the text: the pattern of their lives together within the text declares, there will be no change without progression. The baby, to be called Philip, is a bastard child as Philip was. The man whose failure as a minister was assured by his lack of conviction before he took a church, this man who failed, also, as a writer will now sell books, with his wife as much a force behind this career as the last. Mrs. Bentley plans to stay away from the store, maybe in the fall to give a recital: against his awkwardness in the practical world, she sets her art. She assures the structure of their lives together will remain the same, even while planning out and extolling the virtues of change.

Structural transformation such as Mrs. Bentley envisions is based upon a fixed notion of gender, wherein the female nurtures and creates the conditions for change, while the male provides the force and knowledge that make changes come about. But her ambivalence in regard to her own gender, as well as her husband's, precludes the possibility of transformation. Repeatedly she ascribes to herself the characteristics of weakness and passivity accorded by convention to her sex. Yet time and again she defies the very stereotype she holds to be true, and then cowers with shame or exults, depending on whether her breach of convention is public or in private. Their poverty, the mark of Philip's failure as a traditional provider, she wears in public as a burden, but at home she wields as a weapon against his self-respect. She understands too well what society demands of her as a woman, and not at all what Philip needs of her, not what she as a woman needs of herself.

Mrs. Bentley proclaims, in her journal entry for *Tuesday Evening, March 5*: "I've fought with myself and won at last" (p. 154). She has decided to adopt Judith's baby: outsiders will see it as a gracious and maternal gesture; she sees it as the transformation of shame to triumph; for Philip, it is a humiliation in which his identity will be virtually overwhelmed. In winning because, as she says, "I want it so" (p. 165), she loses.

This is one side of the world, born out of Mrs. Bentley's bicameral mind: the male is a failure as an existential hero; the female's structuralist reality threatens to collapse. This is one way of seeing things, and the text offers numerous motifs to affirm its viability. Two in particular stand out for their compatibility with gender stereotypes: the horse and the garden. Neither motif is static; both develop in parallel with the narrative. Horses are early in the text associated with coming to manhood, and then with masculine sexuality. At the Kirby farm they become an emblem of infidelity, quite literally, and eventually horses come to represent Philip and his affair with Judith, while in one particular scene the string of broncos in a sketch admired by Mrs. Bentley and Paul casts over their relationship, in Philip's eyes, at least, an ominous cloud of suspicion. It is in the unforgettable image of the frozen carcasses, however, that Philip's affair with Judith and its aftermath are brought into chilling focus: the two horses stand where they died, "too spent to turn again and face the wind" (p. 153). Philip, as his wife declares in naming the child of his indiscretion after him, means "lover of horses". The association and its implications are difficult to ignore.

For Mrs. Bentley, the garden is an emblem of gender, as ambivalent in her regard for it as she is in respect to herself. She relates to it with a sort of plaintive desperation that recalls to her an earlier garden and its associations with the child she lost (p. 44). Her struggle to make that garden yield an array of flowers, not food but beauty, was a link with Philip's struggle to write: and its failure both echoed the death of their child and parallel - ed Philip's failure as a writer. Still, she determines to seek refuge in another garden. Inevitably these flowers die as well, in the wind and the dust and sun, and she gives up on it. She has worked against proprieties of gender to water, weed and care for her garden, doing men's and women's labour both, and her garden withers; and with it, her connections with the earth, with maternity, natural beauty and her husband's existential being. She has invested her garden with so much of herself that its failure seems her own.

. . .

It is in the ambiguities of gender sustained by the text that opposing ontologies are freed of a fixed association with one character or another, one sex or another. Mrs. Bentley places herself in what amounts to a structuralist cosmology, and sees her husband as the existential protagonist in a phenomenological context. But the text affirms her own existential function, and insists that Philip is at least as readily accommodated by a structuralist context. The bicameral mind of Mrs. Bentley sustains either set of extremes, and a multiplicity of possibilities between. While Philip's gender and his wife's demands on him push him towards the existential, his own nature, experience and desire insist that he more comfortably inhabits and animates a structuralist reality. And Mrs. Bentley, contrary to the impress either of gender or wilfull intent, is a far more convincing existential protagonist than her husband.

Philip's consciousness of the world is dominated by form, in spite of what his wife may think or wish. There is little continuity between his experience, as a minister or as a man, and his values. For him, the church provides a sustaining structure to his life, but no meaning. His chosen text for his first sermon, "As For Me and My House We Will Serve the Lord", is not a declaration of faith, as Mrs. Bentley takes it, but a statement of purpose. The theological, social and domestic mythologies associated with the ministry give shape to the Bentley's presence in Horizon, but within the strictures of his function serving community and church Philip leads a separate life as an artist and solitary man.

We are never given the words of his sermons, and rarely their subjects. Yet numerous works of his art are described in detail. Words do not express Philip's condition in the world, nor his understanding of it. He is the antithesis of Paul, the philologist, a marvelous figure in whom words are reduced to meaning alone, without context or syntax, so that meaning becomes meaningless. He is far more like Judith, whose purity of voice lifts the words she sings to soar beyond their meaning. Significantly, Judith responds to drawings of herself with an exclamation on the quality of their likeness, then with silence. The affinity between Philip and Judith is reinforced by their similar defiance of gender conventions, while still being fully representative of their sexes, a point made manifest in their eventual affair. Paul, when he sees Philip's art, interprets it, reduces it to explanation. Paul, like Mrs. Bentley, relates to reality through words; Philip, like Judith, in spite of them.

At one point, and the context is irrelevant, Mrs. Bentley says of Philip, "I took my place beside him, and as he groped for words began explaining the situation as it really was" (p. 73) There is no break for her between how things seem and how they are. Words, her words, declare the continuity between experience and reality: they mean what they say. For Philip, words are a barrier. To penetrate it and make the way things are accessible, is only possible through perceptions of form. In models devised within his art, he searches out the hidden meanings of reality. The real is in the shape of things, not the things themselves. The real is in relationships, structures; in the syntax, not the words. Mrs. Bentley tries to understand his art, but succeeds only in understanding its content, and cannot see the function of its form. In the following passage, both the struggle for Philip's art to emerge from a welter of words, and the struggle of Mrs. Bentley to reduce it once again to words, are in striking evidence:

> He had been drawing again, and under his papers I found a sketch of a little country schoolhouse .... You see it the way Paul sees it. The distorted, barren land- scape makes you feel the meaning of its persistence there ... suddenly like Paul you begin to think poetry, and strive to utter eloquence.
>
> And it was just a few rough pencil strokes, and he had it buried among some notes he'd been making for next Sunday's sermon.
>
> According to Philip it's form that's important in a pic- ture, not the subject or the associations that the subject calls to mind; the pattern you see, not the literary emo- tion you feel; ... A picture worth its salt is supposed to make you experience something that he calls aesthetic excitement, not send you into dithyrambs about humanity in microcosm. (p. 80)

Here quite clearly Philip's structuralist conception of art is shown in confrontation with his wife's phenomenological perception of things. Herein lies the crucial conflict of the novel — not a dialec- tic, but the struggle between two mutually exclusive conditions of mind; and ultimately the mind containing both is Mrs. Bentley's.

Mrs. Bentley insists on her guilt for having forced Philip to aban- don his art for the ministry. She willingly accepts responsibility, as the proof of his affection. She readily accepts blame for the instability of their lives, since each new move seems evidence to her that Philip "still must care a little for his dowdy wife" (p. 10). Because her guilt is the measure of her husband's love, she cultivates the tawdriness and improprieties that cause it. This ac- counts for her acceptance of the discrepancy between her estima- tion of his love and his expression of it. When finally the discrepancy cannot be reconciled with experience, Mrs. Bentley seizes control of their lives, determined to change reality.

Working against Mrs. Bentley's will to change, however, is the pattern of Philip's existence; a series of transformations, a story repeated with variations but without fundamental change or progression. He was a bastard child; the natural son of a preacher who belongs in young Philip's mind to the escape world of imagination, and a drab woman who embodied for the boy his sordid surroundings. Philip's adopted son Steve is an outcast in Horizon. His real son, the first one, dies. His other son is a bastard child as well. As a boy, his father's books gave Philip scope to imagine in life more of value than experience allowed, but crushed him by forcing him to realize his personal insignificance. So too with his writing; so too with his art. The ministry at least gives his life structure and purpose; if not meaning. The painful gap between interior and external worlds that characterized his childhood, that recurred with variations at university, is sustained by his role and function as a minister. In her proposed changes, Mrs. Bentley makes no provisions to bridge this gap — which she, tragically, is incapable of recognizing. In an urban bookstore, Philip's ideal world of the imagination will be no closer to the surrounding conditions of his life than it has ever been.

Philip remains locked into a highly structured and discontinuous existence by the text, although his wife would by choice have him otherwise. She, in turn, remains the existential protagonist in a phenomenological continuum. The form of the text as a journal, self-consciously written, is proof enough that she occupies and animates a world in which explanation is everything, in which things mean what they are said to mean. She equates appearance with reality: thus, it is she, in fact, not Philip, who is so concerned about what everyone thinks of them, of her. And it is she, not Philip, who is so concerned about the continuity a child will provide: "It's going to be a boy, of course, and I'm going to call him Philip too" (p. 158). Even her art, her music, has value to her for what it does, and means, as much as for itself. She plays to win Philip, to win Steve; she plays for Paul. She uses music, by her own admission, not to transcend ordinary experience or to elevate it, but to draw it into coherence, into her control.

Mrs. Bentley writes to interpret lives; she yearns towards meaning. She tries desperately to submerge herself in her husband's mythology, while trying as desperately to lift him out of it. She manipulates to gain control of his life, in order to yield control

of her own; to gain possession of both. The creation of her journal is from an existential perspective an act of self-creation. What
she writes, the text, however, is beyond her will. In it, both structuralist and phenomenological conceptions of reality converge.
It is the literal embodiment of her bicameral mind. With the end
of the text, the Bentleys end as well. The novel, however, remains
intact, a perpetual presence in the reader's mind.

Notes

[1] Sinclair Ross, *As For Me and My House* (New York: Reynal, 1941; Toronto,
McClelland and Stewart, 1969), p. 3. This and all subsequent references
in parentheses within the text are to the Toronto edition.

HUGH MACLENNAN

CANADIAN NATIONALISM IN SEARCH OF A FORM: HUGH MacLENNAN'S *BAROMETER RISING*

David Arnason

Hugh MacLennan published his first novel, *Barometer Rising*, in 1941. Since that time, he has become the "grand old man" of Canadian novelists, an assessment that has little to do with his age or the quality of his achievement, but is rather an acknowledgement that the development of a Canadian consciousness is paralleled in the development of his work.

Success did not come easily or quickly to MacLennan. He wrote two novels, *So All Their Praises* (1933) and *Man Should Rejoice* (1937) which were never published. Both were concerned with broad international issues. It was only when MacLennan narrowed his scope and turned to a Canadian subject that he did succeed. That success was marked by the publication in 1941 of *Barometer Rising*, the first novel written in Canada, by a Canadian, in which a peculiarly Canadian consciousness manifests itself.

Since that time, MacLennan has continued to expand his vision of Canada and Canadian consciousness. At the same time, his importance has been recognized, and a growing body of critical study of his work is available. Unfortunately, certain critical clichés have prevented a balanced assessment. The first of these is that MacLennan has, in some incomprehensible way, suffered "a failure of imagination," and the second is that he is a sociologist in disguise. Neither of these views will stand close scrutiny.

A reassessment of *Barometer Rising* must begin with MacLennan's second novel, *Two Solitudes*. In it, he has created his vision of the artist as a young man, in the person of Paul Tallard. Though Paul Tallard comes from a very different background than Hugh MacLennan, he is the young artist who discovers the difficulty of dealing with broad world themes, and turns back to his Canadian roots. The insights, values and ideas that Paul gains in *Two Solitudes* mirror MacLennan's aesthetic and ethical views.

For instance, in *Two Solitudes*, Paul gains an insight into the problem of writing a Canadian novel:

> ... he realized that his readers' ignorance of the essential Canadian clashes and values presented him with a

unique problem. The background would have to be created from scratch if his story was to become intelligible. He could afford to take nothing for granted. He would have to build the stage and props for his play, and then write the play itself.[1]

It is an insight which MacLennan himself shares with his character, and it accounts, in part, for some of the successes and some of the failures of MacLennan's work.

The basis of Paul's insight is an assumption that the reader will be ignorant of things Canadian. Who then is this hypothetical reader? Obviously, he is not a thinking modern Canadian, or else he should know something of the "essential Canadian clashes and values" and the kind of stage-business that Paul envisions would be superfluous. Is he then some outsider, some American or English, or non-Canadian-Canadian literary creature to whom the author offers his work with built in apologies? This appears to be the case and many of the excesses in MacLennan's work spring from an assessment of his audience that is parallel to the assessment that Paul makes. Why else would a man suffering from shell-shock, obsessed by thoughts of revenge and desperately hungry for love be permitted by his artistic creator to think: "The Citadel itself flew the Union Jack in all weathers and was rightly considered a symbol and bastion of the British Empire."[2]

Why else would a wounded alcoholic doctor, seconds before he is to deliver a proposal of marriage be permitted to pause and contemplate irrelevantly that

> "... Halifax, more than most towns, seemed governed by a fate she neither made nor understood, for it was her birthright to serve the English in time of war and to sleep neglected when there was peace. It was a bondage Halifax had no thought of escaping because it was the only life she had ever known; but to Murray this seemed a pity, for the town figured more largely in the calamities of the British Empire than in its prosperities, never seemed able to become truly North American."
> (BR p. 33)

These examples are typical, and they are by no means isolated instances. Throughout both *Barometer Rising* and *Two Solitudes* action is continually interrupted by contemplations about Canadian society, Canada's place in the world and the forces that operate

in Canada. Usually, these thoughts do not arise as any conse-
quence of the action and seem to exist purely as apologia to the
un-Canadian reader. Sometimes they seem to be meretricious in-
terpolations on the part of the author, a difficulty in form that
arises from MacLennan's inability to handle his narrative with
skill.

In part, though, MacLennan's insight is a valid one. At the time
of his writing *Barometer Rising*, there were not many people in
Canada who thought of themselves as essentially Canadian, and
so some of the stage business is not so superfluous as it might
first appear. Now, thirty years later, when people can refer to
themselves as Canadians without feeling that there is something
embarrassing or pretentious about the use of the word, MacLennan's self-consciousness seems particularly clumsy. In retrospect,
any battle that has been won seems disproportionate to its causes.
Today, we wonder whether Canada, as a nation, can survive.
Thirty years ago the problem was not whether Canada survived,
but whether it existed at all.

Since MacLennan is very much concerned with ideas, it is
necessary to examine some of the ideas that he considers important. That is to say, since MacLennan is building "the stage and
the props for his play," it might be worthwhile to examine them
before we look at the play itself.

First, MacLennan's conception of Canada's possibilities seems
to be based on an idea of corporate spiritual energy invested in
the state. The wars in *Barometer Rising* and *Two Solitudes* are
testimony to the expended energy of the Europeans. The First
World War, MacLennan feels, will leave only madness, contempt,
despair and an "intolerable burden of guilt" in Europe, because
the war is the "logical result" of the Europeans "living out the
sociological results of their own lives." Canada's role in the future
will be to "pull Britain clear of decay and give her a new birth"
(BR pp. 200-201). MacLennan is a bit less overtly didactic and
somewhat more dramatically convincing in his treatment of European decadence in *Two Solitudes*. First, the reader is given a picture of a cultured, wealthy, Parisian woman, the carefully
wrought product of an European civilization caught, fascinated,
waiting for a brutal German to debase her sexually. It soon
becomes apparent, as MacLennan moves toward the lecturer's
tone in which he is most comfortable, that she is an analogue for
one part of Europe and the brutal porcine German is an analogue

for the other. As Paul retraces in his mind the progress of his novel *Young Man of 1933*, we find that an effete, wasted civilization that has abandoned itself to machines and cities and has forsaken God is powerless to resist the resurgence of totemism, magic and brutal atavism, in fact, the whole *danse macabre* that "had burst out of the unconscious" (TS p. 338) and found its focus in Hitler.

Speaking for MacLennan, Paul says "the same brand of patriotism is never likely to exist all over Canada. Each race so violently disapproves of the tribal gods of the other, I can't see how any single Canadian politician can ever imitate Hitler — at least, not over the whole country" (TS p. 362). MacLennan clearly feels that the future is Canada's. In *Barometer Rising* he confidently and optimistically foresaw Canada as "the central arch which united the new order" (BR p. 218). A trifle more subdued in *Two Solitudes*, he sees Canada acting "out of the instinct to do what was necessary" taking the first steps to self-knowledge, aware that she is "not unique but like all the others, alone with history, with science, with the future" (TS p. 4l2). This view of Canada is not, however, as chastened as it may first appear. The war is leading the rest of the world to self-destruction while it leads Canada to self-knowledge.

Against this backdrop of historical inevitability, MacLennan sets his props: his own ideas and attitudes, and his impressions of what are typically Canadian ideas and attitudes. MacLennan clearly distrusts certain aspects of progress. In *Barometer Rising* his characters deplore the mass production of ships, and regret deeply the passing of honest craftsmanship. In *Two Solitudes* Paul sees the machine behind Hitler, "the still small voice of God the Father no longer audible through the stroke of the connecting rod" (TS p. 339). Angus Murray in *Barometer Rising* has a theory that "... this war is the product of the big city" (BR p. 50). Paul Tallard in *Two Solitudes* sees "the new city-hatred (contempt for all things but cleverness)" (TS p. 339) as the foundation for anti-semitism, class warfare and economic jealousy. The conscienceless American engineer of *Barometer Rising* is the typical product of the city.

On the other hand, MacLennan clearly feels a deep emotional attachment to certain aspects of the old order. The simple, God-fearing farmer-fishermen of Cape Breton epitomize for him the enduring values. Tied both to the sea and the land, governed by the natural rhythms of the earth, they are honest and noble. Alec MacKenzie of *Barometer Rising* and Captain John Yardley of *Two Solitudes* function as archetypal figures, symbols of human potentiality against whom the other characters may be measured.

This is not to say that MacLennan is opposed to change. Indeed, there are many things about the old order that he resents — the desperate and cold materialism of men like McQueen, the aristocratic conventions of people like Colonel Wain and the Methuens which lead them to debase the country in which they live and which gives them their living, and the narrow religious bigotry of Alfred Wain and Father Beaubien. Change offers not only the hatred of the cities and the brutality of the machine, but also the possibility for growth and renewal, for the fulfilling of destiny and the achievement of self-knowledge. The drastic and accelerated changes occasioned by the war are the flames from which Canada will arise, Phoenix-like, to take its rightful place in the world.

Canada, as MacLennan sees it, and presumably as Canadians themselves think of it, is the product of two cultures. On the one hand, it is tied to England and "a world without England would be intolerable" (BR p. 54). On the other hand it is tied to the United States by "a frontier that was more a link than a division." Uniquely, it partakes of the two cultures. MacLennan clearly sees a dialectic at work, and Neil Macrae expresses it: "... if there were enough Canadians like himself, half-American and half-English, then the day was inevitable when the halves would join and his country would become the central arch which united the new order" (BR p. 218). The same kind of dialectic functions in *Two Solitudes* in which Paul Tallard becomes the synthesis of the French-Canadian and English-Canadian cultures. Here, though, the symbolic form of the dialectic functions against MacLennan's thesis that the cultures are in fact solitudes and must co-exist rather than merge. The title of the novel is from a poem by Rilke, and is part of a definition of Love, another example of MacLennan's incurable optimism.

There is one more significant idea that must be mentioned, and that is the sense of geography that MacLennan feels is part of the Canadian vision and which becomes, in his novels, an important device. In *Two Solitudes*, Heather paints a picture and asks Paul to comment on it. When he sees it, he (or else the author — there is some confusion) notices "... she had missed the vastness of such a scene, the sense of the cold wind stretching so many hundreds of miles to the north of it, through ice and tundra and desolation" (TS p. 307). It is an error that MacLennan has no intention of making. The sun that sets on Halifax makes long shadows in Montreal, glints on the prairies and beams down from high noon on Vancouver. MacLennan seems determined to create a vision of Canada as at least a geographical reality if not a social one, and he loses no opportunity to tie a description of a particular place into a vision of the whole continent.

A set of ideas provides the stage and the props for MacLennan's play: the background is an historically inevitable achievement of destiny and self-knowledge by a young and vigorous country pulled from the outside by two cultures and from the inside by two cultures, caught between the old and the new. The props are certain attitudes and representative characters. Against this is to be set a play which will be an artistic whole, and which will utilize this stage and these properties. Obviously enough, since a nation is a composite of its individuals, the play will concern itself with the achievement of individual destiny and self-knowledge.

It is fashionable to claim that the failures in MacLennan's novels are the result of a failure of imagination. This is not an adequate assessment. The failures that occur are usually the result of a failure to handle with skill the technical form of the novel and sometimes the result of the misapplication of an unbalanced talent.

First, every novel must have a voice, a presumed narrator who tells the story. In the case of *Barometer Rising* the voice is that of an omniscient author who sees everything, who can move about at will and permit the reader to share the thoughts, feelings, and vision of various characters. At times, he exists independently of any character and observes and comments for himself. Like the characters themselves, he is limited to a present and retrospective vision, and none of the unfortunate dramatic ironies of the "dear and gentle reader" school of omniscient author intrude themselves. When the voice speaks for itself, and when it operates at some distance from the characters, it is observant, acute, and incisive. When it moves closer, though, it runs into problems. Too often we begin with the description of a character's thoughts, and find that the anonymous voice has taken matters out of their hands and is commenting itself. For example, on page 67 of

Barometer Rising we discover Wain contemplating Alec MacKenzie. "Wain puffed a lungful of smoke against the windowpane"; at this point the anonymous voice is watching from outside. "MacKenzie was the only man in the world capable of upsetting his apple-cart, of cancelling out all the patient work he had done in Halifax since his return from France" — now we have moved into Wain's mind and are observing his thought. "But the big man had no notion of this" — so far, so good. "When he had accepted the job and brought his wife and family to Halifax he had never guessed that it had been Wain's motive to make him a dependent." By this point there is some considerable doubt as to whether Wain is thinking or the narrator has taken over.[3]

The result of this unsureness in the handling of point-of-view is that the characters are blurred. At times the thoughts of the characters are authentic and individual; at other times they are not. Penny, for instance, is distinctly feminine much of the time, but when she contemplates the Nova Scotian scene, an anonymous voice intrudes. She could be Neil Murray or anybody else:

> Her eye wandered back to the freighter sliding upstream: a commonplace ship, certainly foreign and probably of the Mediterranean origin, manned by heaven knew what conglomeration of Levantines, with maybe a Scotsman in the engine-room and a renegade Nova Scotian somewhere in the forecastle. The war had brought so many of these mongrel vessels to Halifax, they had become a part of the landscape. (BR p. 17)

Besides blurring the identity of the characters, the authorial voice also blurs the action and interferes with the dramatic power of the narrative. MacLennan's chief skill lies in his ability to write sustained passages of descriptive narrative. This is obvious in his powerful description of the events leading to the explosion and the chaotic action thereafter. He chooses to dissipate this power by his refusal, in the first half of the book, to sustain his focus on any action. As the action approaches a climax, the focus shifts and the dramatic tension created is lost. To be sure, this shifting focus is obviously intentional. The unfulfilled nature of the characters calls for unfulfilled action, and provides a striking contrast to the sharp decisive nature of the action in the latter part of the book, as the cathartic effect of the explosion impels the characters to self-knowledge and the fulfillment of their destinies. In theory, it is a fine idea, and as an outline for a novel it has a compelling symmetry. Unfortunately, in practice it is unsatisfying, and even more unfortunately, MacLennan is incapable of supplying any richness of imagery and metaphor to make up the deficiency.

It is frequently pointed out that the explosion in *Barometer Rising* operates as a kind of *deus ex machina* which dispenses an arbitrary, though poetic justice. It interferes with the action, and prevents the confrontations that the early development of the book would seem to demand. For instance, Neil does not encounter Geoffrey Wain until he is safely dead, and the triangular relationship between Neil, Penny, and Angus creates none of the difficulties inherent in the situation. This is quite simply explicable, though, in terms of MacLennan's aesthetics. Just as Canada itself must work out its destiny in terms of individual self-knowledge, so must each of the characters in the novel.

Confrontation leads to victory or defeat, but not to the kind of self-knowledge that MacLennan wants to delineate. The explosion prevents Neil from confronting Colonel Wain and Angus from confronting Neil. Instead, it makes each confront himself and learn to understand himself. At the end of the novel, each of the characters is oddly isolated and self-contained. There has been no development of relationships; but then, that is not what the novel is about. Though Penny and Neil are reunited physically as they ride together on the train, each is completely separate and distinct; that is to say, no communication goes on between them. Neil does not even know that he is a father when the novel ends.

This argument does not absolve the novel of weakness in its close. The process of self-discovery is not particularly convincing, and MacLennan's refusal to permit relationships to grow and change limits the novel and is frustrating to the reader. The argument does absolve MacLennan of much of the charge that his imagination is limited. He does not fail to develop interpersonal relationships because he cannot envision them, but because he chooses to concentrate on the individual's relationship with himself.

Another defect in the novel occurs as a result of MacLennan's use of characters in his novel both as props in his stage setting and participants in the action. The characters are too obviously symbolic. Colonel Wain and Alec MacKenzie represent two facets of the old order, Angus Murray represents the transition and Neil and Penny represent the new order. MacLennan makes the mistake of overestimating the obtuseness of his readers, and to make sure that nobody has missed the point, he allows Angus Murray to sum up the symbolic action in a neat little précis:

> There was Geoffrey Wain, the descendent of military colonists who had remained essentially a colonist himself, never really believing that anything above the second rate could exist in Canada, a man who had not thought it necessary to lick the boots of the English but had merely taken it for granted that they mattered and Canadians didn't. There was Alec MacKenzie, the primitive man who had lived just long enough to bridge the gap out of the pioneering era and save his children from becoming anachronisms. There were Penny and Neil Macrae, two people who could seem at home almost anywhere, who had inherited as a matter of course and in their own country the urbane and technical heritage of both Europe and eastern United States. And there was himself, caught somewhere between the two extremes, intellectually gripped by the new and emotionally held by the old, too restless to remain at peace on the land and too contemptuous of bourgeois values to feel at ease in any city.

All in all though, struggling under the symbolic load they must carry and with their thoughts continually being wrenched away from them by the author, the characters do remarkably well for themselves. Angus Murray is not a very convincing alcoholic, and is perhaps a bit too clear sighted, but he does seem motivated by genuine concerns, and his responses are convincing. Penny Wain does not convince us of her brilliance, but does convince us of her femininity. Colonel Wain, though a megalomaniac is not much more a parody than many real-life colonels. Alec MacKenzie, though a bit too good to be true, is acceptable. Neil number one is indecisive and paranoid, and his actions confirm this. Neil number two is smugly selfish and competent, as is shown by his handling of things after the explosion. The difficulty is that it takes an unusually powerful ability to suspend disbelief to be convinced that the two are one, and that is a chief flaw in the book. We have seen no flashes of the old Neil or the Neil to

come in the shuffling character of the first part of the book, and
so we are not convinced at his change. The peripheral characters
— Aunt Maria, Roddy and the rest who have escaped the symbolic load and who don't do much thinking are all quite delightful.

Style is as much an aspect of form as it is of thought and it is
in respect of style that the novel has its chief virtues and its chief
faults. MacLennan's greatest strength is in pure narrative description. His point-by-point description of the Halifax explosion is
as good as anything of its kind in Canadian literature, or any other
literature, for that matter. His description of the details of the landscape are deft and sure and he can characterize people with swift,
sure and precise detail. Where he is weakest is in his handling
of metaphor, and his novel loses strength from his inability to
make vivid and animate comparisons. His ear for dialogue is not
particularly good. The speech of his characters is a bit bookish
at best, and collapses at moments of deep emotional stress, as
may be seen by the stilted conversation between Neil and Penny
at their first confrontation. John Yardley's accent in *Two Solitudes*
is chiefly the result of his inability to pronounce the "a" in "that,"
though he can pronounce the same sound well enough in other
words. Finally, a tendency to prefer latinate forms, possibly as
a result of his training in the classics, leads MacLennan at times
to such infelicities of expression as "she welcomed the lassitude
as an anodyne to thought" (BR p. 11).

In the end, a novel is not judged by weighing its strengths and
weaknesses and drawing up a balance sheet. It must stand on
its own, apart from the author's intent and its significance as a
philosophic document. On these terms, *Barometer Rising* is a
limited success. MacLennan has taken the subject of national consciousness in Canada and given it a form that is convincing. Unfortunately, the novel is weighed down by a lot of stage business
that reduces its immediacy and vitality. The clutter is in part a
weakness in MacLennan's writing, but another part of it is sheer
historical necessity. An evolving Canadian consciousness found
its first firm voice in MacLennan, and if that voice is a bit self-
conscious, surely that is understandable.

In a conversation between Margaret Laurence and Robert
Kroetsch in a book called *Creation*, an interesting passage occurs:

> L: You know, I read Kipling, and what the hell did
> Kipling have to do with where I was living? And

that isn't to say that we shouldn't read widely, but it is a good thing to be able to read, as a child, something that belongs to you, belongs to your people. And you and I might have sort of sub-consciously had a compulsion to set down our own background.

K: I've suspected that often. We want to hear our story.[4]

Laurence and Kroetsch speak of "our people" and "our story," and unselfconsciously regard themselves as Canadians. I don't think it is too much of an overstatement to say that their easy acceptance of the Canadian fact owes something to the ground broken by Hugh MacLennan.

Notes

[1]   Hugh MacLennan, *Two Solitudes* (Toronto: MacMillan of Canada, 1969), p. 365. All further references to the novel will be indicated by the abbreviation TS.

[2]   Hugh MacLennan, *Barometer Rising* (Toronto: McClelland & Stewart, 1969), p. 6. All further references to the novel will be indicated by the abbreviation BR.

[3]   See pages 133-134, page 197, and pages 200-201 for similar examples.

[4]   Robert Kroetsch, ed., *Creation* (Toronto: New Press, 1970), p. 63.

OF CABBAGES AND KINGS: THE CONCEPT OF THE HERO IN *THE WATCH THAT ENDS THE NIGHT*

Elspeth Cameron

In November 1952, MacLennan made the sweeping statement, "As Hemingway goes, so goes writing in our time."[1] It was the publication of *The Old Man and the Sea* which prompted this remark, but it was not in any way tossed off glibly as a book reviewer's means of drawing attention to his subject; it was, and had been for some time, a deeply held belief of MacLennan's. "To those like myself who discovered Hemingway at the end of the 1920's," he would later recall, "English prose as they had known it seemed suddenly stale and dull ... reading Hemingway was pure excitement. He was so fresh then, he so perfectly combined poetry with meticulous accuracy of fact, that for a time he overwhelmed the literary world."[2]

MacLennan's view of Hemingway as "the bell-weather of our flock these past twenty-five years"[3] was of crucial importance in the emergence of the novel he had begun two years earlier in the fall of 1950 — a novel that would not ultimately see publication until 13 February 1959 — for it was through his struggle to define his personal relationship as a writer to the fiction of Hemingway that his unique concept of the hero would emerge in *The Watch that Ends the Night*.

Hemingway did "overwhelm the literary world," as MacLennan observed, by speaking directly to the young men and women growing up in the shadow of the First World War. But not every reader of Hemingway was affected as intensely as MacLennan was. He was utterly enthralled by *The Sun Also Rises* (1926), *A Farewell to Arms* (1929) and *For Whom the Bell Tolls* (1939), novels that were appearing at the very point at which he himself turned from writing "modern" romantic poetry to attempt fiction in the late twenties.

In many ways. MacLennan was exceptionally ripe for the kind of impact Hemingway's fiction was making. His situation virtually guaranteed identification with the youthful North American expatriates Hemingway depicted. As a student at Oxford from 1928-1932 travelling during his "vacs" on the Continent, he fancied himself an "internationalist", observing and comparing the customs of other nations, picking up a smattering of French and much more than a smattering of German, acquiring drinking habits that openly transgressed the teetotaller ethics of his Nova Scotia background. In fact, Hemingway's characters provided ready models for what would soon develop into outright rebellion against the excessively Victorian upbringing he had endured.

His subject at Oxford was classical literature, a study he had pursued under the direction of an overbearing father since boyhood. Not that MacLennan disliked the Classics; on the contrary, Greek and Latin myths had nurtured his early notions of the heroic and Homeric adventures had prepared him to accept their modern counterparts with ease. Now, in Hemingway's bullfighters and soldiers, he saw classical exploits brought to life in contemporary terms; the First World War, of which he had vivid memories from boyhood himself, was a welcome replacement for the Trojan War as a stage for life's important conflicts.

Furthermore, for a young man in his early twenties existing in what he himself called the "monastic"[4] world of Oxford, Hemingway's women must have seemed delectable. Above all, perhaps, the zeal with which he was throwing himself into rugger and tennis year round as an outlet for his various frustrations as a student, offered a perfect entrée to Hemingway's world of sport and violent activity. This was a heady mixture for MacLennan, and he drank down Hemingway's works in draughts so strong that they became the model outright for his first novel, begun in 1921.

That novel — "So All Their Praises"[5] — was never published, partly because of the effect the Depression had on publishing in general, but also because MacLennan unwittingly had chosen as a model a writer with whom he was at odds in a fundamental way. The rejection of his novel by several publishers forced him to re-assess his talents and begin the process of defining his own theories of fiction. By March 1935, in the midst of a second novel "A Man Should Rejoice"[6], he over-reacted to Hemingway with a disapproval as forceful as his initial idealization: "Inside a few years," he wrote to a friend, "the Hemingway school will be a back number. It is now in process of apotheosis, which is evidence for my statement. The apotheosis of Shaw took place around 1928, and now he is a joke. I believe that by the time we are fifty the Hemingway crowd will be studied as examples of stupidity and derangement." Indeed, he extended his indictment to include all American writers who were, in his opinion, "swimming up and down sewers saying how tough they were." American fiction seemed to him to be unduly concerned with "the succulence of mortified flesh."[7] These were strong words from a writer whose main character in "So All Their Praises" had claimed Hemingway-style that "bawdiness and art are inseparable."[8] Since traces of Hemingway's influence persisted well into MacLennan's second novel (to such a degree that the novel's ending is strongly reminiscent of A Farewell to Arms), his diatribe in 1935 probably owed more to anger at not finding a publisher than to any well-reasoned evaluation of Hemingway. It would be a long time before he could free himself of the spell Hemingway's work had cast over him. Nonetheless, as even the title of his second novel — "A Man Should Rejoice" — suggests, Hemingway's profound disillusionment with what he called the "obscenity" of abstract words like "honour" and "duty" (in a passage which especially intrigued MacLennan)[9] did not jibe with his own sense of the modern world.

The borderline rejection of MacLennan's second novel in 1937 was traumatic. In his painful recognition that something was seriously amiss, he hit on an insight that was to pave the way to success with his third manuscript, Barometer Rising. Publishers' reports had indicated that there was considerable confusion over the novel's point of view; it seemed neither British, nor American, yet it was English. Where had it come from? Eventually, MacLennan realized that his "Canadianness" (or rather the absence of any recognizable "Canadian" tradition of fiction to prepare the way for his work) was an obstacle. As a Canadian attempting to imitate Americans (and in his second novel he had branched out to include Sinclair Lewis's Babbitt as a model), he was running against the grain. As he would later describe it, "Suddenly I realized that no matter how hard they may try, few writers can escape their own environment. They are stuck with their own country whether they want it or not .... Hemingway may have used Italy, Spain or Cuba for most of his settings; but ... Spain and Italy are always seen through American eyes."[10] Once Barometer Rising was published in 1941, he was convinced that he had been right to give up attempting to become "a Canadian Hemingway."[11] Nonetheless, he had not entirely laid the ghost — or rather the all-too-alive presence — of Hemingway to rest.

How did MacLennan's sense of the modern world differ from Hemingway's? He worked this out in a series of essays and articles written in the fifties while he was working on *The Watch that Ends the Night*. He agreed with Hemingway that the First World War had been a cataclysmic turning point in history. But whereas for Hemingway (as for the majority of so-called "modern" writers and painters between the wars) the War marked a total disillusionment with the Victorian ideals which had fostered it, to MacLennan it represented the ultimate expression of those ideals in a form so extreme that a new age was called for. The post-war years of the twenties and thirties, in MacLennan's eyes, had been "the most prolonged and violent transition human society has suffered since the fall of the Roman Empire,"[12] a transition which had held him "prisoner".

Specifically, these years had been "transitional" in his personal life. Especially between 1932 and 1935, when he had endured a great misery and frustration complying with his father's ambition that he get a Ph.D. from Princeton, MacLennan had felt like a "prisoner". So great had been his despair that the thought of suicide had occurred to him. Eventually, however, the Second World War, which for Hemingway and others would simply spawn further disillusionment, marked the regaining of balance for MacLennan: in 1949 he claimed that there had been "a crystallization of the spirit which possessed England in the summer of 1940 (later he would date this specifically as 10 June 1940[13] when Neville Chamberlain resigned and Churchill took over)" by which he meant generally the rallying speeches in which "Churchill used great words like duty and honour, staked his life on them and restored them to dignity."

In clear opposition to the leading writers and painters of the day, MacLennan went on to state, "the world at large was not as supine or infected as T. S. Eliot and the avant-gardists thought it was. It did not end with a whimper, and those who tried to end it with a bang suffered the greatest military defeat in history."[14]

These observations helped MacLennan identify those aspects of Hemingway's work with which he could not agree. Although he was willing to grant that Hemingway was "a concise, polished craftsman" who, being sensitive, quite rightly had portrayed a violent reaction to the trauma of World War I, he could not condone "his total, his almost nihilistic pessimism." "His desire for honesty," MacLennan explained in an essay called "Changing Values in Fiction", "made life appear worse and more sordid that

it actually is.''[15] He used a novel by Tom Lea called *The Brave Bulls*
to illustrate how the romantic realism of Hemingway was now
developing away from nihilism toward an affirmation of life more
representative of the times. In contrast, he mentioned Norman
Mailer's *The Naked and the Dead* as a deplorable example of the
impasse which could result when Hemingway's "nihilism" was
taken to extremes.

A decade older than when he first read Hemingway, and happily married to Dorothy Duncan, MacLennan now found Hemingway's women inadequate: "they are almost never real women:
they are at best lyric emotions."[16] Indeed, to MacLennan "the
history of literature never saw a period in which women were
treated with a more incredible contempt and indifference than
they were by the best writers of America   between the years 1920
and 1940."[17]

Thus, by 1950 when he began writing *The Watch that Ends the
Night*, MacLennan had clarified his position on Hemingway
without entirely dispensing with him. There remained an emotional attachment to the first contemporary writer to strike his
imagination that he could not shake off. Long before Hemingway
committed suicide, he seemed "unbalanced" or deranged to
MacLennan, who somewhat clumsily dragged in Freudian
references to "the death-wish" to describe Hemingway's most
fundamental drive. His ambiguous feelings about Hemingway
centred on the passion in Hemingway's work: on the one hand,
it was moving, even thrilling; on the other hand, it was
dangerous, undoubtedly destructive. As he wrote in 1948, "Canadians might enjoy the books of Hemingway and Faulkner, but
we couldn't help regarding them as extreme; and, in the bottom
of our hearts we felt that both men were unsound because they
both so obviously lacked commonsense."[18]

It is evident from a long letter MacLennan sent to his friend
and editor at Macmillans, John Gray, that almost as soon as he
had begun drafting scenes for *The Watch that Ends the Night* late
in 1950, the whole question of the nature of the hero perplexed
him. One aspect of his musings — which had arisen naturally
out of the service his previous fiction had done for the growth
of Canada's national identity — centred on the relationship between the nation and its citizens, particularly its important citizens
or leaders. "It is a fact today," he argued,

    ... that the destinies of millions of people are not af-

fected by their own characters at all, but by the policies
of nations. The novel of civil life, one might say,
becomes indistinguishable from the novel of the private
soldier in the army. And this theme — the soldier as
victim of a huge, blind, inhuman organization — has
been done to death.

On the other hand, where individual character was
destiny before, national character seems to be destiny
now. I have felt this deeply for a long time, ever since
before World War II began. And it was this feeling, probably more than anything else, which was responsible
for the nature of at least two of my novels before *Each
Man's Son*. People who don't feel this way about national character naturally have thought that a book like
The Precipice was cold and intellectual. At any rate it
was a relative failure.

But if you look back on the great dramatic characters —
Oedipus, Faust, Hamlet, Lear, Othello, Macbeth — only
Hamlet is credible today, assuming Hamlet to be a
modern man. No modern man could ignore so blindly
the warning signs of impending danger as did the
others unless he were mad, in which case he would not
be tragic. The last great tragic heroes were Capt. Ahab
[*Moby Dick*] and Rubashov [*Darkness at Noon*], and it is
significant that Rubashov was not so much the symbol
as the incarnation of communistic intellectualism. But
any other man intelligent enough to be a great general
(Macbeth and Othello), or a great king (Oedipus) would
inevitably have enough sophistication, enough
knowledge of society and psychology, to withhold his
decisive actions until he had verified the evidence. At
least, any modern civilized man would so act.

On the other hand, this is not true of nations. Nations
are apparently as incapable of heeding warning signs as
were primitives like Othello and Oedipus. Nations succeed or fail according to their characters, and in the case
of nation after nation, the indirect tragic flaw has
brought them to visible ruin before your eyes. Germany
was Faust (the ablest and blindest of all the tragic
heroes). The flaw in France is *La peur d'être dupe* – the overtrust
in the intellectual which enables France as a nation to be satisfied

if she can analyze a situation in such a way to uphold her intellectual vanity even at the cost of her existence. The flaw in the United
States is the flaw of adolescent pride, which is constantly at war
with the good side of that same adolescent who has received a
very moral upbringing and can't understand why everyone
doesn't like him, who doesn't want to grow up and – oh, God,
the United States is so complicated and yet so transparent!

But a country like ours, at least up to the moment, is at best
a sort of Horatio to Hamlet – though the U.S.A. is not much
of a Hamlet.[19]

Behind these remarks hovered the Korean War which for the
last six months had been much on everyone's mind. To MacLennan, it had special significance because it threatened to disprove
his theory that the Second World War had marked a strenthen-
ing of moral optimism and that a new (and better) age was imminent. Judging from his literary comparisons, he was now ignoring Hemingway (possibly because Hemingway's *Across the
River and Into the Trees* had attracted critical scorn that year) and
turning instead to Shakespeare (whose tragedies had been held
up by both his father and his Oxford friends as supreme example of the heroic) in his search for models. Certainly his own personal experience had militated against his accepting any notion
that character is destiny: a wilful father, the Depression and two
world wars — to mention only the salient examples which might
have sprung first to his mind — had moulded his life regardless.
What he groped for, as if in the dark, was a hero that would both
be as "great" and "tragic" (and as "famous") as Shakespeare's
heroes, but who also would reflect the modern age more accurately than most so-called "modern" protagonists. "It is no accident," he maintained to Gray, "that the best contemporary
novels have narrowed the field so that they deal with only a few
individuals and probe the depth of those characters, yet have,
on the whole, been unable to make the claim that these characters
are "great" enough to be genuinely "tragic."[20]

To complicate matters, after getting his knuckles rapped by
Canadian critics for straying south of the border in his third
published novel *The Precipice*, he was more convinced than ever
that he must write out of and reflect the Canadian scene if he
was to be successful. That meant that his hero must also be

quintessentially "Canadian". Since Canada seemed to him (in that comparison suggested by an image from a poem by Douglas LePan, "*Coureurs de bois*" (1948)) much more like the minor character Horatio than the flamboyant hero Hamlet, the dilemma seemed impossible to resolve. Overlooking Horatio's sterling qualities for the simple reason that he was not centre-stage, MacLennan wrestled with the contradiction he saw between the need to create a modern hero of real stature and the necessity of reflecting a national character that was far from heroic.

Fortunately, the new job he took up at McGill in the fall of 1951 gave him the security he needed to ponder these issues. Gone was the insistent desperation with which he had churned out *Each Man's Son*, a novel which had, in his opinion, "become narrow, cloistered and bitter"[21] in the writing. Teaching courses on the history of English prose and modern fiction, both of which included Hemingway, were just what he needed to allow his mind free range on literary matters and to give time a chance to pass.

Six months later, he looked once again at the world in general and at Canada and literary matters in particular and put forward his views in an address for the University of New Brunswick called "The Present as Seen in its Literature".[22] Although he spoke of the artist at large, his remarks were highly personal:

> The literture of doom and despair - its eloquence and sombre beauty has filled our minds and interpreted our emotions from 1914 to the present time. And now, quite suddenly, its mood has been fractured. Any one who writes books today feels as if he were in the unnatural calm which lies in the cone of a typhoon. The hour is midnight and all around him the winds are whirling. He knows they are there, but suddenly he can't hear them, he can't guess what their direction will be when they strike again. Since the atom bomb fell on Hiroshima; more particularly since the world split into two opposite camps between east and west; the shape of things to come has been obscured. The artist, like everyone else, feels the iminent presence of tremendous events. But what their nature will be — above all what direction these events will take — the artist cannot even guess. Not only are signs lacking. Familiar symbols have become inadequate .... Since 1945, most of our literature has lost the power to use the symbols of its

trade to mediate between men and the corrosive force of their undefined emotions .... It may very possibly mean that the moral climate has changed for the better.[23]

With reference to Hemingway, T. S. Eliot, Faulkner, Mailer and others, MacLennan described the literature of the first half of the twentieth century as one of "frustrated heroism", the high point (or rather the low point) of which was "the suicidal mood of the 1930's"[24] best represented by Hemingway. MacLennan singled out a novel by the South African writer Alan Paton, *Cry, The Beloved Country,* as an example of what he thought was a shift from nihilism to affirmation: like Hemingway, Paton "shrinks from nothing," but his hero, the black parson Stephen Kumalo, is a "symbol which will have, for later writers, a power of attraction greater than that of any hero of Hemingway" because he demonstrates that love is "more enormous" than hate.[25]

And what of Canada's potential role in this moral edification? MacLennan rose to rhetorical heights as he expressed his renewed faith in a Canada that had been changing apace: "Canada has been uniquely fortunate in the past forty years. She entered this century as narrowly innocent as a puritanical adolescent .... She, too, has undergone prodigious psychological changes, but instead of being ground down into the mud, she has only been splashed with it by passing cars. She has lost her innocence and with its loss the symbols of childhood have lost their power and use .... More and more we are becomng a nation of city-dwellers. More and more have we become involved directly and past recall in international affairs."[26]

As MacLennan indicated here, Canada was evolving into a position that would render her *especially suited* to represent the spirit of the new age. Canadian writers and painters alike, according to him, were already busy exploring "in their own quiet way" the "frontiers of the spirit." Gone was Canada's earlier Victorian notion of "virtue" as equivalent to "good" (a subject he had treated in *The Precipice*; at last the time was ripe for the treatment of evil in relation to love. With new confidence, MacLennan baldly claimed, "I predict that twenty-five years from now the literature and art of Canada will have developed so far that it will be recognized as an integral part of the literature and art of the English-speaking world."[27]

Within a year, he had refined these ideas into the single statement that was to be the bedrock of his aesthetic theory from then on: that the artist had the responsibility "within a framework of truth to make compensation for the human predicament."[28] In other words, great art must show that good triumphs over evil, that the force of love is more powerful than that of destructive hate.

Although this speech shows that MacLennan had resolved national matters for his own purposes as a writer, it reveals that he was still having difficulty settling on a hero. "The mercury is still wavering in the glass," he admitted. "The compasses are still swinging in wild and contradictory directions."[29] A scan of the many articles and essays he wrote for journals during the 1950s suggests the crux of his problem: he was torn in his notion of the "heroic". On the one hand, he greatly admired sheer physical strength, but on the other hand, he respected moral strength, a strength of character which might be termed stoic. The former arose directly from his boyhood love of boxing, tennis, sailing and other sports and was reinforced in much of the literature he enjoyed — Homeric adventures or the *Boys Own Paper* and *Chums* escapades; the latter resulted from his admiration of his father who set his son an example of stoicism by his great powers of endurance which MacLennan — especially in completing the long education his father chose for him — imitated through the habit of self-denial, an attitude also reinforced by literature, mainly explicitly Christian.

These two concepts of the "heroic" were not entirely compartmentalized for MacLennan — his father encouraged his tennis, for example — but for his purposes as a writer, they were not easily reconciled. His articles during the decade frequently concerned athletic heroes: baseball stars like Ty Cobb,[30] hockey players like Maurice "Rocket" Richard,[31] tennis champions like William Tilden[32] and sailors like Joshua Slocum[33]; a fascination which culminated in an essay called significantly "The Homeric Tradition" (1955).[34] In this piece, MacLennan admitted that his favourite writers (judged at least by the amount of time spent reading) had been the sports columnists in the newspapers. He confessed at once that the "celebration of champions" in modern sports columns was exclusively male fare, but went on to justify his enduring interest by tracing the genre right back to Homer's *Iliad*. Such heroes display "enough physical, mental and moral capacity to offer a real challenge to destiny.'' For most readers, he concluded, ''physical prowess, the perfect control of the nervous system, the body and the mind, the absolute dedication to performing a difficult action supremely well, is worth any man's life-time effort.'' Successful athletes provide modern men with ''a larger-than-life'' hero.

Although MacLennan stoutly defended this view of the ''heroic'' with some consistency, and even claimed that it put demands on the intelligence that equalled the physical, he knew better. The truth was that the kind of intelligence he saw in sports was closer to the cunning of Ulysses than to any civilized wisdom. ''The better an athlete is,'' he said elsewhere, ''the less he knows about what he is doing .... His performance rushes right out of his subconscious so that he seems possessed by a power greater than his own.''[35]

The instinctive man of action, he knew, had limitations: too often such men could degenerate into mere brutality. Shakespeare's heroes, he observed in contrast elsewhere, Hamlet in particular, represented man as ''noble, like an angel, the paragon of animals,''[36] since heroes like Hamlet were more likely to think and debate than act. MacLennan, intellectually at least, was more likely to agree that Shakespeare's heroes were more truly ''great'' and ''tragic'' than Hemingway's. Emotionally, though, his attraction to the heroic splendour of men of action persisted, not least in his continuing admiration of Hemingway.

In an essay that obliquely throws considerable light on this matter, ''Modern Tennis — A Study in Decadence'',[37] he defined decadence in sport by referring to Hemingway's description of the development of bull-fighting in Spain: ''decay sets in when an art, once satisfying, begins to magnify certain aspects at the expense of the activity as a whole.'' His argument eventually carried over into the realm of writing. Just as he saw tennis being destroyed by the ''mania for speed,'' so also he saw that Hemingway's need for ''immediate and constant tension''[38] had chipped away at the integrity of the ''hero'': Hemingway's ''heroes,'' he was saying by 1954, ''are generally monosyllabic primitives in search of dream girls and combat for the sake of the muscle-flexing and excitement it gives them''; they are ''incomplete ... as human beings.''[39]

If MacLennan saw so clearly the limitations of the physical hero, if he really believed that the heroes of most modern literature

(Hemingway's in particular) were adolescent, incomplete, even decadent, and if he truly wished to opt for the quiet maturity he considered representative of the new era in general and of Canada especially, why did his attachment to the physical style of heroism persist? One simple answer might be that he had not entirely outgrown those adolescent fantasies he claimed to deplore. But there is another reason more important to his craft as a writer. Although he did not see it fully himself, he sensed that the physical hero demanded fast action writing, and that fast action writing was more dramatic and interesting for readers of fiction. To put it another way, ever since his success with the powerful description of the Halifax explosion in *Barometer Rising*, he had felt most at ease writing about violent action. Physical conflict had always called forth his best talents. And it was this that he continued to admire in Hemingway. The master's heroes might be brutal goons, but the descriptive prose their antics elicited was matchless.

By 1954, by which time he was well into the writing of his own novel, he was finally able to separate Hemingway's content from Hemingway's style. In "Homage to Hemingway", the only original essay in the collection *Thirty and Three* which Dorothy Duncan assembled that year, MacLennan praised "the morning freshness of his style," the power of his language and his fidelity to the world of the five senses.[40] "The undeniable fact remains," MacLennan maintained, "that each time we encounter the prose of Hemingway himself (divorcing it from any ideas we may expect it to convey) we recognize it as the work of a master in its ability to move us and expand our perceptions."[41] But that parenthetical qualification was crucial:

> Since his interest is to make us feel, he can seldom
> allow us to think. He dare not use characters who are
> thoughtful men, for if he did they would ruin the bare
> perfection of his style by speaking in a dialogue full of
> abstract words .... Thoughtful men cannot help living
> on mental levels that are distinct from physical ones.
> They are too rational, or too engrossed with the need of
> earning a living, to go to Africa to shoot lions or to
> Spain to watch bulls being killed. Liquor is apt to dull
> their perceptions instead of heightening them, as liquor
> seems to do for Hemingway's heroes. Rational men
> discuss their own neuroses, they are interested in

science, they become involved in a multitude of activities for which the Hemingway style lacks an adequate vocabulary. They argue about communism and
democracy, are concerned with the high cost of living
and getting on in their jobs, they worry about their
children's education and the danger of another depression. They show an interest in women as personalities,
not as mere embodiments of a sensual dream. Their
sexual lives are not ritualistic. In short, their minds,
their ambitions, their awareness of themselves as
coherent, complex personalities involved in a mundane
existence makes them entirely unsuitable as catalysts for
Hemingway. Such men are even apt to wonder at times
how they can save their souls.[42]

Because Hemingway had reduced men to the level of animals and
influenced others to do the same, MacLennan judged him "to
a considerable extent responsible for the unhappy condition of
the novel at the present time."[43]

By the spring of 1955, this view of Hemingway had firmed into a doctrinaire stance: "Hemingway's very genius," he told a
gathering of the Royal Society of Canada, "has put him in a strait-
jacket .... Educated men do not talk like Hemingway
characters."[44] From now on, MacLennan would associate Hemingway with derangement by using the image of the "strait-
jacket" to describe what his style did to content. "The novel must
return to people again," MacLennan confidently asserted in what
was implicitly a description of his own contrasting aims with his
current novel, "must prove its power to celebrate and judge their
lives, must believe in their value, and must respect the
audience."[45]

To whom could MacLennan now turn for models of "heroism"?
Shakespeare, as we have seen, had been lurking in the back of
his mind since 1950 in relation to his theory of the "tragic flaw"
in nations. In his letter to John Gray, he had decided that among
Shakespeare's heroes, he could imagine only Hamlet taking part
in any modern dilemma. It seemed since then that he had abandoned them as models, but now, five years later, he re-read
twenty-two plays of Shakespeare with some view to evaluating
those heroes once again.

To his astonishment, he found that "more than any writer who
ever lived, Shakespeare took it for granted that decent men are

dull. Worse still he assumed they were all dupes. He does not offer a single truly religious person in the whole folio, none who is at once steadfast, intelligent and competent."[46] Like the heroes of Hemingway, Shakespeare's men seemed incomplete to MacLennan; like Hemingway, Shakespeare seemed to know "that ... even an attempt to tell the whole truth about his characters would spoil the fine theatrical effects he wanted"; like Hemingway, Shakespeare was foremost a "magician" skilled at "incantation".[47]

The only thoughtful heroes MacLennan could locate in contemporary literature were those of the British novelist C. P. Snow who seemed to have appropriated the authority of science for the world of fiction,[48] but somehow — although they commanded his respect — Snow's novels left MacLennan a little cold: "But what of books like these?" he wrote to John Gray. "Is knowledge and insight and analytical power enough? Somewhere the soul rebels .... Reading Snow reminded me of the passage in Lucretius about the joys of standing on a promontory and watching the sailors struggling in the sea."[49] Ultimately, MacLennan abandoned the search for a model hero, and turned instead to Conrad and Tolstoy for inspiration in the realm of theme and form. He would have to work the matter out on his own.

In an essay exploring this quandary, called "The Death of the Hero"[50], MacLennan continued to chart the direction he himself must take. Neither in life nor in literature were there heroes to emulate: "With the resignation of Winston Churchill from active life," he wrote, "it has become a time without heroes above the level of the sports arena .... The few literary heroes remaining, Eliot, Hemingway, Faulkner, are tired old men .... There are no heroes any more, either in books or in the world of letters itself." Recognizing that "heroes can exist only when men have some fairly clear idea of what they think life ought to be," he concluded that "literature ... must continue to nudge closer and closer to the truth of life, deal with more reality and less magic and the incantation of words."

Considering that MacLennan had been struggling hard to work out his own theory of the heroic at the same time he was incorporating those notions into his novel, and that he had already created heroes in four previous novels, it must have irked him to read in a learned journal "that Canada has produced no great writers because ours is a country without a single literary hero

— the argument being that greatness in a literary man depends on his ability to create characters."[51] This remark prodded him into further action, however. Two months later, in an essay called "The Transition Ends" (1955), he appears to have considered and accepted this premise and to have focussed many of his previous thoughts about the present situation in literature:

> If it is in the character of the fictional hero that an age reveals its inner meaning, it seems to me the best proof that the temper of society has changed is that these solitary, neurotic, haunted heroes of the past fifty years are already beginning to look like historical characters. What manner of man the new hero will be cannot yet be seen, but it is almost certain that he will be more intelligent than the haunted men of the transition, less desperate, less neurotic, and more willing to accept life as it is. As it is with men, so it is with nations. Only by accepting their own limitations can they become wise; only by facing their own fears can they be happy. [52]

"The world of art," he maintained in an image from his earlier speech about watching the "typhoon" of the modern world, is "barometric"[53], since it reflects society. Because "the conditions which produced the attitudes of 'modernists' like Eliot, Picasso, James Joyce, Proust, Dos Passos and Hemingway have changed out of all recognition," a hero more typical of the "quiet accents" of the "new age" is called for. As MacLennan now saw it, the "ferocious neuroticism" that characterized the heroes of the age of transition "developed into the psychoses of fascism, communism and naziism" with the result that "the literary heroes of the transitional age became increasingly more desperate and still more solitary." For examples he referred to Andre Malraux's *La Condition Humaine* and Arthur Koestler's *Darkness at Noon*. It was now the ordinary man, the "little man" [as in *Little Man, What Now?* by Rudolf Ditzen] that typified that 1950s. In an article only three months later, "Will TV Produce a New Breed of Canadian Hero?"[54] he concluded that the absence in Canada of "hero-worship" for any Superman (which he dismissed as "the oldest recurrent dream of the mentally ungrown") signalled national maturity. As for Canada's adulation of athletes, he excused this on grounds that it provided a healthy "emotional safety-valve" for man's innate aggression.[55]

Although MacLennan's deliberations about the nature of the hero were not the only problems with which he was wrestling during the first half of the fifties (considerations of form, time and theme also plagued him), it was primarily of his own heroes that he was thinking when he confessed to John Gray in 1954, "I'm still hoping to get the novel ready for a fall publication in 1955, but this is one book I simply can't afford to rush. Which doesn't mean the writing — that in itself is no longer a problem to me — but grasping the meaning."[56]

Grasping the meaning of casting an ordinary man or "little man" as his hero was indeed difficult. As he recognized, "it is not the new age, but the transition to it that stirs the passions."[57] How was he to make a quiet, little, ordinary man as interesting as those shocking, even scandalous heroes of the transition had been?

The resolution of this challenge came gradually through the merging of an opinion MacLennan had long worked on independently and the theories of psychology which had by now filtered into common parlance. As far back as 1949, MacLennan saw the use to which psychology might be put in the service of fiction. Neither television nor movies, he argued, could "probe deeply below the surface of the individual mind .... The inner scene of a novel — the one that counts — is more private than a confessional box, for it is both the conscious *and* unconscious of the individual character .... The more public our outer lives are, the more private our inner lives have become .... It is to this privacy, this solitude within the apparently uniform crowd, that the novelist of today addresses himself."[58]

By 1956, that vague "search for the frontiers of the spirit" which had been the keynote of his address at New Brunswick in 1952 had become much more precise. "In the human subconscious," as everyone these days is supposed to know," he wrote, "sadism and masochism are constantly at grips. Between the hunter and the hunted, the slugger and the slugged, the subconscious bond is profound."[59] The truly dramatic conflict of the mid-twentieth century for MacLennan as he worked through this theory was the one that took place within every individual between the contradictory impulses that made man the unique creature he is. Fascinated as he had always been at the tension between man's urge to create and his compulsion to destroy — a concern that lay behind the best essay he wrote during these years "Joseph

Haydn and Captain Bligh'"[60]—MacLennan absorbed the popular
psychology of his day and created for his fourth published novel
a protagonist whose response to inner conflict illustrated his
heroic mettle.

With George Stewart in *The Watch that Ends the Night*, MacLennan illustrated his theory of the hero. A man of no extraordinary
talents, not even possessed of that "life-force" he envies in both
his friend, the surgeon Jerome Martell, and his own wife, the
painter Catherine, George embarks on a heroic odyssey of the
soul. The circumstances of his life compel him to respond, and
he does so with innate nobility. Like Marlow in Conrad's *Heart
of Darkness*, one of the books MacLennan was teaching at McGill
and which in its psychological theme was one model for his own
book, George plumbs the depth of human despair and feels every
lust and murderous impulse of which man is capable. He travels
down into the evil in his own soul, knows chaos, and, despite
the temptation to commit suicide in the face of nihilism, chooses
form, morality and love. At the novel's climax, George faces the
crippling knowledge that Catherine must die — and fairly soon
— of the embolisms caused with increasing frequency by her weak
heart. Furthermore, he must come to grips with this under the
enormous stress of knowing that Jerome, the man Catherine has
passionately loved and married before himself, although long
thought dead, has returned and visited her in his absence.
"Then," as George puts it, "comes the Great Fear .... There was
no discharge in this war. There was only endurance. There lay
ahead only the fearful tunnel with nothing at the end. Could I
or could I not — could she or could she not — believe that this
struggle had any value in itself?"

For a time, George weakens and yields to the destructive impulses in himself, an experience which is mirrored by MacLennan in one of the very few passages that approach stream-of-
consciousness in his work:

> My subconscious rose. The subconscious — the greedy,
> lustful, infantile subconscious, indiscriminate and un-
> critical discoverer of truths, half-truths and chimaeras
> which are obscene fusions of foetal truths, this source of
> hate, love, murder and salvation, of poetry and destruc-
> tion, this Everything in Everyman, how quickly if it
> swamps him, can it obliterate the character a man has
> spent a lifetime creating!

Then a man discovers in dismay that what he believed to be his identity is no more than a tiny canoe at the mercy of an ocean. Shark-filled, plankton-filled, refractor of light, terrible and mysterious, for years this ocean has seemed to slumber beneath the tiny identity it received from the dark river.

Now the ocean rises and the things within it become visible. Little man, what now? The ocean rises, all frames disappear from around the pictures, there is no form, no sense, nothing but chaos in the darkness of the ocean storm. Little man, what now?

The resolution comes from deep inside himself; somehow he finds the strength to cope:

... And the earth was without form, and void; and darkness was on the face of the deep.
... And the spirit of God moved upon the face of the waters. And God said: *let there be light*: and there was light.
Here, I found at last, is the nature of the final human struggle. Within, not without.[61]

Although it is possible to criticize MacLennan for casting his hero's revelation in words from the Bible rather than his own, or to fault his artistry for leading us up to this tremendous insight only to admit that he finds it impossible to describe such a struggle in words, his representation of a type of heroism suited to contemporary times is clear. And it could not be further from Hemingway. Indeed, it is a total rejection of those ''greedy, lustful, infantile'' impulses that, according to him, motivated his former idol's heroes. As George comments elsewhere in the novel, ''there it was, the ancient marriage of good and evil, the goodness of this day and compulsive evil people must see and know, but the sky dominated in the end. Pale and shining, it told me that our sins can be forgiven.''[62] As the novel's original title — ''Requiem'' — suggests, MacLennan intended to pay tribute in a way more appropriate to the 1950s to his own ''lost generation.''[63]

The extraordinary thing about *The Watch that Ends the Night* seems to be MacLennan's inclusion of a character such as Jerome Martell in a novel that relegated Hemingway and his heroes to the back seats of modern fiction. At first glance Jerome is a hero remarkably similar to Hemingway's men: physically strong, animalistic and instinctive, full of that "explosive" life-force that more often than not causes chaos, a man attracted to war (even to the Spanish Civil War in which Hemingway's Robert Jordan had fought), his essence seems to be caught in the name he has taken from his adopted parents — Martell "the hammer". According to MacLennan, he flowed directly from a dream into his imagination in the winter of 1956, complete with the episode (so reminiscent of Hemingway) in which he escapes down-river in a canoe from a man bent on destroying him. In fact, he would later single Jerome out as "the key figure of the novel:"[64]

> By what strange guidance was he nameless? Why that scene in New Brunswick .... Ostensibly he had no part in the novel I was blundering along with, but some force caused me to know this was integral, and I spent a winter on it.[65]

For MacLennan, the character Jerome had come to him as a flash-back to "the prehistoric origins of original sins"; "if the public," he could later claim, "can't feel any sympathy or pity for Martell, all I can say is that they refuse to look into their own souls."[66] Tracing Jerome's revolutionary tendencies right back to the first rising of man against the father, MacLennan created a character who seems to be taken wholesale from Hemingway.

However, although Jerome is portrayed in much the same way as a Hemingway hero, and is manifestly a protagonist of what MacLennan called the "transition", he is fundamentally different from Hemingway's men: the great "spirit" in him that expresses itself destructively also shows itself in the *creative* drive to heal others through his extraordinary powers as a surgeon. Ultimately, it is Jerome whose mere presence in her hospital room calls Catherine back from the brink of death: "He is," MacLennan would later explain to John Gray, "in some ways, a great man. The same force which gives life also destroys it, and then rebuilds it.'"[67] The hammer is not only a weapon, it is also a *tool*; the Biblical Jerome may have been militant, but he was also a soldier *of God*. It is true that MacLennan emphasizes Jerome's destructive capacities, but it is important to note that he illustrates that it is *circumstances* beyond the control of the individual (in this case that "transition" of the thirties which included the Spanish Civil War) that are responsible for this. It is man's prerogative, however, within any particular arena, to choose the direction his energies take: every man has the opportunity to resolve within himself the great conflict between his destructive urges and his creative powers.

Jerome is not a Hemingway-style hero; he is simply George Stewart writ large. Both men share with all men and women[68] the same dilemma, and to MacLennan that dilemma was the fundamental nexus of the human condition. Circumstances might vary from one person to the next and the inner strength of one individual would never be exactly the same as that of another, but for MacLennan, as he described it in a CBC talk later published as "The Story of a Novel"[69], "somehow I was going to write a book which would not depend on character-in-action, but on spirit-in-action. The conflict here, the essential one, was between the human spirit of Everyman and Everyman's human condition." This, he explained, meant rejecting both Shakespeare's external action (as both "inaccurate and inadequate") and the heroes of modern novels (who were "outcasts ... men excessively primitive ... excessively criminal").

In *The Watch that Ends the Night*, MacLennan managed to have his cake and eat it too. Not only did he create in George Stewart a hero who was truly representative of the modern age, whose inner conflict seemed both "great" and "tragic", but he managed in Jerome Martell a "larger-than-life" hero who could be represented in Hemingway-style fast action prose without endorsing Hemingway's "pessimistic nihilism." MacLennan portrayed the variety of "Everyman's human condition" by showing these two men side by side. For George, a cruel personal fate imposes itself from without; Jerome is swept up on the wave of mindless passion that war had always seemed to MacLennan. Each of them pits that "human spirit of Everyman" against his own particular "human condition", but the struggle is at heart the same. And the resolution is the same: the power of good (or the creative drive) ultimately triumphs over the power of evil (or the destructive drive). Why? Because for MacLennan the will to survive is stronger than despair.

From his personal experience, MacLennan was predisposed to view the world this way. Not only did his intensely Christian upbringing have its effect, but his own struggles to overcome despair[70] — both in the 1930s at Princeton and again in the 1950s when his wife's existence hung teetering in the balance — also marked him. The aesthetic philosophy of affirmation which he developed theoretically during the fifties and incorporated into *The Watch that Ends the Night* reflected a temperamental necessity.

As he wrote his novel, his choice for a personal hero, as described in his essay "Triumph: the Story of a Man's Greatest Moment" (1957)[71], was Handel. An unlikely choice at first glance, but the pattern was the same: a life that was a sequence of disasters, temporary despair, forbearance derived from Christian revelation, a drying up of artistic inspiration, despair; and then, in a burst of glory, the creation of the *Messiah*. Overcoming the urge to destroy oneself, faith that life is worth living, patience while waiting for creativity to flare up again — this was for MacLennan the truly heroic enterprise of man, and one which he was watching firsthand during this decade while his wife — like Catherine — fought for her very life as a series of embolisms broke her strength but not her creativity. Despair might haunt the darkest watch that ended the night, but the rising sun of affirmation was sure to follow.

In dramatizing the "subconscious bond" between the creative and destructive aspects of man, MacLennan's fiction took a giant step forward. In *Each Man's Son* he had tried to illustrate each of these impulses in separate characters: the brutal prizefighter Archie MacNeil and the humanitarian doctor Daniel Ainslie. But even in those two characters there were hints that personality could not be that simple. Despite MacLennan's confidence in the almost god-like powers of doctors, Ainslie has more than a touch of granite in his will; and Archie somehow enlists our sympathy in a way no outright goon ever could. In *The Watch that Ends the Night*, these undertones blossomed into full understanding. Through battling with the theory of a hero for modern times, MacLennan had seen that all of us are potential bullies and possible healers; the two were never mutually exclusive.

MacLennan used the work of Hemingway as a springboard to launch a hero he thought reflected the new age. George's maturity would represent a development beyond those adolescent heroes of the twenties; his "quiet accents" would replace the "ferocious neuroticism" that had characterized the "suicidal" thirties; above all, his inner battle to overcome the destructive demons called forth by despair would transport readers across the frontiers of the spirit. Although the splendid Jerome might seem remote from the lives of average readers because his particular "human condition" was unusually dramatic and his "human spirit" remarkably strong, George Stewart was a man with whom any reader could imaginatively trade places in order to see the importance, the depth and even the beauty of the age-old pattern.

Notes

1   H.M., "The View from Here", *Montrealer* (Nov. 1952), p. 58.
2   H.M., "Hemingway, Hunter and the Hunted", A Writer's Diary, *Montreal Star* (21 Sept. 1963), p. 4.
3   H.M., "The View from Here", *Montrealer* (Nov. 1952), p. 58.
4   H.M., letter to his mother, 4 Dec. 1929, property of Frances MacLennan.
5   H.M., "So All Their Praises", unpublished ms., McGill Collection, box 3, part 1, folders 1-2.
6   H.M., "A Man Should Rejoice", unpublished ms., McGill Collection, box 3, part 2, folders 3-9.
7   H.M., letter to George Barret, 5 March 1935, McCord Museum, Montreal.
8   H.M., "So All Their Praises", p. 147.
9   This passage, found in *A Farewell to Arms*, is quoted and analysed at some length by MacLennan in "Changing Values in Fiction", *Canadian Author and Bookman*, 25, No. 3 (Autumn 1949), pp. l3ff.
10 H.M., "The Discovery of Canada as a Literary Scene", unpublished address, University of Rochester (1935), McGill Collection, box 1, part 1, folders 3, 1-9. See also "Literature in a New Country", *Scotchman's Return and Other Essays*, (Toronto: Macmillan, 1960), pp. 140-1.
11 H.M., "Culture, Canadian Style", *Saturday Review of Literature*, 25 (28 March 1942), p. 18.
12 H.M., "Fifty Grand", *Montrealer* (May 1957), p. 38.
13 H.M., "The Present World as Seen in its Literature", Founder's Day Address, University of New Brunswick (18 Feb. 1952), p. 8.
14 H.M., "Changing Values in Fiction", p. l4.
15 *Ibid.*, p. 13
16 H.M. probably took this idea directly from an essay on Hemingway by Edmund Wilson in 1941; see "Hemingway: Gauge of Miracle", *The Wound and the Bow* (London: Methuen, 1961), p. 199, where the lovers in *A Farewell to Arms* are described as "the abstractions of a lyric emotion."
17 H.M., "Changing Values in Fiction", p. 15.
18 H.M., "The Future Trend in the Novel", *Canadian Author and Bookman*, 24, No. 3 (Sept. 1948), p. 5.
19 H.M., letter to John Gray, 7 Dec. 1950, Macmillan Collection.
20 *Ibid.*
21 H.M., letter to John Gray, 5 Jan. 1953, Macmillan Collection.
22 H.M., "The Present World as Seen in its Literature", Founder's Day Address (18 Feb. 1952).
23 *Ibid.*, pp. 5-6.
24 *Ibid.*, p. 7.
25 *Ibid.*, p. 11.
26 *Ibid.*, p. 12
27 *Ibid.*
28 H.M., "The Artist and Critic in Society", *Princeton Alumni Weekly*, 53 (30

Jan. 1953), p. 91.

[29] H.M., "The Present World as Seen in its Literature", p. 11.

[30] H.M., "The View from Here", *Montrealer* (May 1952), pp. 58-9.

[31] H.M., "Cinerama 'Nightmare'; Spirit of Hockey", *Saturday Night* (26 Feb. 1955), pp. 9-10.

[32] H.M., "Modern Tennis — A Study in Decadence", *Montrealer* (Nov. 1953), pp. 54-5.

[33] H.M., "A Great Story Reborn", *Montrealer* (May 1953), pp. 54-5.

[34] H.M., "The Homeric Tradition", *Montrealer* (Sept. 1955), p. 21, p. 23.

[35] H.M., "The View from Here", *Montrealer* (May 1952), pp. 58-9.

[36] H.M., "The View from Here", *Montrealer* (Nov. 1952), pp. 58-9.

[37] H.M., "Modern Tennis — A Study in Decadence", p. 54.

[38] H.M., "Changing Values in Fiction", p. 15.

[39] H.M., "Homage to Hemingway", *Thirty and Three* (Toronto: Macmillan, 1954), pp. 86-7.

[40] *Ibid.*, p. 86.

[41] *Ibid.*, p. 87

[42] *Ibid.*, pp. 94-5.

[43] *Ibid.*, p. 95.

[44] H.M., "The Challenge to Prose", *Transactions of the Royal Society of Canada*, 49, Series 3, Section 2 (June 1955), p. 53.

[45] *Ibid.*, p. 55.

[46] H.M., "Shakespeare Revisited", *Montrealer* (May 1955), p. 23.

[47] *Ibid.*, pp. 23-4.

[48] H.M., "Death of the Hero", *Montrealer* (June 1955), p. 25.

[49] H.M., letter to John Gray, 21 Dec. 1951, Macmillan Collection.

[50] H.M., "Death of the Hero", *Montrealer* (June 1955).

[51] H.M., "The Homeric Tradition", *Montrealer* (Sept. 1955), p. 23.

[52] H.M., "The Transition Ends", *Montrealer* (Nov. 1955), p. 27.

[53] *Ibid.*, p. 25.

[54] H.M., "Will TV Produce a New Breed of Canadian Hero?" *Liberty* (Feb. 1956), pp. 32-3, 52, 54.

[55] This was an idea he explored elsewhere, notably during the same year in "Confessions of a Wood-Chopping Man", *Montrealer* (Nov. 1956), pp. 22-4. Characteristically, he saw his own athletic endeavors as serving the same purpose.

[56] H.M., letter to John Gray, 6 July 1954, Macmillan Collection.

[57] H.M., "The Transition Ends", p. 25.

[58] H.M., "Changing Values in Fiction", *Canadian Author and Bookman*, p. 25, No. 3 (Autumn, 1949), p. 18.

[59] H.M., "Will TV Produce a New Breed of Canadian Hero", *Liberty* (Feb. 1956), p. 54.

[60] H.M., "Joseph Haydn and Captain Bligh", *Montrealer* (July 1953), pp. 50-51.

[61] H.M., *The Watch that Ends the Night* (New York: Scribners, 1959), pp. 342-3.

[62] *Ibid.*, pp. 168-9.

[63] "The title came to me the other day, and the requiem is only incidentally for Dorothy. As I see the novel, it is for our whole generation." (H.M., letter to John Gray, 15 June 1957).

[64] H.M., letter to John Gray, 28 Jan. 1958, Macmillan Collection.

[65] H.M., letter to John Gray, 4 Feb. 1958, Macmillan Collection.

[66] H.M., letter to John Gray, 9 March 1958, Macmillan Collection

[67] *Ibid.*

[68] Although this paper deals only with MacLennan's male heroes, the same truths are demonstrated in Catherine who is both creative painter and "spiritual vampire".

[69] H.M., "The Story of a Novel", *Canadian Lit.*, 3 (Winter, 1960), pp. 35-9.

[70] H.M., "Fifty Grand: A Semi-Centenarian Takes Stock", *Montrealer* (May 1957), pp. 37-41.

[71] H.M., "Triumph: The Story of a Man's Greatest Moment", *Montrealer* (March 1957), pp. 53-6, 58.

ELISABETH SMART

ELIZABETH SMART'S LYRICAL NOVEL: *BY GRAND CENTRAL STATION I SAT DOWN AND WEPT*

Lorraine McMullen

Elizabeth Smart's *By Grand Central Station I Sat Down and Wept* is an unusual novel. Closer in many ways to a symbolist poem, an impressionist painting, or a piece of music than to the traditional novel, it is most aptly termed a lyrical novel. When pieced together, events of the novel strike us as ordinary, perhaps even mundane. A young woman falls in love with a married man and has a brief affair with him; he returns to his wife and she finds herself alone and pregnant. Magazine racks are filled with stories of such unhappy love affairs, but the classics, too — Shakespeare, Ovid, Euripides, Wagner — all give us tales of ill-starred romances. The mode of expression, not the plot line, dictates whether a work is a world classic or pulp magazine fiction. Elizabeth Smart is aware of the paradox that what may appear sordid and disreputable in one form may appear lyrical and magnificent in another. She is aware also that the experience which is central to her novel encompasses the sordid and the marvellous, the sacred and profane; and her language is devised and structured to reflect these polarities.

Smart has divided her novel into ten short parts. The first three, set in California, encompass the meeting of the lovers and the consummation of their love, complicated by the presence of the lover's wife and the sense of guilt her presence engenders in the narrator-protagonist. In Part Four, the lovers are stopped by police at the Arizona border and questioned about their relationship. In Parts Five and Six, the woman returns to her Ottawa family and acquaintances, all of whom prove unsympathetic. In Part Seven, she travels to New York to meet her lover and finds him hospitalized after attempting suicide. In Part Eight she awaits his hoped-for return in a dingy New York hotel room. In Part Nine, she is once more on the west coast, now alone, pregnant, in growing despair. In Part Ten, in New York, facing her desertion, she awaits the birth of her child.

The novel begins with the first meeting of the protagonist with her future lover and ends with her realization that the affair is ended. While the novel involves a circular journey tracing a path from west to east, north to Canada, south to New York, west again and once more east, it is also, and more importantly, a voyage of mind and heart, which traces the complex graph of the protagonist's emotions throughout the affair. The novel is created of this emotional voyage. While we have come to expect a novel to concern itself with events and character development, in this lyrical work, events and character are subordinate to effect. Using words less as a language of communication than as an expression of emotion, the novel directs itself to rendering the texture of experience. "I was trying to say that this is how it is,"[1] the author explains. "How it is" — the inner reality — is the focus of this work.

As a lyrical novel, *By Grand Central Station* is something of a hybrid, combining aspects of two genres. Time, place, character, and event still exist: events occur within the space of a year; setting shifts from west to east and back; three characters interact. At the same time, much as in lyrical poetry, incantatory rhythm, lyrical and evocative language, daring and extravagant imagery heighten emotional expression. While novels are associated with storytelling, and the reader expects to find a character with whom he can identify and a plot in which he may become involved, in this novel emotional experience rather than external experience or individual character is central. The skeleton of barely identifiable events exists so that the resulting emotional effects can be expressed. Narration is subordinate to lyricism. Because it is the voice of the unmarried woman protagonist that we hear, from her perspective that we enter into experience, and her emotions that we share, the fictional world of the novel is her internal world. Events and individuals become aspects of the poetic vision, raw material for imagery. The protagonist shapes the world she sees to the expression of feeling. Objects, scenes, characters exist as images within the protagonist's lyrical subjective point of view, while the underlying plot fuses the array of disjointed images. Intensely emotional and lyrical, hence romantic in expression, the language of feeling is never out of control. Analogies and conceits, however exaggerated and even startling, are never ill-conceived or inappropriate. Literary allusions link the love affair with expressions of love throughout the ages, and biblical allusions underline its essentially sacred and eternal nature.

Interior monologue can be used to present realistic details filtered through an individual consciousness. To some extent this is what Smart does in seeking to describe "how it is". But because the reality she seeks to present is the protagonist's sensibility, the point of view is lyrical and confessional. A design of images and motifs takes form from the loose, disjointed series of events, recollections, conversations, displacing the external world or shifting from the external to the internal world to reveal the protagonist's mind and heart. Her emotional journey becomes a quest in which she abstracts impressions from the concrete world and refashions them into the texture of lyric poetry.

Characters exist to serve the lyrical intentions of the novel. The protagonist is the lyrical "I", as in a lyric poem; others are image-figures with which she interacts. Neither the protagonist, nor her lover, nor his wife, is named: all three remain shadowy figures in the lyrical acting out an archetypal pattern. Nor is any of the three described except for a few evocative details. On first meeting, the wife is seen first by the waiting protagonist, before the husband, as indication of how she is to continue to stand between the two. As the traditionally-termed injured party, the wife is portrayed as trusting and vulnerable, appealing in her very helplessness. It is her eyes that first strike the protagonist and which come to represent her innocence: "But then it is her eyes that come forward ...: her madonna eyes, soft as the newly-born, trusting as the untempted."[2] She is compared to a nymph: "... she leans over in the pool and her damp dark hair falls like sorrow, like mercy, like the mourning-weeds of pity" (p. 25). In a technique of reversal, not uncommon in this paradox-filled novel, this married woman, compared to a madonna and a nymph, appears virginal. She is associated with the fragility and innocence of flowers and birds. Her innocence is both childlike and saintly: "... the gentle flowers, able to die unceremoniously, remind me of her grief ... more angels weep for her whose devastated love runs into all the oceans of the world" (p. 27); "... her pathetic slenderness is covered over with a love as gentle as trusting as tenacious as the birds who rebuild their continually violated nests" (p. 25); "She knows nothing, but like autumn birds feels foreboding in the air ... but less wise than the birds whom small signs send on three thousand mile flights, she can only look vaguely over the Pacific ..." (p. 29).

When first seen, the protagonist's love "... fumbles with the tickets and the bags, and shuffles up to the event ..." (p. 17). "Shuffle" and "fumble" are hardly the action verbs one associates with a long-awaited romantic hero. Nor does he ever prove to be particularly heroic. This man is even more imprecisely described than his wife; in fact, he never becomes more than a silhouette or a shadow. Neither his appearance nor his personality is important. What is important is his effect on the protagonist: "... he, when he was only a word, was able to cause me sleepless nights and shivers of intimation" (p. 20). The ambivalence with which the lover is viewed is a reflection of the conflicting emotions with which the protagonist experiences her love affair, an affair she anticipates from its beginning will bring sorrow as well as joy, "I do not beckon to the Beginning, whose advent will surely strew our world with blood..." (p. 22), she says, saying at the same time of her future lover, "His foreshortened face appears in profile on the car window like the irregular graph of my doom, merciless as a mathematician, leering accompaniment to all my good resolves." The word "shadow" recurs insistently: "When his soft shadow which yet in the night comes barbed with all the weapons of guilt, is cast up hugely on the pane, I watch it as from a loge in the theatre, ..." (p. 22). As he takes her hand in the darkness of the car, she says, "... but now that hand casts everywhere an octopus shadow from which I can never escape" (p. 23). From the protagonist's lyrical point of view, the lover appears as a spectral, fateful, and often threatening figure.

The protagonist herself is passive. Her own personality is even less clearly drawn than that of her lover or his wife. Like them she is a figure in a drama which she watches unfold. She, too, serves the lyrical intention of the novel. The closer to the heart of the experience, the less concretized the individual. The protagonist remains only a voice.

Setting takes on the texture of imagery. Like the characters, it is mirrored through the eyes of the protagonist as an adjunct to emotional expression. The lush California setting presides over the lover's apotheosis, imaging its eroticism, its ecstasy, and its dangers. Like the protagonist's love, the setting appears excessive, larger than life: "Up the canyon the redwoods and the thick-leafed hands of the castor-tree forebode disaster by their beauty, built on too grand a scale" (p. 19). Menace is hidden within the beauty of the landscape: "But poison oak grows over the path and over all the banks, and it is impossible even to go into the damp overhung valley without being poisoned. Later in the year it flushes scarlet, both warning and recording fatality" (p. 19). The description underlines the sensuousness of the surroundings: "Round the doorways double-size flowers grow without encouragement: lilies, nasturtiums in a bank down to the creek, roses, geraniums, fuchsias, bleeding-hearts, hydrangeas. The sea booms. The stream rushes loudly" (p. 19). As the lush and sensuous flowers grow without encouragement, so does emotion, and it is in the lush and sensuous, and at the same time menacing, valley that the love is first consummated, a love which is to contain at least as much agony as ecstasy: "And I lay down on the redwood needles and seemed to flow down the canyon with the thunder and confusion of the stream, ..." (p. 26).

In similar, though less lyrical, fashion, the Canadian winter mirrors the response of family and acquaintances, "... how sympathetic the frozen Chaudière falls seem under the December sky, compared with these inflexible faces. ... They, who talk of a greater love, what is under the long cold of their look?" (p. 68). "Remember Ottawa in New Year's Eve sulking under snow" (p. 69). Finally, the all-night café at New York's Grand Central Station, a hangout for derelicts, where the novel ends is equally appropriate. Here the protagonist sits alone, deserted: "These tables are topped in leather on which the blood has never dried" (p. 119).

A lyrical novel is itself a paradox in its combination of features of two genres, its use of elements of the novel for lyrical purposes. In *By Grand Central Station* the aesthetic arrangement of the traditional elements is designed to express the pleasure and pain of love in a paradoxical structure, with motifs and symbols designed to show the existence of the polarities of joy and sorrow. The protagonist sees the world and experience in terms of paradox. While joyously embracing her experience, she is always aware of its dangers and of the inevitability with which sorrow follows happiness. She accepts love as "a happiness which, like birth, can afford the blood and the tearing" (p. 26).

The first words of the novel create oppositions which mirror the dialectic within the mind and heart of the protagonist. Awaiting her first meeting with her future lover, she says, "... all the muscles of my will are holding my terror to face the moment I most desire." By linking the two seeming contraries, "terror" and "desire", she sets the stage for the continuing paradoxical structure of the novel and her own ambivalent, sometimes contradictory, emotions. In the next sentence, with the words,

"Apprehension and the summer afternoon keep drying my lips
....," she links emotion with physical sensation, fusing the two
worlds, the emotional and the physical, as she will continue to
do throughout the novel.

All elements of the novel contribute to the tension of opposites
within the experience. As the effects of love and joy, of grief,
ecstasy, and despair, birth and death are the opposites to which
the narrator returns obsessively, so blood and water, the central
symbols to which she returns insistently, are paradoxical. Blood,
while associated with birth, is also linked with passion, suffering, sacrifice, and death. Water, most often linked with life and
creativity, is also associated with death.

Love is viewed by the protagonist as a flood on which she is
borne, by which she may be swept away, and in which she might
drown. "I thought [love] would be like a bird in the hand, not
a wild sea that treated me like flotsam" (p. 41); "I flow away in
a flood of love" (p. 41); "Where are we all headed for on the
swollen river of my undamned grief?" (p. 118); "I am going to
have a child, so all my dreams are of water, across which the ghost
of an almost accomplished calamity beckons. But tonight the child
lay within like the fated and only island in all the seas" (p. 118).
Through the water image, the child is linked with love.

Blood, associated with sorrow and death, is also linked with
birth: "Will there be birth from all this blood, or is death only
exacting his greedy price?" (p. 34). "Lucky Syrinx, who chose
legend instead of too much blood!" (p. 26). "He also is drowning in the blood of too much sacrifice" (p. 127); "Not all of the
poisonous tides of the blood I have spilt can influence the tidals
of love" (p. 41). The association of blood with "tidals of love"
fuses the two central images, blood and water as do the words,
"But the sea that floods is love, and it gushes out of me like an
arterial wound. I am drowning in it" (p. 118), an image which
at the same time links love with death. The flood of love on which
the protagonist is borne does become the flood in which she
drowns: "The drowning never ceases. The water submerges and
blends, but I am not dead. I am under the sea. The entire sea
is on top of me" (pp. 118-19). The emotion which carried her to
ecstasy carries her to despair.

Birth as a motif is linked with love from the novel's beginning.
"Will there be a birth from all this blood, or is death only exacting his greedy price?" "Is an infant struggling in the triangular

womb?'' (p. 34) the protagonist asks as the affair begins. The birth motif embraces several kinds of birth, linking three levels of experience: the birth of a passionate love affair, the birth of a child, the creation of a lyrical work.

The narrator turns to the classics and the Bible for analogies and symbols adequate to express her passion. She makes of herself and her love archetypal figures acting out their love in the world of myth and legend. Their experience and emotions rise above the temporal and parochial to become constituents of the eternal and the infinite. By their association with gods and heroes, the lovers are mythologized. The protagonist links herself with others loved by gods: "O lucky Daphne, motionless and green to avoid the touch of a god" (p. 24), of the nymph transformed into a bay tree to escape Apollo; "Jupiter has been with Leda, I thought, and now nothing can avert the Trojan wars," she says of their first union (p. 27). Implicit in the classical allusions is recognition of the inevitability of the protagonist's acceptance of love and of the unhappiness, even disaster which will be its inevitable result. She associates herself with other women involved in tragic love situations, such as Ophelia and Isolde. When deserted by her lover, the protagonist associates herself with Dido, the queen of Carthage who committed suicide when deserted by Aeneas: "By the Pacific I wander like Dido, heaving such a passion of tears in the breaking waves, that I wonder why the whole world isn't weeping inconsolably" (p. 108). With this analogy, the narrator also lends cosmic significance to her experience, a significance amplified by association of herself with the natural world and translation of her experience into hyperbolic and dramatic metaphor and symbol: "I am the same tune now as the trees, hummingbirds, sky, fruits, vegetables in rows. I am all or any of these. I can metamorphose at will" (p. 45); "Take away everything I have, or could have, anything the world could offer, I am still empress of a new-found-land, that neither Columbus nor Cortez could have equalled, even in their instigating dreams" (p. 47); "... but can I see by the light of a match while I burn in the arms of the sun?" (p. 28).

Along with the cosmic significance which such metaphors, analogies, and classical allusions lend to the love affair, there are important religious overtones. The biblical cadence of the novel's rhythms contributes to the love's apotheosis. The most dramatic of the biblical allusions underlining the religious dimension is the use of verses from the Song of Solomon which, in the voice of the protagonist, are counterpointed with the crude questioning of the police who stop the couple at the Arizona state border. This counterpointing of voices points out the dichotomy between the two ways of looking at the experience: for the protagonist, her love is sacred and lyrical; for the police, as outsiders, it is adulterous and sinful.

The interweaving of the lyrical, cadenced biblical language with the direct and brutal words of the interrogators also recalls to the reader the inextricable link between the sensual and the spiritual; the sensual is not denied but made transcendent, the marvelous is shown to exist within the corporeal. In her use of the Song of Solomon, Smart comes full circle: the lyrically erotic language which in the Old Testament was transposed to express a divine love, to image a transcendent world which can only be expressed through the concrete, now is turned back, still carrying its sacred implications, to add to an erotic experience the resonance of the spiritual, to underline one of the main paradoxes of the novel, that to be human is to be both flesh and spirit, human and divine.

The intermeshing of the spoken words of the police with the silent discourse of the protagonist is achieved by the use of parenthesis for the silent discourse. In the conjunction of the exterior dialogue (which is actually a dramatic monologue, since only one side of the conversation is given) with the interior monologue, the impression is created of the spoken words entering the protagonist's consciousness, the dialogue entering the monologue frame. An ironic tension is created and developed between outer appearance (the words of the police) and inner reality (the protagonist's recitation from the Song of Solomon). While to some extent the effect may be compared to that of an aside in drama, the emphasis remains with the interior monologue. The opposition of the views expressed by the two voice levels underlines the impossibility of communication:

> Did you sleep in the same room? (Behold thou art
> fair, my love, behold thou art fair: thou hast dove's
> eyes).
> In the same bed? (Behold thou art fair, my beloved,
> yea pleasant, also our bed is green).
> Did intercourse take place? (I sat down under his

shadow with great delight and his fruit was sweet to my taste). (p. 51)

As the grilling is continued by a police matron, the protagonist's reaction remains the same:

> The matron says: Give me your bracelet, no jewelry allowed. (My beloved —). At once. And your ring. (My beloved —). And your bag ....
> The eyes of the jealous world peer through the peephole in the door, in the eyes of the keeper. But still the only torture is in his absence. (p. 52)

While such other voices impinge upon the consciousness of the lyrical "I" through whose sensibility the world is filtered, we never hear, directly or indirectly, the voices of the lover or his wife, the two other figures central to the lyrical experience. Distanced from the reader, they remain shadowy figures in the experience of the narrator-protagonist, acting out their parts in an elemental pattern. Other voices heard directly are those of secondary figures, largely unsympathetic, acting as a kind of chorus. These voices express an attitude and a reaction antithetical to hers. Through them, the world in general is shown to be unsympathetic, capable of viewing the affair only from the most superficial level, but capable, nevertheless, of passing judgment.

Brief comments of family and acquaintances, directly reported as scattered bits of conversation recalled by the protagonist, tend to isolate her further: " 'Love? Stuff and nonsense!' my mother would say, 'It's loyalty and decency and common standards of behaviour that count' " (p. 67); "... the well-meaning matrons who, from their insulated living say, 'My dear, I think you would regret it afterwards if you broke up a marriage, ... when you felt it about to happen the right thing would have been to have gone away at once,' 'If he needs money why doesn't he get a job?' 'What does he know of Love that lets his country down in her Hour-of-Need?' " (pp. 67-68). The clichés spoken by these observers reflect the conventional and unthinking views of onlookers to any adulterous affair.

For the most part, the novel consists of the present tense discourse of the lyrical "I" which is overheard by the reader. Verbalization is synchronized with action or experience. In the course of the interior monologue, the lyrical "I" conveys to us what she is doing and what is happening to her, and what she is feeling.

Present-tense discursive language lends a sense of directness and immediacy as the reader overhears the lyrical "I" in the act of responding to her situation.

There are times when the monologuist addresses her thoughts to others, human or divine. When considering her feelings of guilt at injuring her lover's wife, she addresses God: "God, come down out of the eucalyptus tree outside my window, ..." (p. 33). After her recitation from the Song of Solomon, she addresses Solomon in language ironically more appropriate to her crude interrogators: "Get wise to yourself, Solomon, lay off all that stuff. Join a club. Get pally with the gang" (p. 54). She apostrophizes the angels, "What was your price, Gabriel, Michael of the ministering wing?" (p. 38). Travelling to rejoin her lover she addresses him as "you" (pp. 74-77). Such make-believe communication further underlines her loneliness and isolation.

While most of the novel is narrated in the present, that present shifts in its mode of operation. We think of the present in its most common use, expressing immediate action, emotion, or response, but there are times when the present becomes a timeless present shifting to the expression of a generalization, as in these thoughts of the monologuist:

> And over the fading wooden house I sense the reminiscence of the pioneer's passion, and the determination of early statesmen who were mild but individual, able to allude to Shakespeare while discussing politics under the elms. No great neon face has been superimposed over their minor but memorable history. Nor has the blood of the early settlers, split in feud and heroism, yet been bottled by a Coca-Cola firm and sold as ten-cent tradition. (p. 63)

At times too, the present modulates from instant present to habitual present to indicate a repetition or a longer duration. Such uses of the present contain, at least implicitly, such adverbs as whenever, sometimes, always, never. The monologuist says, for example, "Like Anteus, when I am thrust against this earth, I bounce back recharged with hope" (p. 62); of her lover's wife, she says, "I see she can walk across the leering world and suffer injury only from those she loves" (p. 18); and "How can she walk through the streets, so vulnerable, so unknowing, and not have people and dogs and perpetual calamity following her?"

In keeping with these varied modes of present tense, are the paradigmatic scenes, which, while they are in themselves individual scenes, are representative of other similar scenes. Such a scene occurs in the home of the Wurtles, a couple with whom the lovers stay for a short time:

> When we tear ourselves out of the night and come into the kitchen, Mrs. Wurtle says, "Romance, eh?" but she smiles, she turns away her head, and when we kiss behind her back as we help her dry the dishes, she says, "Oh, you two love-birds, go on out again!"
>
> What is going to happen? Nothing. For everything has happened. All time is now, and time can do no better. Nothing can ever be more now than now, and before this nothing was. There are no minor facts in life, there is only the one tremendous one.
>
> We can include the world in our love, and no irritations can disrupt it, not even envy.
>
> Mr. Wurtle, sitting on the sofa late at night, says, with a legal air, "Then I have it from you there is such a thing as Love?" I lean upon the cushion, faint from this few hours separation, but I sigh, "Yes, oh, yes, ..." (p. 43)

Here the present tense shifts from a brief scene in the instant present to expression of a generalization in the timeless present, and shifts back to another instant moment in another brief scene. The impression created is that of the lyrical "I" speaking to herself while involved in these scenes.

While the present tense in its various modes is used most, a recurrent feature of this monologue is the manner in which from time to time shifts are made to other tenses. For example, while the protagonist's thoughts remain in the present as she travels home, the next episode, in which she considers the unsympathetic and uncomprehending attitude of family and friends, takes place in the past tense. This section begins: "As I sat down in the swivel chair in my father's office, with his desk massively symbolic between us, I realized that I could never defend myself" (p. 67). Recollected words of others are then interjected in present tense direct discourse in a dramatization of recollected attitudes. In such a situation, present experience giving way entirely to a remembrance of incidents and attitudes, the narrator's monologue becomes a memory monologue. In similar fashion, the episode with the police, which begins with the counterpointing of interior and exterior voices, continues in past tense narrative. When the past tense is used, it is never simply to narrate what has occurred but rather to comment upon past situations as in the episode with the police, and as earlier, when the protagonist recalls her feelings for her lover before they met, ''… he, when he was only a word, was able to cause me sleepless nights and shivers of intimation, …'' (p. 20).

In the final and most emotionally wrought part of the novel, the monologue shifts rapidly from present to past to future in a surreal structure. Bits of action and event are interwoven with lyrical effusions, and the protagonist shifts from speaker to listener to speaker, and from interior to exterior, in a kaleidoscopic shifting of scene and tense:

> By Grand Central Station I sat down and wept:
>
> I will not be placated by the mechanical motions of existence, nor find consolation in the solicitude of waiters who notice my devastated face. Sleep tried to seduce me by promising a more reasonable tomorrow. But I will not be betrayed by such a Judas of fallacy: it betrays everyone: it leads them into death. (p. 117)
>
> I race disaster down Third Avenue. It shimmers in the Hudson River. When I dare to look up for a sign of comfort the neons flash relentlessly.
>
> No, no one will pity you here where failure is the same as shame, and tears anachronisms, out of place even in cinemas.
>
> "Sure, kid. We all got troubles. Buck up. Take it on the chin."
>
> If you can smile now you might become a great success in the advertising business. Brave little woman … Quite a gal. Her saucy repartee conceals alluring tragedy. Once she could feel, she could weep. Once she too was human. But you see what can be done? Why, she's making $15,000 a year. (p. 120)

In its handling of voice and language *By Grand Central Station* is a remarkable accomplishment. Even more remarkable is that it is the first novel of a very young woman, and was written in 1941. In 1941, Canada's best known writers were Frederick Philip

Grove, Hugh MacLennan, Morley Callaghan, and Mazo de la Roche, then still writing her Jalna series. That year Sinclair Ross's *As For Me and My House*, published in the United States, received scant attention in Canada. Equally remarkable is the history of *By Grand Central Station*. Appearing first in England in 1945, during the last months of the war, it was an underground success, but was not widely known until 1966 when it was republished with an introduction by Brigid Brophy hailing it as one of "half a dozen masterpieces of poetic prose in the world" (p. 5). It was still almost unknown in Canada. It is said that Elizabeth Smart's family blocked its importation into Canada. The first North American publication, the Popular Library edition in 1975, finally brought the novel to attention in Canada. Now at last *By Grand Central Station* joins the list of Canadian classics.

Notes

1   "Psalm of Love," Radio Times, December 1978, p. 19
2   Elizabeth Smart, *By Grand Central Station I Sat Down and Wept* (London: Edition Poetry, 1945; rpt. New York, Popular Library, 1975), p. 17. Page references in parenthesis are from this edition.

AN APPETITE FOR LIFE: THE LIFE AND LOVE OF ELIZABETH SMART

John Goddard

A pair of black doors with frosted windows block the midday driz-
zle and workaday world from the French House pub, cramped
hang-out of the offbeat literati in the heart of London's Soho. Inside, the air is blue, and rife with raucous babble — a witty put-
down of a new play, a smutty anecdote from a late-night party.
The patrons share a vaguely artistic air, but each is distinctive:
an arch young man with deep-set eyes and pointed shoes; a lo-
quacious woman with shredded hair, dyed pink at the ends; a
thin man of shy demeanour wearing a pale-green bow tie.

At one end of the bar is Elizabeth Smart, nursing a Bloody Mary
and waving a cigarette as she talks. Her hair, slightly flattened
by the rain, is still honey-blonde and thick, belying the years that
show on her face. Her accent is compromised by forty years
abroad — the r's and h's still distinct but the o's elongated, the
a's softer. "Why don't we go somewhere else?" she says after
breaking off the conversation with the others. "It's far too noisy
in here."

She was born in Ottawa in 1913, lived among the Establishment and next door to William Lyon Mackenzie King. Then she
rebelled. She made love to a woman to defy her mother, lived
on a commune in Big Sur long before the beatniks, had four
children by British poet George Barker (who was married to someone else), and, when the going got rough, wrote her slim
classic, *By Grand Central Station I Sat Down and Wept*, the story
of a self-defeating passion that is smouldering still. She has spent
the past fifteen years in a remote cottage in Suffolk, a wild spot
one hundred and sixty kilometres east of London, accessible only through a gravel pit and cow pasture. Now, belatedly free of
maternal responsibilities, she is back in circulation, reading at
poetry festivals, going to parties, and "looking in" at the French
House when in London. Soon (August 1982), she is to end the
long estrangement from her native country by becoming writer-
in-residence at the University of Alberta in Edmonton.

"I feel terribly excited about going back to Canada," she says,
settling down on the sofa in her son's flat, away from the French
House din. "It has always been on my mind to return." She had

lost touch for a while, to the point of not knowing that modern Canadian literature existed. But when *Grand Central* was republished by Popular Library in 1975 and made available in Canada for the first time, Canadian writers began seeking her out, sending her books in thanks for her hospitality. "I was much amazed when I read these, mostly women actually: the Margarets, Alice Munro, and even earlier books like *The Double Hook*. I felt a total kinship with them. Even the rhythms of the sentences and so on. It's something I don't understand, why Canadians are Canadians and Americans are Americans. Is it something about the wind blowing over the prairies or something?"

She still considers herself very much a Canadian and has set her new novel in the Canada of her childhood, a novel she plans to complete in Edmonton, adding to a collection of three slim books: *Grand Central* in 1945, a book of poems; *A Bonus*, in 1977; and another novel, *The Assumption of the Rogues and Rascals*, in 1978.

"And we *did* have a wonderful childhood," one paragraph of the new work reads, as it appeared recently in *Harper's & Queen*, a London magazine, "thrilling to the frothing surf on the bland sea of Brackley Beach, Prince Edward Island; or making leaf houses in the woods by the lake at Kingsmere; going for walks with Daddy, begging to be thrown into flat round juniper bushes, just prickly enough for ecstasy; finding enchanted flowers in Flower Ben on early cold picnics; taking the adventurous first trip up to the cottage, wondering if we could get there, because of the congealed snow on the road, packed down in old drifts, and patches of ice. Then we roared with joy and spring. How we must have driven our patient father frantic, bellowing out of tune, loud, excited, *A Hundred Blue Bottles*, from one hundred relentlessly down to one."

Her father was Russell Smart, a pioneering patent-and-trade-mark lawyer who was "retained by Coca-Cola and Kellogg's to fight Pepsi-Cola and Shredded Wheat, things like that." He was a kind, patient, generous man who continued to send Elizabeth a monthly allowance long after she left home, and who sponsored twenty-two boat trips to Europe during her adolescence. "One would think up a project and if it were reasonable he would finance you. I would say that I wanted to study music, and my sister would say she wanted to study sculpture." And off they would go, with a governess in the early days, later by themselves.

Her mother was an engaging hostess who kept perpetual open house, or so it seemed. In winter the parties were at home in Ottawa, where Elizabeth met young Mike Pearson and diplomats who later helped her in London when, pregnant with her second child, she fled the man she loved. In summer the activities moved to the cottage at Kingsmere, next to Mackenzie King's estate, where as a child she played in the leaves with Eugene Forsey and as a young woman, provocatively beautiful in photographs, she drew the attention of young men: "I was one of three sisters, lively girls and, you know, men were always sort of nosing around the way they do."

But casting a shadow on the frivolity was the other side of her mother's character. "I loved her very much, but ..." She was bossy, domineering and reproachful. She tolerated the trips abroad but stopped the girls from going to university, keeping them dependent while the son studied law. Elizabeth wanted to be free.

On one trip to England, while browsing in the little magazine and book shops on Charing Cross Road, she got an idea. "There was a wonderful shop called Better Books; I think that is where I found George Barker's and I thought they were marvellous. By that time I knew a few people, and I'd say, do you know George Barker, because I'd like to meet him and marry him. I didn't know he was married you see."

By that time Barker was on his way to becoming known. He'd been singled out by W. B. Yeats as promising, and was a close friend of Dylan Thomas and David Gascoyne — the three of them generally considered to be the best British poets of their generation. But Elizabeth and George didn't meet for another two years. She returned to Ottawa in 1938, to a job on the Ottawa *Journal* against her mother's wishes: "Every morning my mother would say, 'Stay in bed today, don't go in,' and she'd bring me breakfast in bed."

After six months Elizabeth did quit, fed up because the *Journal* wouldn't pay her a living wage — only $2.50 a week because she lived at home. She went to New York, slept on her sister's sofa, worked in art galleries, and tried to sell the manuscripts she had been writing since age ten. "I had written a novel by then and lots and lots of poems. I sent them to an agent and she thought they were very shocking. She sent them back with a reproachful note. The novel was about male impotence and, you see, those things were not discussed in those days. It wasn't explicit like *Fear of Flying* or anything, it was just a little too frank." It was never published.

Elizabeth also sent poems to London and Paris and struck up a correspondence with Lawrence Durrell. From Durrell she learned George Barker was broke and willing to sell his manuscripts to collectors. She wrote to Barker and he sold her one, but the correspondence ended there. She went to Mexico City, then to California, had a lesbian affair, and wrote a novel about it called *Dig a Grave and Let Us Bury Our Mother*. It, too, was never published.

In 1940, while she was still in California, Barker sent her an urgent message. He was teaching at Imperial Tohoku University in Japan and sensed war coming. Could she send him money for passage to California — for two passages, one for him and one for his wife — and get immigration papers? She sent him savings she had earned as a maid and some borrowed money, but the documents were more difficult to come by, requiring sponsorship from a millionaire. She engaged the help of Christopher Isherwood, who was working for MGM in Hollywood at the time and knew Barker's work. Finally all was set. Barker and his wife sailed to California and took a bus to Monterey. Elizabeth was waiting for them, as she describes in the opening line of *Grand Central*:

> I am standing on a corner in Monterey, waiting for the
> bus to come in, and all the muscles of my will are
> holding my terror to face the moment I most desire.

The book is not straight autobiography, she says. She has trouble remembering now which were the true events and which the fiction. But she found a wooden hut for them at Big Sur, a virtual wilderness in 1940. She thought the three of them could all just be friends but, as the book describes, the inevitable happened: "Under the waterfall he surprised me bathing and gave me what I could no more refuse than the earth can refuse the rain."

The triangle broke up after a few months. Barker and his wife left for New York; Elizabeth retreated to an abandoned school house in Pender Harbour, British Columbia — pregnant — where she wrote sequences of *Grand Central* in longhand, out of order, building the edifice brick by brick: "I wrote the border incident last," she says of the passage she most often reads to an audience.

It is a fictionalized account of how she and George are detained at the California-Arizona border and charged under the Mann Act — a law ostensibly prohibiting couples from crossing state lines to fornicate but also a ruse for police in those days to detain suspected gangsters and spies. The passage has a rude American cop interrogating the heroine, who replies with verses from the *Song of Songs*: "Did intercourse take place? (I sat down under his shadow with great delight and his fruit was sweet to my taste)."

"At the time I wrote it, I was terribly pregnant," she says, "and I remember, oh, the boredom of it and looking up the Bible to get the bits I wanted. I didn't feel like doing research but I wanted to get the book done in case I died in childbirth. Well, people used to you know."

She didn't tell her parents she was having a baby — they were already against her for not helping in the war effort — but George knew. He visited her briefly. When he tried to visit a second time, he was stopped at the border. Elizabeth's mother "had harangued the ambassador or something" to keep him out of Canada. To be near him, Elizabeth used her former Ottawa ties to get a job at the British Army Office in Washington.

"I was still in love. I was pretty much in love for about nineteen years, really, but I saw early on, I mean I really started trying to leave him early on, because I saw it wasn't a working proposition. I never expected him to be of any help because I wouldn't have been so silly. I saw there wasn't anything he could do and I didn't expect him to. I just thought I could do it. I was working as a filing clerk and had the lowest salary you're allowed to have in America, and George would say that his wife had gone away and we were going to go to Reno and then, I don't know, there were all sorts of excuses, all very, very, very believable stories. Then I'd get suspicious and look in his pockets and I'd find a laundry list with her writing on it. So then I'd say, Go, I'm not seeing you again, and he could always make jokes and get around my resolution and then I'd let him in again. This went on for ages. But then it was too horrible and awful so I decided to get myself to England."

In 1943, in wartime, pregnant with her second child, she waited three weeks in New York for a ship and crossed the Atlantic in a convoy. Three of the ships went down. She didn't leave a forwarding address, "but of course he got himself over and found me and there we were." They had a third and fourth child, but he had no money. He lived with his mother and went on to have more children by other women. *Grand Central* was published but in a printing of only 2,000 copies. An Ottawa book store imported six of them; Elizabeth's mother bought them all and burned them, using her influence again to prevent more copies from coming into the country.

The book circulated in New York, however, and was praised by the beat poets. Jay Landesman, now head of Polytantric Press in London (Elizabeth's publisher), was editor in the late 1950s of the underground magazine, *Neurotica*. "*Grand Central* is an historic book," he says, "way ahead of anything written at the time. It was a forerunner of Kerouac's *On the Road*, and Elizabeth and George were the forerunners of that kind of living. They broke down traditions completely, broke down the standards of morality. Kerouac and those guys broke it down in the 1950s when it was easier. Elizabeth and George did it in wartime, that's the exciting thing. They were in pajamas when the rest of the world was in uniforms."

Landesman first met Barker in New York in the late '50s at a gathering of beat poets. "Allen Ginsberg was at George's feet. They were in awe of him. They were aware of what Elizabeth and George had done." Inspired by such meetings, Landesman wrote a musical that played on Broadway in 1959 called *The Nervous Set* about Kerouac, Ginsberg, Barker, and a few others. Kerouac was played by Larry Hagman — the J.R. of *Dallas*.

Grand Central influenced a new generation after Panther Books published it in paperback in Britain in 1966. "It was one of the cult books," says Helen Dennis, professor of American literature at the University of Warwick. "The late '60s was a time of great optimism among young people, a time to break social and political conventions, and this book seemed to be an expression of that spirit."

British novelist Brigid Brophy called the book "a masterpiece of poetic prose" in her introduction to the 1966 edition: "*By Grand Central Station* is one of the most shelled, skinned, nerve-exposed books every written ... a cry of complete vulnerability ... transformed into a source of eternal pleasure, a work of art."

For all its anguish and torment, however, the book is ultimately hopeful and forgiving. "Inspiring, truthful and very feminine," says Ann Barr, features editor at *Harper's & Queen*, and a close friend of Elizabeth's. "It's one of the books everyone has read,

more so than *Ulysses*, which everyone only says they've read.''
Everyone in her circle might have read *Grand Central* but the book
did not attract a mass readership, possibly because, like poetry,
its dense, lyrical style demands concentration.

Meanwhile, Elizabeth had to make a living — for herself, her
two boys and two girls. She got jobs on various women's
magazines, as a music editor and fashion writer, and later worked in advertising. Bob Johnson, now production manager at
Harper's & Queen, shared a cubicle with her in the mid-1960s when
the magazine was called simply *Queen*. ''She always seemed to
be at least half on the way to being smashed,'' he says. ''She
needed something to keep her going all the time, what with four
kids, getting older, the whole George Barker thing, and just the
business of getting through life. In the absence of anything else
she would grab a can of Cow Gum (layout paste). She's the first
person I ever   heard of sniffing glue.''

At *Queen* she wrote book reviews, but her main job was laying
out fourteen pages of fashion, writing the intros, and making the
captions fit. ''She was tremendous at it,'' says Ann Barr. ''Her
pages were like concrete poetry. When she went into advertising she was the highest-paid copywriter in London.''

But her literary career was in limbo. She regrets her skimpy
output as a writer, but babies, she says, are part of being in love.
''It's a natural feeling to want to have a baby when you're really
in love. Every woman feels it and I think men do too when they're
really involved. A woman is a man with a womb, that's what
the word means. It's not a man without something, its a man
with something and that something is a womb. I wanted these
female experiences.''

At age fifty, with her children grown, she was ready to start
writing again seriously. But problems she doesn't like talking
about obliged her to raise two infant grandchildren. She retreated
to a cottage in Suffolk, channelling her creative energies into a
one-acre garden, cultivating a wilderness that must have resembl-
ed in some ways her childhood playground at Kingsmere. There
was some literary activity. She continued to write the occasional
newspaper and magazine piece and in 1977 published *A Bonus*
— forty-four pages of poetry collected over the years. The book
isn't available in Canada, although Deneau Publishers is interested in it. Deneau also plans to publish a hardcover edition
of *Grand Central* in late 1982. *The Assumption of the Rogues and*

Rascals was published in 1978, a slim book of 120 pages. The reviews in Britain were favourable, but the book never attracted the following of her first. Eleanor Wachtel, reviewing *Rogues and Rascals* for *Books in Canada*, called it "an elliptical novel, a gathering of reflections, stories, bits of memoir, journal entries and so on that … lacks the first's drive, just as survival seems somehow less forceful than love."

After the grandchildren in her care had more or less reached adulthood, Elizabeth was in danger of great-grandmother problems and decided enough was enough. At a poetry festival in Cambridge she met poet Patrick Lane, writer-in-residence at Edmonton for 1981-82. He suggested she succeed him, and the university later sent her a formal invitation.

By the time I heard Elizabeth Smart's life story, I had spent time with her at her son's flat, in restaurants, in cafés, at parties, at her cottage, and at poetry readings, including one she gave at the opening of the cultural centre at Canada House in London. She revealed herself as a warm, kind, giving person. But what was George Barker like? What made him worth pursuing so? Elizabeth alternately describes him as fascinating, selfish, interesting, badly behaved, and a marvellous poet. The nicest thing most of her friends had to say was that he was cruel. "He'll charm you," said Ann Barr.

I phoned him and was invited for Saturday night to his home in Norfolk, near the sea. Elizabeth phoned Saturday morning to say she would be there — they were still in touch, meeting occasionally at poetry readings. I was first to arrive — after dark by train, bus, and taxi — at an Elizabethan stone building said to be haunted by a little girl in the study and by an old sea captain upstairs. Saturday night, it turned out, is drinking night, and George was in the drinking room.

"Come in young man," he said, beckoning with one hand. At sixty-nine he retains luminous blue eyes, is lean and tall despite a slight stoop of the shoulders, and, yes, sexy-looking in a turtleneck sweater, blue jeans, and dirty white running shoes — cliché garb for a poet except that he probably invented the look. We talked about the weather for fifteen minutes, a conversation his wife, Elspeth, thought silly. She is a soft-spoken, forty-year-old Scot anyone would at once call beautiful, even in Wellington boots and country woollens. She has been with George for nineteen years, has five children by him, the youngest aged seven, and is considered George's fifth wife, counting Elizabeth. George has fourteen "conspicuous" children, as Elizabeth puts it, though he has boasted as many as thirty-five, she says.

Elizabeth arrived with a friend via three pubs. More drinks were poured, then the fireworks began.

"You cow," George said to Elizabeth in his gravelly voice. "Your face looks like the back of Auden's hand. I love you."

"I love you too but that's irrelevant."

"You loathsome Canadian. You're like something out of Ibsen, horrible. You have no versification."

"I know."

"It was I who taught you the word *eye* is spelled with one letter."

"I know."

And so it went.

Elspeth took me aside to balance the effect, speaking softly. "He's shy. He's a wonderful person and I love him. We sit up in bed sometimes in the early morning, propped up on our pillows, in our own particular darkness, drinking tea, with the light from the windows and the electric fire flashing off the posts and the knobs of the brass bed. He becomes so articulate and poetic."

To quiet the others down, Elspeth read Matthew Arnold's "Dover Beach" to the group, hauntingly, until George complained she read like a waitress. Someone phoned to invite us all to a party and we were off, shouting at each other, singing Presbyterian hymns and getting lost along the way. We finally arrived at an old stone country house that seemed to be full of well-dressed women in their late twenties, and George soon had a clutch of them around him.

"What's his magic?" I asked.

"He's sixty-nine and still very sexy," said one.

"He's just very special," said another.

"He's so overt in his rudeness, he challenges you," said a third. "You keep coming back for more."

"What's your opinion of *Grand Central*?" I asked Barker at one point.

"The best thing since *Wuthering Heights*," he said. "And I hate *Wuthering Heights*. Women don't have souls."

It was clear that Barker and Elizabeth still have strong feelings for each other. It was also clear the encounter was painful for them

— certainly for Elizabeth, who showed pain on her face, in her voice, and in her submissive responses. "So much pain," she said late one night in Soho, in a slightly different context. She had been eating with friends in an Oriental restaurant on Frith Street, talking, joking, by all appearances having a good time, when she abruptly got up, said goodnight, and walked out. Intercepted on the street, she said something ambiguous about pain being hard to bear.

But pain is a prime motivator, a key tool, for Elizabeth Smart the writer. Brigid Brophy touches on the point when she says *Grand Central* is a cry transformed into a work of art. Elizabeth, in fact, has developed a theory about the relationship between love, pain, and art. She wrote about it in the February issue of *Woman's Journal*, in a piece called "How to Mend a Broken Heart" in which she gives advice to spurned lovers. "Pain is, can be, useful," she writes. "But only if you use it. You have to be willing to suffer. You have to accept it ... because if you fight against pain you augment it .... So say: Come dear pain. Come, be welcome. Please overwhelm me ...."

"Examine yourself," she advises. "Perhaps it was the bastard in him that triggered your susceptibilities. It looked like glamour, then, and you only saw the shiny side. You responded joyfully .... And now you have the beginning of wisdom: the price of love is pain."

She warns against bitterness: "It was a rich experience. Don't deny it. Don't denigrate it. Don't say If Only. Suffer. If bitterness comes creeping in, nip it in the bud. A bitter person has failed as a human being .... A consenting adult cries in private, takes the pain, acknowledges it, praises the experience, blames nobody.

"A consenting adult moves on."

ETHEL WILSON

MAGGIE'S LAKE: THE VISION OF FEMALE POWER IN *SWAMP ANGEL*

Donna E. Smyth

In the hands of Nell Severance, the Swamp Angel gun is a dangerous, beautiful, wicked, wonderful thing. Nell has been a juggler and an artist who, in retrospect, describes her performance:

> ... when I think how I used to be able to keep them moving so fluid and slow — how you had to work to get that timing! ... and then the drums beginning, and faster and faster — all timed — and the drums louder and louder — a real drum roll ... and I'd have the three guns going so fast they dazzled, one behind my back and one under my elegant long legs (such lovely legs!), and one out as if out towards the audience and then crack-crack-crack and the audience going crazy and me bowing and laughing like anything ... how I loved it.[1]

For Nell the gun is a charged symbol, an iconic link between herself, the past and Philip Severance. She fondles and strokes it when she needs comfort. She uses it to deflect Eddie Vardoe's murderous anger when he discovers that Maggie has left him. She sends it to Maggie when she can no longer be the guardian of the gun.

In the end, Maggie, as the new guardian, can throw the gun into "her lake" because she has no need for it. She knows she is performing "a rite of some kind" (p. 156) and she throws it, like Excalibur, in a great arc:

> It made a shining parabola in the air, turning downwards — turning, turning, catching the sunlight, hitting the surface of the lake, sparkling down into the clear water, vanishing amidst breaking bubbles in the water, sinking down among the affrighted fish, settling in the ooze. (p. 157)

Restored to the great reservoir of symbols from whence it was derived, the gun, as an object, has played its part. Yet its name dominates the book. Something angelic, full of light, growing out of the muck, out of a swamp. What is potentially destructive becomes energy used to create a human community.

Before Maggie can manifest this vision, she must find herself. Her first act is a refusal. To say No, as Camus knew, is the beginning of rebellion.[2] In Maggie's case the refusal is a rejection of a loveless marriage, and it means she must find a way to make her own living. She has to step outside the traditional women's culture, and unpaid work, into the male preserve of sport fishing. "Brought up from childhood by a man, with men" (p. 30), Maggie, in fact, is an artist in her own right. She ties fishing flies, creating out of bird feathers and a hook, something beautiful and deadly.

From the beginning, Maggie is associated with fishing; she is a Fisher Queen on a quest for self-knowledge and self-healing. The end of that quest is restoration of harmony, not only for herself but for her community.

Maggie times her escape carefully. In her unholy marriage with Eddie, time has been "out of sync", space has shrunk to the prison of a house. Driving away in the taxi, "She exulted in each small sight and sound, in new time, in new space, because she had got free" (p. 23). She takes her own symbols with her: her fishing rod and the yellow Chinese bowl;[3] wand and grail receptacle, male and female, yin and yang, balanced as they are in Maggie's hands. As a grail symbol, the yellow bowl connects several levels of the novel. Yellow is a sacred colour and is related to its Chinese origins, not only on the religious level, but as part of the Chinese connection which is an important link for Maggie between herself and her vision of human community. When she looks at Joey, her taxi driver, "She thought that she understood him ... in a way that seemed open to her" (p. 27). This balance between an old culture and a new, between East and West, is essential to the founding of Maggie's small Utopia in the Canadian wilderness.

Once Maggie has left Eddie, she gains a new name, or rather, her old, true name is restored to her. Maggie Vardoe becomes Maggie Lloyd. It is clear from Maggie's memories that her first marriage to Tom Lloyd was a holy one: that is, mutually loving and balanced. The old, new name is part of the restoration.

Her first stop-over on her flight from Eddie and the City is a small motel cabin at Chilliwack. Here she is "as free of care or remembrance as if she had just been born ..." (p. 34).

Reborn, Maggie passes through the portentously named but real town of Hope on her journey to the interior of British Columbia. The narrator comments:

> Make no mistake, when you have reached Hope and
> the roads that divide there you have quite left Van-
> couver and the Pacific Ocean. They are dispropor-
> tionately remote. You are entering a continent, and you
> meet the continent there, at Hope. (p. 36)

Maggie's own interior journey is subsumed within the
geographical framework. Her next step is to restore the harmony
between herself and nature symbolized, for her and Ethel Wilson,
by fishing. She retreats into isolation by the river where she is
one element in the cosmic picture as is the doe who comes to
gaze at her without fear. Maggie fishes: "In the pleasure of casting
over the lively stream she forgot — as always when she was
fishing — her own existence" (p. 38). Forgetful of self, she also
struggles with remorse and guilt but, through meditation in
Nature, is restored:

> ... the scent of the pines, the ancient rocks below and
> above her, and the pine-made earth, a physical languor,
> her solitude, her troubled mind, and a lifting of her
> spirit to God by the river brought tears to her eyes. I
> am on a margin of life, she thought, and she
> remembered that twice before in her own life she had
> known herself to be taken to that margin of a world
> which was powerful and close. (pp. 39-40)

Maggie remains at the Similkameen cabins for three days and
nights, the mythic time for death and rebirth. At this point, the
narrator is quite explicit:

> These days had been for Maggie like the respite that
> perhaps comes to the soul after death. This soul
> (perhaps, we say) is tired from slavery or from its own
> folly or just from the journey and from the struggle of
> departure and arrival, alone, and for a time — or what
> we used to call time — must stay still, and accustom the
> ages of the soul and its multiplied senses to something
> new, which is still fondly familiar. (p. 40)

Three Loon Lake is Haldar Gunnarsen's dream which Maggie,
through her strength and healing powers, makes possible and
manifest in this world. The fishing lodge is a way of living gently off the land and with the land. It integrates the human and

the natural. It depends on human love and hard work.

The germ of potential destruction is present in Vera Gunnarsen who is not happy in the wilderness and whose strength is taxed almost to breaking point by the lodge. Vera becomes jealous of Maggie and Haldar, not understanding that Maggie is now wedded to a place: "Maggie's union with Three Loon Lake was like a happy marriage (were we married last week, or have we always lived together as one?)" (p. 84).

Vera and Hilda Severance are traditional counterparts to Maggie and Nell who have both chosen non-traditional roles. Vera makes her life a martyrdom because she does not know any better. Ambivalent about Maggie's strength and competency, she finally succumbs to her own dark night of the soul when she attempts to drown herself in the lake and fails. Like a child, she then turns to Maggie who holds her: "Maggie, bending drew Vera up and held her strong and softly in her arms until the trembling and crying went quiet" (p. 147).

Hilda rebels against her unconventional mother and chooses as conventional a life as possible for herself. Once married to Albert Cousins, she will find fulfillment as a wife and mother. Nell's true spiritual daughter is Maggie to whom she entrusts the Swamp Angel. She also gives Maggie her knowledge of a lifetime, her spiritual wisdom. In their brief visit at Kamloops, Nell finds an image for her vision:

> "... I look back and round and I see the miraculous interweaving of creation ... the everlasting web ... and I see a stone and a word and this stub," and she threw down the stub of her cigarette, "and the man who made it, joined to bounds of creation ...." (p. 150)

It is up to Maggie to put the vision into practice. With her woman's knowledge and her father's training, she becomes the power centre for the group at the lodge. Haldar relies on her; Alan loves her; Vera comes to depend on her; Angus, the young Chinese boy, works well because she is there. Yet Maggie is not the "boss" in the traditional male sense. She is building a community based on work, love and trust; the Loon Lake lodge is a tangible expression of the "everlasting web".

If Maggie were ambitious, in the patriarchal sense, she would have taken up Mr. Cunningham's offer of a job. Instead, she chooses to stay where her "love service" is needed. She is a secular saint who fulfills herself through giving of her strength to others. When such a gift is placed on demand, as it was in her marriage with Eddie Vardoe, the gift itself becomes a perverted form of life. The narrator defines this perversion: ''... Maggie Lloyd, with no one to care for, had tried to save herself by an act of compassion and fatal stupidity. She had married Edward Vardoe'' (p. 16).

By freeing herself from a false relationship, Maggie is free to form true ones. The Gunnarsens become her adopted family but the lodge community also includes Angus and, implicitly, others who will come to share in the dream and the work. Beyond the nuclear family model, this community cuts across race, age, class and gender bias. The worldly world might look at them and see: a run-away wife, a crippled man, his neurotic wife, his bewildered little boy, a Chinese boy. In the context of the novel, however, we see them as: a redeeming angel, a man with a big dream, a woman and her little boy in need of love, a young man who will become a leader.

The natural setting for this community is an important aspect of its meaning. Eddie Vardoe, the fast-talking salesman, would never survive in this wilderness. He belongs where time is money and relationships are mutually predatory. By contrast, time in nature slows down, becomes a seasonal, cyclical rhythm. The novel opens with an image of migrating birds returning in the spring. This image prefigures Maggie's own flight to her true home. The novel concludes with the image of fish flickering around the Swamp Angel at the bottom of Maggie's lake. Plucked from its human symbolic context, the gun is now part of the natural order. Maggie has become the true Swamp Angel.

Nature restores, but it can also destroy. Balanced against the fawn and kitten image is that of the eagle and the osprey. Balanced against the images of water as a healing power are those of water's potential destructiveness. Maggie imagines herself as a strong swimmer but the narrator slips in a warning in brackets: "She could never sink, she thinks (but she could)" (p. 100). Vera tries to drown herself; Mr. Cunningham is nearly drowned.

The human relationship with the natural world is tempered by experience and caution. Ethel Wilson preserves the distinction between nature and human nature. Her view of human nature is, however, a profoundly female one.

The two poles of strength in the book are Nell and Maggie. Be-

tween them is spun the "everlasting web" of human con-
nectedness. There are sympathetic male characters (Albert
Cousins, Haldar, Henry Corder) but their roles, compared to the
women's, are minor. Power is defined in female terms: not hierar-
chically but co-operatively structured; not domination but shar-
ing and serving; not trying to possess or exploit Nature but trying to live in harmony and balance with the natural world.

The spiritual vision is female and so is the narrator's godlike
eye which sees just how Maggie would buy a big roast so as to
leave leftovers for this husband she despises. The narrator who
sees with some compassion how Vera has been worked beyond
her strength and so welcomes Maggie's arrival:

> She was almost happy. Her load seemed for a time to
> slide away. Only a woman who pulls too heavy a load
> for her strength and skill could know Mrs. Gunnarsen's
> emotion. Not even a horse. (p. 74)

Who sees, with amusement, proud Nell Severance bowing her
head to wear a hat to her daughter's wedding. Who creates for
us the "close fabric" of these women's lives with an understanding based on experience of the traditional women's culture and
roles which have shaped these characters' lives.

Ethel Wilson is not a feminist writer in the conscious, political
sense of the term but she thoroughly explores women's experiences within the dominant male culture. Some of her women
characters transcend their roles and, in so doing, transform
themselves and make possible the transformation of others.
Wilson also understands and respects women who choose the
more traditional roles of wife/mother. She understands too the
economic and social pressures upon these women, most of whom,
like Maggie and Nell, have had little or no professional education or training. For such women, the conventional career choices
are simply non-existent. They either find a non-traditional escape
route or a man to support them. In this sense, most of the
characters in her fiction come out of a 1940's -1950's Canadian
context (with the exception of those in The Innocent Traveller) and
their lives reflect the larger social/political forces of that period
described by writers such as Betty Friedan.[4]

Yet Maggie and Nell are also avatars; they belong to and derive
from the powerful mythic structure of the female psyche, not as
described by males, but as experienced by women. Nell is the

wise Old Woman, grandmother of our soul. Maggie is the
Woman-Self who finds and heals herself. Her woman's power
allows others to heal themselves. Her element is the transfor-
mative one: water. Literally, sexually, and symbolically, the lake
belongs to her but, belonging to her, is shared with others. The
Fisher Queen restores the land, and her fish flick triumphantly
over the discarded gun.

Notes

1   Ethel Wilson, *Swamp Angel* (Toronto: New Canadian Library, 1962), p. 64.
    All further quotations will be taken from this edition.
2   "What is a rebel? A man who says no: but whose refusal does not imply
    a renunciation. He is also a man who says yes as soon as he begins to
    think for himself." Albert Camus, *The Rebel*, trans. Anthony Bowen (Lon-
    don: Peregrine Books, 1967), p. 19.
3   David Stouck, "Ethel Wilson's Novels", *Canadian Literature*, No. 74
    (Autumn, 1977), p. 85, refers to the symbol "of the grail in Maggie's
    yellow Chinese bowl."
4   Betty Friedan, *The Feminine Mystique* (New York: Norton, 1963).

INNOCENCE AND SOLITUDE: THE FICTIONS OF ETHEL WILSON

George Woodcock

Ethel Wilson always stood somewhat outside the general currents of Canadian writing in her time or any time. She was a great deal older than most of her contemporary novelists, and belonged by experience as well as birth to an earlier generation. She did not publish her first short story until she was forty-nine in 1937, when "I Just Love Dogs" appeared in the *New Statesman*, and her first novel, *Hetty Dorval*, appeared in 1947, when she was fifty-nine. Her career, after that, was remarkably short, for the last of her six books, *Mrs. Golightly and Other Stories*, appeared in 1961, and the last of her contributions to literary periodicals in 1964. Though Ethel Wilson lived long afterwards, until 1980, she withdrew in her later years into the silence of bereavement and sickness. The two items that represented the end of her career as a published writer, both appearing in the autumn of 1964, were a short story in *Tamarack Review* ("A Visit to the Frontier") and a slight autobiographical essay ("Reflections in a Pool") in *Canadian Literature*.

Thus Ethel Wilson's career as a writer lasted only twenty-seven of her ninety-two years, and her books all appeared within an even briefer period of fourteen years. In terms of publication she was the junior contemporary of much younger writers like Hugh MacLennan and Sinclair Ross, both of whom published first novels six years before *Hetty Dorval*, but in terms of age and experience she was the contemporary of writers we regard as belonging to much older generations. She was three years younger than D. H. Lawrence and six years younger than Virginia Woolf and James Joyce; she was six years older than Aldous Huxley and J. B. Priestley, and as a child she had known Arnold Bennett. When she reached Vancouver, she and the city were both in their early teens, youthful and growing, and when King Edward VII died she was a young woman in her early twenties.

I suggest that in this temporal disjunction between experience and creation lie many of the clues to the special character of Ethel Wilson's writing. For, as I remarked in an earlier and briefer essay, "She had retained, I realized, an Edwardian sensibility, but she had developed a contemporary ironic intelligence, and it was the interplay of the two that gave her books their special quality."[1]

When she began to write, Ethel Wilson carried with her — in terms of personal memories and family traditions — the rich past to which she gave fictional form in *The Innocent Traveller*, that intriguing chronicle in which the history of the young city of Vancouver is interwoven with the group biography of a transplanted Victorian family. At the same time, coming of a literary lineage (Matthew Arnold as well as Arnold Bennett haunted its past) she had remained aware of what was happening in the literary world of her time, and in her correspondence she showed a sensitive appreciation of the special qualities of novelists as varied in time and kind as Defoe and Proust.

The breadth of Ethel Wilson's literary sympathies extended to her Canadian contemporaries, and she followed with enthusiastic interest the upsurge of writing in this country during the 1950s and the early 1960s. She expressed her admiration for the achievements of Gabrielle Roy, Morley Callaghan and Robertson Davies, and recognized the originality and the lyrical power of a novel so unlike her own work as Sheila Watson's *The Double Hook*. Her very use of the adjective "dissimilar" when she talked of these writers implied that she did not need to identify herself with them. Indeed, one of the aspects of the literary calling she always emphasized was the fact that it was solitary and hence individual. In a late essay, "A Cat Among the Falcons" (*Canadian Literature* 2, 1959), she talked of her misgivings about Creative Writing courses, and went on, discussing the writers she admired:

> ... I am impelled to think that most of them — equipped with their natural and varied gifts and their early acquired processes of language — travelled their own legendary way. I cannot avoid the conviction that a writer who can already handle his tools and write, is thereafter self-taught by writing (how the view opens out), and thus a literature is made .... It is possible that a preference for early and thorough familiarity with the language, for privacy of intention, and the individual road in the matter of "creative writing" (I borrow the term, it is not mine), is a personal idiosyncrasy only; but as I look over the wide reaches of writing and at the highly personal art and act of writing, I don't think so.[2]

Clearly Ethel Wilson saw her own writing in this way — as an activity that in its creative phases was private, individual, unruled by any collective imperative. In the same essay she talked of how, in her experience, the act of creation went beyond the conscious direction even of the writer herself.

> There is a moment, I think, within a novelist of any originality, whatever his country or his scope, when some sort of synthesis takes place over which he has only partial control. There is an incandescence, and from it meaning emerges, words appear, they take shape in their order, a fusion occurs.[3]

It was this passionate sense of the personal and unconsciously motivated development of original literary works — a far cry from the doctrines of art breeding from art that Northrop Frye developed out of Oscar Wilde's *Intentions* — that made Ethel Wilson distrustful of fashions in fiction and intent on going her own way and — as she put it — "simply writing." This made her appreciate writers unfashionable among the literary intelligentsia who handled their medium lovingly and carefully. Writing to Desmond Pacey, she defended Arnold Bennett against what she regarded as Virginia Woolf's blindness to "his view of poor persons, poor houses, poor places, mean streets, and their relative beauty to those concerned — both dwellers and observers."[4] And in the *Canadian Literature* essay already cited she took up the defence of another writer often despised by academic critics and cultural snobs.

> Somerset Maugham does not pretend to sit upon Olympus, but I wonder if there is any novelist anywhere in the English-speaking world today who can write a straightforward story like *Cakes and Ale*, full of humanity and dextrous exposure.[5]

In Ethel Wilson's approach to literature there was a great deal of what she called "innocence" when she applied it to her characters — the power to look at the world with clear eyes and live with what one sees. Once she talked of the "artlessness" that is "very artful indeed," and it is this quality that is evident not only in her writing but also in her perceptions of the qualities in other people's writing that she admires. Writing about some of the writers she most admired — again to Desmond Pacey — she remarked that "my taste runs to economy in writing — with some glorious exceptions,'' and went on to say of the novelists she liked:

> I would say that the limpid style of most of them, the lack of pretentiousness, the fact that these people have something to say, with skill, with good heart, often with deep feeling yet with some cynicism, their detachment as well as their involvement, give one inexpressible pleasure. They have *style*, each his own, and without style ... how dull.[6]

Ethel Wilson did not pretend to be a critic, though at times she wrote with great insight about her craft, and for the purposes of this essay it is not important whether what she says about her favourite writers is objectively correct, though generally speaking I believe it is. The point is that in delineating the qualities of others she seems to speak of her own aims in writing, and certainly what all her works strive at — without invariably attaining — the limpid and unpretentious style, involvement distanced by detachment, irony without the loss of feeling.

Ethel Wilson was not one of those novelists who regarded critics as vermin on the body of literature. She saw the value of the critic as mediator, but she was as unhappy about fads in criticism as she was about fads in fiction, and though she herself handled symbolism sparingly but skilfully, she was especially perturbed by any broadly symbolic interpretation of her work. The critic who discusses Ethel Wilson's work should be guided by this preference on her part, for her great virtue lies in her power to record experience, not literally, but faithfully, and it is out of this recording and out of her extraordinarily clear observation of peoples and places that her symbolism and the formal structure of her novels emerge by natural extension; one never has the feeling that any symbol appearing in her books is deliberately invented, either for its own sake or to evade the difficulties of clear and direct expression.

I talked a moment ago about the clear observation of ''people and places'', and in that phrase, it seems to me, is contained the dual pattern that gives so much of its interest to Ethel Wilson's work. For she presents the unusual combination — especially in Canada — of the novelist of manners and the novelist concerned in a lyrical way with the natural world and man's place in it. She is greatly interested in the details of daily life and the modes of human behaviour and intercourse, and in representing them she has something of the wit and playfulness of a Congreve or a Peacock as well as the wry understanding of a Jane Austen. Yet she is so intensely open to the appeal of the natural setting, of the places she and her characters inhabit, that she writes of them with a shimmering intensity that reminds one — though it in no evident way imitates him — of the young D. H. Lawrence, the Lawrence of *Sons and Lovers* and *The White Peacock* celebrating the English countryside.

It is significant that what Ethel Wilson found intriguing in Proust was not so much his more obvious and celebrated preoccupation with Time, but his concern with Place, from which, as she once said, "he took his text". For her, Proust writing on Paris and Combray and Balbec seemed to be reaching the universal through a regional awareness, which she was careful to point out was something quite different from provincialism. She was willing to admit that there were some writers — and good writers — who were not affected by Place. But for her it was so essential that, with all her awareness of the universal implications of literature and of the intense privacy of the act of creation, her writing must be centred where her life had mainly been experienced. As she said in another late essay ("The Bridge or the Stokehold", *Canadian Literature* 5, 1960):

> ... I am not consciously aware in my personal act of writing (how could one be?) of "the Canadian novel" or "the English novel" or "the American novel", as the critic or the critical reader must be aware, and as I am aware when I transfer to the position of the critical reader. When I think of the universal yet private and, I hope, critical approach of a working writer to his novel itself, the happier I am — free, and devoid of personal or national self-consciousness, which is the way I like it. Self-consciousness is a triple curse. But in retrospect I see my Canadianness, for example, in that my locale in a sustained piece of writing (that is, in a book) has to be British Columbia. There are other places that I know and love, but none that I know, and feel, and love in the same way. But I did not choose it. It chose. It is very strong.[7]

In stressing that Ethel Wilson is so intent an observer of human behaviour, and so sensitive to the setting where her novels or stories are mostly placed, I do not suggest she is ever a mere recorder, for the inventive imagination works strongly as she melds together the detail out of which her fictions are constructed. However authentic their lives may be, her characters seem rarely to be taken largely from life, and sometimes it is clear that they have sprouted and grown from a very small germ of actuality. In the essay I have just quoted, Ethel Wilson tells us:

> A novel of mine or its main character, grew directly from a few words dropped almost at random in a previous book. The words were, "... formed other connections". What connections? I had never seen and did not know the girl in question. She did not exist in my knowledge any more than a fly in the next room, but I considered certain aspects and likelihoods, and wrote a book called *Lilly's Story*. On the way, characters multiplied, their outlines at first dim, later clear. I cannot imagine willingly employing even a marginal character without knowing his outside appearance so well that he could be identified in the street by myself and for my own purposes.[8]

This imaginative construction of her characters to the point of actually visualizing them is related to the economy Ethel Wilson has been able to achieve in the text as well as in the structure of her concise yet complex novels. If she is not excessively concerned with the process of symbolization, she has always been skilful in tense, evocative writing that stimulates the mind's eye; this allows her to dispense with lengthy passages of explication and at moments to achieve the visualized shorthand of a kind of prose imagism, as in the brilliant and counterbalancing sentences that open and close *Swamp Angel*:

> Ten twenty fifty brown birds flew past the window and then a few stragglers ....[9]
> When all was still the fish, who had fled, returned, flickering, weaving curiously over the Swamp Angel. Then flickering, weaving, they resumed their way.[10]

By such simple means the whole novel is looped into its environment.

....

In the first part of this essay I have been relating what I see as the essential qualities of Ethel Wilson's fiction to her personal attitudes towards the art of fiction, which are those of an acute, honest and somewhat ironic self-observer. The appearance of simplicity which her work offers demands, I suggest, this approach. We must have some idea of her general strategy to understand how the imagination uses this limpid style, this illusion of glittering verisimilitude, this deceptively didactic manner of narration which implies more than it ever states. Now I shall suggest how this strategy is translated into the tactical patterns of her various novels.

Hetty Dorval, the first of these novels, is perhaps the most striking example of the combination of a Victorian sensibility and a modern ironic consciousness that I have noticed as especially characteristic of Ethel Wilson. Indeed, it is the failure of these two aspects of her literary persona to coalesce at this point that makes it less than perfect, though an extraordinarily pleasing book. Ethel Wilson herself described it as an "innocent novella", and indeed it is based on the encounter of two kinds of innocence — that which grows into experience in the sense of embracing and seeking to understand the collective life of humanity, and that which does not.

The plot is a simple one, with strong elements of the conventional Edwardian romance. A beautiful but mysterious young woman, Hetty Dorval, arrives to occupy a bungalow on the outskirts of Lytton, a small town in the British Columbian interior at the confluence of the Fraser and the Thompson rivers. Frankie Burnaby, the narrator, is attracted by her charm, and for a few years Hetty weaves in a pattern of coincidences in and out of Frankie's life, a temptress with a shadowy past of which we learn only by vague conversational allusions. In the end, when Hetty attracts a cousin to whom Frankie — now a young woman — is deeply attached, there is a confrontation between them, and Hetty leaves the field and goes off with an Austrian lover to Vienna.

> Six weeks later the German Army occupied Vienna.
> There arose a wall of silence around the city, through which only faint confused sounds were sometimes heard.[11]

Hetty Dorval is a tightly knit little book, simple in plot and written with a kind of casual candour that fits and illuminates

Frankie's character as we watch it developing. In its combination of conciseness and completeness, *Hetty Dorval* is much nearer to a French récit — by Gide or Camus, for example — than it is to the Edwardian romances usually populated by characters like Hetty. Considered in herself, Hetty Dorval seems an improbable *femme fatale*, with her strange and literally two-faced beauty.

> We remained standing there and gazing at the empty sky. Then Mrs. Dorval turned her face on me and I realized all of a sudden that she had another face. This full face was different from the profile I had been studying, and was for the moment animated. Her brows, darker than her fair hair, pointed slightly upwards in the middle in moments of stress and became in appearance tragic, and her eyes which were fringed with thick, short, dark lashes opened wide and looked brilliant instead of serene. The emotion might be caused by pain, by the beauty of flighting geese, by death, or even by some very mild physical discomfort, but the impact on the beholder was the same, and arresting. Ordinarily, Mrs. Dorval's full face was calm and somewhat indolent. The purity was not there, but there was what I later came to regard as a rather pleasing yet disturbing sensual look, caused I think by the over-fullness of the curved mouth and by those same rounded high cheek-bones which in profile looked so tender. Whatever it was, it is a fact that the side face and the full face gave not the same impression, but that both had a rapt striking beauty when her eyebrows showed distress.[12]

Hetty's life is that of an adventuress who becomes involved with men not because she can love them but because they are rich and powerful; at times she turns her charm upon other people, like Frankie and her cousin Rick, and one is never certain whether she is practicing her power or acts out of an indolent unloving good nature. There are times when Hetty's life moves into melodrama, and on no occasion more strikingly than in the scene in which Mrs. Broom, her long-suffering housekeeper, shatters Hetty's illusions of being an orphan without ties of any kind by revealing that she is actually her mother. It could have been the episode that spoilt the book, but Ethel Wilson handles it with

exemplary skill and locks our attention with a final memorable
visual image.

> And Hetty did exactly what Hetty would do. She did
> not speak to her mother. Without a word or a look she
> rose and slowly went out of the room, closing the door
> behind her, and left her mother standing there, looking
> after her with a ravaged face.
>
> Mrs. Broom had forgotten me. She now looked down
> at her hands, and so did I. Her hands, with the
> pressure upon the table, were red and looked swollen
> and congested. She held up her hands and regarded
> them strangely, turning their roughness this way and
> that to the light. What she thought as she regarded her
> worn hands so strangely I could only guess.[13]

If one makes the leap of credulity and accepts Hetty as
something near to an allegorical figure, then the novel takes on
two aspects. It is first, as I have suggested, a study in two kinds
of innocence, and secondly a fascinating study of the process of
growing up, in which flesh-and-blood Frankie becomes the central figure and Hetty becomes a foil to Frankie's changing attitudes
to existence.

Hetty's innocence is the negative kind that manifests itself in
a failure to feel for or with other people, and, more than that,
a dominant desire to remain untouched by them. Hetty is not
wholly insensitive; she responds with deep feeling to the wild
geese in whom she sees made manifest her own desire to fly for
ever free. But she is incapable of developing loves or loyalties.
"People only existed when they came within her vision. Beyond
that she had neither care nor interest."[14] She has no malice, as
Frankie observes, but she resents attachments that limit her
freedom or interfere with her "self-indulgence and idleness." "It
is preposterous, the way other people clutter up and complicate
one's life," she says. "It is my own phobia ...."[15]

Thus Hetty's innocence takes the form of an inability to proceed beyond the self-bound world of the infant, an inability to
acknowledge herself "a piece of the Continent, a part of the maine
...." Frankie, on the other hand, has been taught by her mother
the truth of John Donne's statement (which is the epigraph to
the novel) that "No man is an Island, intire of it selfe ..." and
so she shows the natural growth from innocence into experience.

John Donne was to Ethel Wilson much more than a convenient source of epigraphs. "My own discovery of John Donne, almost before he has again entered the Re-Establishment, dazzled me,"[16] she remarked in "A Cat Among the Falcons", and there is no doubt that Donne's central statement about the unity of all mankind continued to be an inspiration throughout her writing life, so that her characters can be divided between those who through love move into the world of experience and realize that they are irrevocably "involved in Mankinde."

It was less the spiritual content of Donne that Ethel Wilson absorbed than his abounding sense of the reality of existence and the unity of all beings. She pays tribute to the pious, like the mystical and saintly Annie Hastings in *The Innocent Traveller*, but it is the people who belong to the visible rather than the invisible world that she portrays with the greatest understanding and involvement. Life as she projects it in *Hetty Dorval* no less than in her other novels is the whole world in which we live, including the human communities to which we belong, as Frankie belongs to Lytton and the country around it with its mixed population of whites and Indians and Chinese, but also the whole environment, for everything that happens in the human heart finds its echoes and correspondences in the natural world.

This is why Ethel Wilson's precise and lyrical description of the country of sagebrush hills and great rivers in which so much of *Hetty Dorval* takes place is so important. We read it not merely for its evocative representation of the natural setting but also because we are aware of being offered a kind of mirror in which the human condition is illuminated, just as Frankie's room in Vancouver contains a mirror in which she sees the mountains framed into forms whose power she had never realized before. Frankie herself recognizes the importance of the "genius of place", and remarks:

> My genius of place is a god of water. I have lived where two rivers run together, and beside the brattling noise of China Creek which tumbles past our ranch house and turns our water wheel, and on the shore of the Pacific Ocean too — my home is there, and I shall go back.[17]

And water does indeed play a constant and varying role in Frankie's existence. A sea voyage to England marks the begin-

ning of her growth into maturity; she leaves Canada a girl and
quickly in Europe becomes a sophisticated and responsible young
woman. And perhaps the most potent image in *Hetty Dorval* —
an image generating a vast symbolic power — is that of the confluence of the two rivers, the Fraser and the Thompson, and the
Bridge from which one sees them; it is an image to be repeated
in Ethel Wilson's best novel, *Swamp Angel*, which shares so greatly
the terrain of *Hetty Dorval*. She describes it thus in her first novel:

> At the point where the Thompson, flowing rapidly
> westwards from Kamloops, pours itself into the Fraser,
> flowing widely and sullenly southwards from the
> Lillooet country, is the Bridge. The Bridge springs with
> a single strong gesture across the confluence of the
> rivers and feeds the roads and trails that lead into the
> northern hills which are covered with sage, and are dot-
> ted here and there with extravagantly noble pine trees.
> The way to my own home lay across the Bridge.
>   Ever since I could remember, it was my joy and the
> joy of all of us to stand on this strong iron bridge and
> look down at the line where the expanse of emerald
> and sapphire dancing water joins and is quite lost in the
> sullen Fraser. It is a marriage, where, as often in mar-
> riage, one overcomes the other, and one is lost in the
> other. The Fraser receives all the startling colour of the
> Thompson River and overcomes it, and flows on un-
> changed to look upon but greater in size and quantity
> than before. Ernestine and I used to say, "Let's go
> down to the Bridge," and there we would stand and
> lean on the railing and look down ... at the bright water
> being lost in the brown, and as we walked and laid our
> own little plans of vast importance for that day and the
> next, the sight of the cleaving joining waters and the
> sound of their never-ending roar and the feel of the fre-
> quent Lytton wind that blew down the channels of both
> the rivers were part and parcel of us, and conditioned,
> as they say, our feeling.[18]

The image — like all potent images — can be read in several
ways. It can stand in potent isolation, like the image in a haiku,
suggesting everything, stating nothing. It can be read as a rendering of direct experience, and, given the plot of the book, as a por-

tent of what follows, for soon Ernestine will be destroyed by the "sullen Fraser" when she plunges in to try and save a dog (thus providing the extreme contrast to Hetty's persistent non-involvement with other beings). It can be read symbolically. Rivers run together and all rivers run into the sea, which means much the same as Donne's imagery of islands and continents. Lives run together, as rivers do, so, irrevocably, something from Hetty's life (the brown of the Fraser or the blue of the Thompson?) has flowed into Frankie's life. Or, finally, we can return to our concepts of innocence and experience, and learn that no life continues forever in the innocent blueness of origins; experience muddies and hides it, just as Hetty's sparkling and careless beauty in fact flows into a river of murky consequences.

The Innocent Traveller is a more complex and also a more ponderous book than *Hetty Dorval*, mainly because it attempts to be two things, the life-story of an eccentric personality and the history of a family. In both respects it is highly readable and conducted with wit and wisdom, but the fusion is incomplete.

The novel begins in Staffordshire, Ethel Wilson's ancestral county, and there is no doubt that family traditions and her own memories have contributed to its content, just as one of the younger members of the fictional family, Rose, shares much of Ethel Wilson's youthful experience and perhaps also her point of view.

The innocent traveller is Topaz, at the beginning of the novel a small child, "innocent as a poached egg," telling Matthew Arnold with embarrassing enthusiasm about the newly installed water closet in the Edgeworth house that goes "Whoosh! Whoosh!" She ends far away in space and time from that Staffordshire home, for she has passed a hundred when, in Vancouver, she finally dies, as self-centred, as avid, as innocent, as she had always been.

> Topaz is dying, there is no doubt of that. She — gay, volatile, one hundred years old, the last of her generation, long delayed — is uneasy. She is very restless. She shows no fear and yet she seems to be in some kind of anguish. Plainly she is awaiting something, an affirmation or release. What is that she is saying? She wants to go, she says. She is being prevented. The poor volatile bird.

"Let me go immediately ... immediately ..." she murmurs in her imperious way. "A hundred years ... I shall be late ... me, the youngest." Then the small face lightens. "Quick, get me some fresh lace for my head, someone! I'm going to die, I do declare!" Evidently she is pleased and confident. What an adventure, to be sure!

Away she went. Now she is a memory, a gossamer.[19]

Topaz becomes "a memory, a gossamer" because she had no love and no true attachment. Yet, thanks to circumstances and especially to the love of others, she has been able to live out her life with happiness and zest and to retain to the end the special kind of innocence that enables her to survive in emotional insularity until death gathers her in to the continent of the one experience that, after birth, all mankind must share.

In this way, of course, though it reads as a very different kind of book, much busier and more crowded, *The Innocent Traveller* is an extension of *Hetty Dorval*, presenting the comic rather than the tragic face of innocence. If Topaz is incapable of love, she has an extraordinary zest for living, yet in her own strange way she remains immune from the effects of experience, which leaves her unchanged while it moulds and modifies the other major characters in the novel. The very innocence that keeps her from forming deep personal attachments also enables her to confront each encounter in life with an open kind of enthusiasm. It also makes her tolerant, so that she suffers neither from snobbery nor from any other prejudice and is willing to accept people as she sees they are. Conventions and conventional distinctions mean nothing to her, and she is as devoid of prejudice as she is — like Hetty — lacking in malice.

One of the crucial scenes in the book concerns the black man, Joe Fortes, an actual figure in Vancouver's history who used to teach the children to swim at English Bay and who rescued many from drowning. A woman taught by Joe is presented for membership of the Minerva Club, and a "pudding-faced lady" asserts she has been "seen more than once in a public place, bathing in the arms of a black man."[20] Topaz valiantly defends both Joe Fortes and the maligned woman, who is elected to the club with acclamation, and when she gets home tells her saintly sister Annie and her niece Rachel. And Rachel, who has often been annoyed with Topaz, listens to the tale, and then remarks: "I have never heard you say an unkind thing about anyone. I have never heard you cast an aspersion on anyone. I really believe that you are one of the few people who think no evil."[21]

What Rachel says takes on its full meaning only if we think of it in relation not only to Topaz, but also to Hetty, that other innocent incapable of self-denying love. For Topaz is able to retain and nurture the honesty and fairness that represent the positive side of her innocence only because she has been brought up and protected to the end of her days in the warm nest of the family. Hetty seems less kind and more devious because she has never lived in the emotional shelter a family like the Edgeworths provides. The only relative she knew — and she did not know until the end that this was a real relative — had been Mrs. Broom, the mother masquerading as a servant, and all her years since girlhood had been a long campaign to gain the life of ease she desired without sacrificing the freedom that made the wild geese almost her totem birds. In one poignant scene on an Atlantic liner, Hetty approaches Frankie and her mother, and begs them not to reveal what they know about her, because she hopes to achieve a marriage that will bring her the security she had never known. Topaz's innocence has always flourished in security, and so it has manifested itself in genial eccentricities and a fearless acceptance of life.

Topaz could never have survived as she did, mentally and physically, without the support of that family, some of whose members understood better than she the reality of love. But the family could have survived without Topaz, and in the reader's eye it takes on a life of its own, as a kind of collective character that provides the other stream of interest in the novel.

We encounter the Edgeworths in the first chapter as a solid Staffordshire pottery family which has made money on teapots admired by Queen Victoria at the Great Exhibition and on chamber pots which an African tribe ordered in large numbers, reportedly for use as headgear. The Edgeworths are cultured enough to be the guests and associates of local politicians, though they have remained chapel folk, true to the Methodism that was the militant cult during the industrial revolution.

The Victorian patriarchs die, the children spread over the Empire, to die in India, to prosper in Australia and South Africa and Canada, and finally the remaining nucleus of the family — the saintly Annie, her daughter Rachel and the feckless Topaz, emigrate to Canada. Once again, a sea voyage brings a change of perspectives, and the Edgeworth women find in the new land a place where their natures can expand into a new fulfilment.

> Topaz had at last reached open country. British Columbia stretched before her, exciting her with its mountains, its forests, the Pacific Ocean, the new little frontier town, and all the new people. Here was no time limit, no fortnight's holiday. Here she had come to live; and, drawing long breaths of the opulent air, she began to run about, and dance for joy, exclaiming, all through the open country.[22]

Vancouver, when the family arrives, is still little more than the rough settlement that sprang so quickly into existence when the C.P.R. reached over the mountains.

> Modest one- or two-storied buildings rose, to everyone's admiration, where the nobler forest had lately been. The forest still was, and winding trails through the woods ended at small hidden shacks, almost within the town itself. Vancouver was only a little town, but prophetically it called itself a city.[23]

Vancouver's growth into a real city is one of the themes of *The Innocent Traveller*, but it is so woven into the experience of the novel's main characters that one perceives it rather as one perceives Balzac's projections of Louis Phillippe's France; as a living fictional entity, with Joe Fortes who was a historical individual and Yow the Chinese cook who was a historical type at home within the half-imaginary, half-documentary but wholly self-consistent world of Topaz and her relatives and their middle-class friends of British origin.

It is not the relative authenticity of the imaginative vision that troubles one in *The Innocent Traveller*. It is rather the awkwardness of the structure. The novel is highly episodic in form. Three chapters, "Down at English Bay" (about Joe Fortes), "The Innumerable Laughter" (about Topaz scaring herself by sleeping out one night in the Gulf Islands), and "I have a Father in the Promised Land" (an ironic and amusing account of a revivalist meeting) were all published separately in periodicals, where they stood happily on their own, as self-contained as short stories. This autonomy of the chapters gives the book as a whole a somewhat jerky motion. It is no great improvement that the cracks which result are often papered over by passages of authorial comment, sometimes too ponderous and sometimes too arch. Occasionally such comment actually serves as a flashforward, telling the reader with clumsy confidentiality the future consequences of acts committed in the present.

Ethel Wilson never again attempted a novel as large or as complicated in structure as *The Innocent Traveller*. She returned to shorter fiction with relatively simple structure and a single dominant line of development. Her next two novels, *Tuesday and Wednesday* and *Lilly's Story*, were in fact so short that they were published in a single volume, *The Equations of Love*, which altogether — with its 90,000 to 100,000 words — is no longer than an average novel.

At first sight, except that each of them is concerned with the varieties of emotion and relationship we bring together under the name of love, these two novels — or novellas — seem very different. *Tuesday and Wednesday* is entirely urban, set in a later Vancouver than the little town where Topaz and her sister first arrived. Its action, leading through comedy into tragedy, is completed in the two days of the title. Its characters have no time to change and grow; they merely reveal their true natures through the harrowing of stress and calamity. *Lilly's Story* encompasses the greater part of its heroine's life. It begins in the city and takes refuge in the country. And its very core is the changing and maturing of a personality. Lilly Waller, the pale girl with taffy-coloured hair who works in Lam Sing's restaurant and arouses the passions of Yow (the Edgeworths' cook) is in the beginning an innocent very much like Hetty Dorval, but she is born into life on a lower level, so that her struggle to survive is necessarily more ruthless and predatory. Experience changes her when she devotes her life to providing the best possible future for the child, Eleanor, whom she has by a passing liaison.

It is curious that no previous critic has linked these two novellas with Ethel Wilson's admiration for Arnold Bennett. For in fact they present just what she thought to be good in Bennett — "view of poor persons, poor houses, poor places, mean streets, and their relative beauty to those concerned ...." They are, apart from a few stories, the only writings in which Ethel Wilson left the middle class to which she belonged and imaginatively entered the minds and lives of people who lived outside the sophisticated world that was her own.

There is no suggestion in these novels that Ethel Wilson had been led to write about the poor by any political imperative. In her inclinations she was indeed liberal, and she had read widely in political polemics ever since she was introduced to the *New Statesman* in the 1920s, but, though politicians appear as characters in at least two of her novels, and she would have agreed that the novelist cannot ignore the political any more than other dimensions of life, the idea of writing to make propaganda for any partisan viewpoint was remote from her view of the role of literature. But to show through the glass of the imagination the true lives of poor people — to show them with compassion and understanding — was to her, as much as it had been to Dostoevsky, a part of the novelist's function, provided it were done in a work of literary art, true to and within itself.

Tuesday and Wednesday carries an epigraph from *Bleak House* — Mr. Chadband asking, "Now, my young friends, what is this Terewth ... firstly (in a spirit of love) what is the common sort of Terewth ..." And, somewhat like Jesting Pilate, the novella proceeds to consider how we can judge of human actions, and how the same actions, seen by different people, can seem heroic or despicable, without either viewpoint being objectively correct. Mortimer and Myrtle Johnson (Mort and Myrt) are a feckless working class couple living in an untidy room off Powell Street near the docks in Vancouver. Mort is good-natured, lazy, a born fantasist who turns every gardener's job he loses from idleness into a big landscaping contract. Myrt, who goes out cleaning, is less given to dreaming of this kind, for her small, acrid personality is self-contained and self-fuelling. Losing one job during the days of the novel, Mort almost gets another, and is walking home in a self-congratulatory glow when he encounters his dearest friend, the high-rigger Eddie Hansen, who is — according to his wont — roaring drunk on Powell Street. Eddie forces Mort to accompany him down to the docks on a futile search for a lost suitcase. Eddie staggers over the end of the wharf, and Mort either falls or dives after him — it is never quite clear which — and is dragged to his death by the panic-stricken logger, who cannot swim.

Later, in the Johnsons' flat, various versions of the truth are brought in confrontation with each other. Myrt believes the policemen who tell her of Mort's death. According to them the two men were seen staggering together down the street, and therefore they were presumably both drunk. Myrt thinks only

of herself and bitterly laments what Mort has done to her by getting drunk again with the detested Eddie. But shortly afterwards
her timid cousin, Victoria May Tritt, makes an appearance. On
her way to church Vicky has seen Mort walking soberly along
the street and being accosted by drunken Eddie. On her way back
from church, she has heard Mort's name mentioned by a group
of men talking in the street about the tragedy. On the spur of
the moment, it occurs to her to vindicate Mort's memory by in-
vention, and, reproaching Myrtle with uncharacteristic vigour,
she declares that Mort acted heroically, deliberately diving in to
rescue his drunken friend. Neither version is the whole truth,
but Victoria speaks with the passion of conviction, and Myrtle
in astonishment accepts her story.

> Something grew warm within Myrtle and she saw the
> simple picture of Morty putting his hands together and
> diving in to rescue Eddie Hansen and she became, as
> Victoria May had said, the widow of a hero, and she
> became proud of Morty, but prouder of herself for be-
> ing the widow of a hero. Vicky, seeing what she had
> achieved, expelled a long breath, and relaxed. How sim-
> ple it had been![24]

It is a world of simple, ill-educated people with primitive reactions among whom Ethel Wilson moves, a dripping Vancouver
world where minds are inclined to be as foggy as the skies, and
one wonders, when the equation of Mort's and Myrt's love is
worked out, just how the sum comes out. For underneath the
comic, almost Dickensian masks worn by Myrt and Mort and
Vicky and the self-indulgent Mrs. Emblem, Myrtle's aunt, one
senses emotions of compassion and loyalty and love that are unar-
ticulated or at best articulated in the debased language of the
cinema and the radio. (Television had yet to come.)

Lilly's Story begins in the same depressed area of Vancouver
as *Tuesday and Wednesday*, for the gambling houses where Yow
spends his nights and the café where he meets and becomes
obsessively enamoured of Lilly, a runaway girl working as a
waitress, are not far from the Powell Street areas where the
Johnsons lived.

Yow had already appeared in *The Innocent Traveller*, as lacking
in innocence as Aunt Topaz was full of it, yet capable of love.
He boasted, and probably truthfully, of having killed two men

in China, one quickly and one slowly, but he was devoted to the saintly Annie, Topaz's sister, and he loved Lilly with a ferocity that led to his ruin, for he stole on a large scale from the Edgeworths to win her heart. When Yow was arrested, Lilly — who had never loved in her life — thought only of saving herself from the police, and became a "pale slut who is running through the dark lanes, stopping, crouching in the shadows, listening, hardly daring to look behind her."[25]

If Aunt Topaz stands on one side of Hetty Dorval as the innocent who was sheltered and so saved from having to live in the appalling amorality of endangered innocence, Lilly stands on the other side — the child who never knew even the strange love with which Mrs. Broom had protected Hetty, her unproclaimed daughter. When she flees from the police and disappears to surface again on Vancouver Island, Lilly knows the meaning of love even less than Hetty or Topaz.

> No one had loved her, and she did not even know that she had missed love. She was not bitter, nor cruel, nor was she very bad. She was like the little yellow cat, no worse and no better. She expected nothing. She took things as they came, living where she could, on whom she could, and with whom she could, working only when she had to, protecting herself by lies or by truth, and always keeping on the weather side of the police.[26]

In Nanaimo Lilly goes to live with a Welsh miner, but there is no love. Lilly is still as innocent and uncaring as an animal, as Ethel Wilson suggests in the strangely harsh way in which she describes the relationship.

> Ranny was only a kennel into which a homeless worthless bitch crawls away from the rain, and out of which she will crawl, and from which she will go away leaving the kennel empty and forgotten.[27]

The rest of the novel tells of Lilly's transformation from "a homeless worthless bitch" into a loving and responsible human being, her difficult passage from innocence into experience. With one of those haunting resonances that in Ethel Wilson's work pass on from novel to novel, there is a second echo here of Hetty Dorval. The young Lilly, the taffy-haired girl for whom Yow lusted, may have been a debased counterpart of Hetty, but her later life uncannily resembles that of Hetty's mother, Mrs. Broom. Pregnant by Ranny the miner, she leaves him to have her child, and then assumes another self. She is no longer Lilly Waller, the slut who has an illegitimate child. She gives herself a new name, and with the new name a different history, so that she is now Mrs. Walter Hughes, the widow of a prairie farmer, better bred than herself, who was killed by a horse before their daughter was born. In this guise she sets about finding the circumstances in which she can best bring up her daughter and give her the kind of life she has missed.

To begin she becomes housekeeper to a British ex-officer and his wife at Comox, and there are some idyllic years until Lilly realizes that in the village Eleanor is know as ''the maid's daughter''. She departs and becomes housekeeper at a hospital in the Fraser valley; here she ages as her daughter grows up, and lets her looks fade, and resists the approaches of men, for all she can feel is the possessive love that binds her to her daughter.

The final opening out of that love comes when Eleanor has gone to Vancouver for training as a nurse, has married and herself had children. Lilly, in her hospital, seems to be withering into a loveless existence, when fate and coincidence thrust her back into the stream of life. One day, looking out of the window of her cottage at the hospital, she sees a figure of dread walking in from her past. It is Yow, come to work at the hospital as cook.

> Year after year now she had lived in an obscurity that was so planned and safe that there were times when it seemed that the years of vagrancy had never been. They had become a dream and hardly a dream, yet a recurring dream. Her faked past had almost become her reality. She had forgotten the associates of her vagrant years, and here was Yow, the most dangerous, the most violent of them all.[28]

Reappearing with such melodramatic suddenness, Yow paradoxically liberates Lilly from the life of fear and concealment into which her care for Eleanor has involved her. She flees once again, this time to Toronto, where she works as chambermaid in a hotel. There she meets widowed Mr. Sprockett, and Mr. Sprockett falls in discreet love with her, and Lilly, for the first time since Ranny, accepts a relationship with a man. But this time it is different. Ranny was the unloved provider in whom she found refuge as a fugitive. But Sprockett talks of love, and asks her for love, and Lilly begins to see love as a mutual caring:

> If loving Mr. Sprockett meant looking after him and
> thinking for him and caring for him and guarding him
> from harm and keeping things nice like she'd always
> done for Eleanor and for Matron, then she could love
> him, and she was his, and he was hers.[29]

She senses, in this relationship where she would give as much
as she would be given, "She would be without fear; nothing,
surely, could touch her now." And so, after the long years of
love as sacrifice, Lilly comes to the realization of love as mutual
caring, love as union.

Just as in some ways *Lilly's Story*, that modest and moving
novella, develops elements that had their origin in *Hetty Dorval*,
in other ways it anticipates *Swamp Angel*; perhaps most notably
in the way it develops the correspondences between human life
and the natural world. Its most dramatic scene is one of conflict
between wild creatures, when Lilly and Eleanor, still a child, are
on a little promontory at Comox, with the child's kitten. They
see a robin attacking a tiny snake; the kitten stalks the robin until the shadow of an eagle falls upon it, but before the eagle can
swoop down he in turn is attacked and driven away by a crow
and a seagull. The scene makes Lilly uneasy; she relates it to her
own life, and to her it "seems like everything's cruel, hunting
something." It is beyond Lilly to see — though her daughter
Eleanor may — what Ethel Wilson describes on the next page in
one of her authorial asides as

> The incorporeal presence in air, and light, and dark,
> and earth, and sea, and sky, and in herself, of
> something unexpressed and inexpressible, that
> transcends and heightens ordinary life, and is its
> complement.[30]

Nowhere in Ethel Wilson's work is this sense of a spiritual force
imminent in the natural world more powerfully expressed than
in *Swamp Angel*, the best of her novels. Maggie Vardoe, the
leading character, runs away from her present, as Lilly Waller
had done. She too changes her name to indicate her change of
living, though in her case she takes back an old name, Maggie
Lloyd, which means that she is rejecting the interlude in which
she sought to live according to bourgeois conventions with the
pathetic materialist Edward Vardoe.

Maggie Lloyd is a much more complex figure than the earlier characters with whom one naturally compares her, Hetty and Lilly. She has always known and understood the reality of love, in her relations with her father and later with her first husband, killed during the war. Her love for that dead husband does not vanish, but she married Edward Vardoe for compassion, and only when she realizes that this vain, coarse man is unchangeable does she decide to leave him. Having made her decision, she plans her departure carefully, earning money secretly, arranging her flight with care, and leaving no clues that will enable Vardoe to track her down. In this respect she resembles Lilly saving and planning before she leaves Ranny the miner to have her child.

But Maggie is not really choosing a new way of life. She had been brought up at a fishing lodge beside a lake in New Brunswick, where she helped her father and learnt from him the skill of fly-tying which she uses to finance her flight. It was in that past that she developed the self-reliance, manifesting itself in both resourcefullness and secretiveness, to which she now turns.

> Maggie, brought up from childhood by a man, with men, had never learned the peculiarly but not wholly feminine joys of communication, the déshabille of conversation, of the midnight confidence, the revelation. And now, serenely and alone, she had acted with her own resources ....[31]

There is something uncanny, even slightly repellent about the serenity with which Maggie makes her plans and acts and deals with people. For cruelty is never far from compassion, not only in her view of nature, but also in her own actions. Perhaps compassion has failed with Edward Vardoe, but the way Maggie leaves him, slipping out in the middle of dinner, seems calculated to create the greatest bewilderment and pain, and the same duality exists in her attitude to nature. She loves the wild and the creatures of the wild, yet fishing and all that goes with it are at the heart of her life, and — not being callous — she is aware of the cruelty. After she leaves Vardoe on her flight into the hinterland, Maggie stops for a couple of days beside the Smilikameen River, and fishes there.

> In the pleasure of casting over this lively stream she forgot — as always when she was fishing — her own

existence. Suddenly came a strike, and the line ran out,
there was a quick radiance and splashing above the
water downstream. At the moment of the strike, Maggie
became a co-ordinating creature of wrists and fingers
and reel and rod and line and tension and the small
trout, leaping, darting, leaping. She landed the fish,
took out the hook, slipped in her thumb, broke back the
small neck, and the leaping rainbow thing was dead. A
thought as thin and cruel as a pipe fish cut through her
mind. The pipe fish slid through and away. It would
return.[32]

At the moment of landing the fish, Maggie is as totally and
naturally absorbed in her task and unconscious of its implication
as the osprey she will later watch with such admiration, until the
thought like a pipe fish slips through her mind and separates her
from the world of nature.

Maggie goes on, through Lytton, where the meeting of the
waters is again splendidly described, and on to Kamloops, where,
up in the hills, she gets a job as cook at the lodge run by the Gunnarsons at Three Loon Lake. From now on this is her world and
her life,and she cannot even envisage returning to the city. The
lake, like her, is both cruel and kind. It gives Maggie physical
and mental vigour, but two people are almost killed by it, and
brought back to life by Maggie's care. A strength emerges in her.
She is no longer the discontented powerless wife of Edward Vardoe. She moved to create a life in which her self-reliance can
flourish, a life without attachments, though not without the desire
to help others as she helps the Gunnarsons. But as she helps she
shapes, dealing as capably with Vera Gunnarson's jealousy as
she deals with the practical problems of running and expanding
the lodge. She uses her very decency to impose her will on others,
manipulating them even if it is for their own good, so that in the
end one has a sympathy for poor weak Vera's obsessive feeling
that Maggie is running the Gunnarson's lives. There are times
when her very helpfulness robs other people of their personal
sense of dignity.

In this way the main plot and the sub-plot of *Swamp Angel* come
together and the title is explained. Leaving Vancouver, Maggie
has left not only Edward but also her real friends, Hilda Severance
and her old mother Nell. Hilda's unlikely marriage comes about
and flourishes as Maggie's own marriage with Vardoe ends, and

in the background the eccentric Nell Severance plays with her souvenir of a lost life, the pistol known as the Swamp Angel. For Nell has been a professional juggler in her day and remained romantically attached to the circus world of illusion, yet curiously practical as she now juggles with other people's lives, turning Vardoe aside from his murderous anger towards Maggie, and pushing Hilda into making up her mind to marry Albert Cousins. It is appropriate that when Nell feels the Swamp Angel is a dangerous toy to keep, she sends it to the other juggler, Maggie, and when Nell dies it is Maggie who takes the pistol and throws it into the lake as if it were Excalibur.

> She stood in the boat, and with her strong arm she threw the Angel up into the air, higher than ever Nell Bigley of the Juggling Bigleys had ever tossed it. It made a shining parabola in the air, turning downwards — turning, turning, catching the sunlight, hitting the surface of the lake, sparkling down into the clear water, vanishing amidst breaking bubbles in the water, sinking down among the affrighted fish, settling in the ooze. When all was still the fish who had fled, returned, flickering, weaving curiously over the Swamp Angel. Then flickering, weaving, they resumed their way.[33]

The Swamp Angel, which "in its eighty years or so has caused death and astonishment and jealousy and affection," nevertheless belongs to the temporal world of human artifice, and when it is gone, it will soon be "not even a memory, for there will be no one to remember it." The lake into which it falls represents the timeless world of nature where the fishes flicker and weave a dance that never ends. And so another duality of the novel is projected; we live in time but belong to the timeless, just as the land in which we live is rocks and trees and water but also in other ways a map of the human heart.

Swamp Angel offers Ethel Wilson's most successful structure as a novel, every part tuning with the other, just as Maggie Lloyd is her most developed and most convincing character. Perhaps there is a shade too much of the melodramatic in Nell Severance; perhaps Edward Vardoe is too absurdly contemptible, but otherwise the characters and their relationships exist entirely convincingly in their autonomous world.

Ethel Wilson's last novel, *Love and Salt Water*, was also her least successful. It is a neatly written and well enough constructed book about the growing-up of a middle class girl and her difficulties — which finally end — in achieving the kind of marriage that satisfied her. But the urgency of feeling that burns through the other books is no longer present. The essential plot is perhaps no more unpretentious than that of *Hetty Dorval*, but Ellen Cuppy does not develop through the same sensitively evoked opening of the perceptions as Frankie Burnaby, and there is no enigma in the book as interesting as Hetty. Even the minor characters are less tellingly portrayed as those that crowd *The Innocent Traveller*, and the wit has somehow faded from the narrator's tongue as the irony has from her eye. There is only one point in the whole book at which the reader becomes urgently involved. That is when Ellen takes her little nephew Johnny out in a dinghy in Active Pass to look for seals and they are nearly drowned when the riptide overturns the boat. The feeling of the British Columbia coast and its waters is at times pleasantly recalled, but rarely does it become the commanding environment of *Hetty Dorval* and *Swamp Angel*.

It is perhaps significant that this was the time when Ethel Wilson began to think consciously about her art as a writer, and to write about it almost as a critical outsider. For what is lacking in *Love and Salt Water* is precisely the sense that here is a writer led on half-consciously and only half-willingly by her own creation, which was so strongly present in her earlier books. *Love and Salt Water* is a well-made novel of manners, but the clear flame of feeling and insight one remembers from her earlier books does not shine through the translucency of its prose.

Thus Ethel Wilson's significant novels embrace an even shorter period than the full list of her books suggests. They were published in a mere seven years, from *Hetty Dorval* in 1947 to *Swamp Angel* in 1954, and the period over which they were written was doubtless no longer. But these few short books have an unchallengeable place in the record of Canadian fiction, not only for their own qualities and their influence on younger writers, but also because they were the first successful attempt to bring the physical setting of western Canada convincingly into fiction, so that their comedies of manners and their dramas of feeling were played out against superbly described backdrops of landscape, for Ethel Wilson was unrivalled in her time as a novelist of Place.

Notes

1 George Woodcock, "On Ethel Wilson", in his *The World of Canadian Writing: Critiques and Recollections* (Seattle: University of Washington Press; Vancouver: Douglas and McIntyre Ltd., 1980), p. 122.
2 Ethel Wilson, "A Cat Among the Falcons", *Canadian Literature*, No. 2 (Autumn 1959), pp. 13-4.
3 *Ibid.*, p. 16.
4 Desmond Pacey, *Ethel Wilson* (New York: Twayne Pub., 1967), p. 21.
5 Wilson, "A Cat Among the Falcons", p. 15.
6 Pacey, p. 18.
7 Ethel Wilson, "The Bridge or the Stokehold: Views of the Novelist's Art", *Canadian Literature*, No. 5 (Summer 1960), pp. 43-4.
8 *Ibid.*, p. 46.
9 Ethel Wilson, *Swamp Angel* (Toronto: Macmillan, 1954; rpt. McClelland and Stewart, 1962), pp. 13.
10 *Ibid.*, p. 157.
11 Ethel Wilson, *Hetty Dorval* (Toronto: Macmillan, 1947; rpt. Toronto: Macmillan, 1967), p. 92.
12 *Ibid.*, p. 15.
13 *Ibid.*, pp. 83-4.
14 *Ibid.*, p. 25.
16 Wilson, "A Cat Among the Falcons", p. 14.
17 Wilson, *Hetty Dorval*, p. 57.
18 *Ibid.*, pp. 6-7.
19 Ethel Wilson, *The Innocent Traveller* (London: Macmillan, 1949), p. 275.
20 *Ibid.*, p. 154.
21 *Ibid.*, p. 157.
22 *Ibid.*, p. 122.
23 *Ibid.*, p. 123.
24 Ethel Wilson, *Tuesday and Wednesday* in her *Equations of Love* (London: Macmillan, 1952), p. 123.
25 Ethel Wilson, *Lilly's Story* in her *Equations of Love* (London: Macmillan, 1952), p. 145.
26 *Ibid.*, p. 156.
27 *Ibid.*, p. 164.
28 *Ibid.*, p. 243.
29 *Ibid.*, p. 276.
30 *Ibid.*, p. 194.
31 Ethel Wilson, *Swamp Angel*, p. 20.
32 *Ibid.*, p. 38.
33 *Ibid.*, p. 157.

ERNEST BUCKLER

THE GENESIS OF ERNEST BUCKLER'S
THE MOUNTAIN AND THE VALLEY

Alan R. Young

A year after Ernest Buckler had published *The Mountain and the Valley* (1952), he gave a radio talk in which he mentioned that the novel had taken him six years to write.[1] However, Buckler's correspondence and manuscripts, now deposited in the Thomas Fisher Rare Book Library at the University of Toronto, reveal that the gestation period for this now acknowledged classic of Canadian literature was much longer.[2] My intention here is to trace the course of that gestation and to show how Buckler's comments on the novel, taken in consideration with his early short stories that were reworked into its fabric, collectively provide a unique glimpse of the processes of his creative imagination and at the same time suggest that certain aspects of the novel may hitherto have been overlooked by its interpreters.

The first hint of Buckler's desire to become a novelist occurs in a letter to *Esquire* in 1937 in which he quotes from the novel he himself is supposedly writing:

> ... When David closed his eyes at night, all the strange horde of imagination swarmed, seething, into his brain — the bewildering multiplicity of memory, the teeming variety of perception, the infinite permutations of speech ... the ephemeral, cloud patterns of ideas, constantly recast into a new galaxy, never still enough to have form or meaning or to crystallize and outline themselves in the mold of words; shimmering and wandering, through each other, insubstantial and bodiless, like the interstitial weavings of a puff of smoke.[3]

Here, complete with typical Bucklerian simile, is an intriguing but unconscious anticipation of the inner turmoil of David Canaan which is to become the central concern of the completed novel some fifteen years later. A few months later, in response to another letter to *Esquire* in which Buckler had pretended that his own fiction was superior to that of the magazine's contributors (among whom were Hemingway and Fitzgerald), Burton Rasco, the influential *New Yorker* critic, sent Buckler a telegram praising his "excellent sense and command of vigorous and effective English prose" and expressing his willingness as advisor to a publishing company to see whatever Buckler considered his "best unpublished work."[4] Buckler's bluff had been called for he had little to send, least of all a novel. Nevertheless, in 1939 in a letter to Rasco he mentioned that he was thinking of writing a "farm" novel.[5]

No further references to his plans for a novel occur until 1946. Meanwhile Buckler had been writing plays for the CBC, had managed to move from the correspondence to the fiction columns of *Esquire*, and had begun what was to be a fruitful relationship with *Saturday Night* by publishing a number of poems, articles and stories. However, in 1946, encouraged by these successes, Buckler seems to have returned to the idea of a novel, and he wrote to Edward Aswell of Harper and Brothers (the publishers) asking whether it was "too late for a book which has anything to do with the war."[6] Buckler mentions that "the short stories I did about the war, the ones I wrote from the truest compulsion, got editorial praise but no print." What troubles him is that these stories "are still gnawing at me inside my head, the way only stories you really believed in, but which were still-born, can." Out of this frustration, however, emerged the plan for a novel, for, enclosed with the letter to Aswell, are three stories which, Buckler claims, are "connected, my best, and have in them the foetus of a novel."[7]

Today the three stories are immediately recognizable as the barely-formed "foetus" of *The Mountain and the Valley*. In the letter Buckler explains that his "main theme is embodied in the one, 'The Trains Go By', the frustration of a young man who has to see it all happen to someone else," and his theme is "suggested also in 'Thanks for Listening'." A glance at "The Trains Go By" quickly reveals that the story was later modified and reshaped to form the bulk of Part Six "The Train" in the novel. The story concentrates upon Peter's isolation and frustration and the effects on him of the visit of his sister Martha and her sailor husband David. Whole passages and stretches of dialogue recur in the novel where, of course, the characters' names are changed to David, Anna and Toby respectively.[8] The pattern of the plot is also retained. Peter, who lives alone on the farm, is visited by his sister and brother-in-law prior to this latter's departure for the war. A remarkable understanding develops between the two men, but this is shattered at the end when Peter observes David's departure in the train and realizes the "*It was always someone else,* that was the panic of it. There had been these things while he was alive and young but they had all been for other men. The trains had all gone by and the grey smoke settled on the fields and he was standing there alone, with a hoe."[9]

A sequence of Peter's subsequent bitter reflections follows which reaches a climax when he slashes at his turnips with his hoe. The only basic difference between the novel and the story is that in the latter the two men are meeting each other for the first time and, rather than going hunting in the old orchards (see Chapter XXXVI) as they do in the novel, they walk to the top of the mountain. Presumably Buckler later made these adjustments so that the contrasts between the two men, who know each other from childhood on, could be sustained throughout the book and expanded to symbolize the pervasive dilemma facing David who is torn between his love for the land and his desire to move beyond the limitations of his rural culture. Given the symbolic importance in the novel of David's final climb up the mountain, which suggests his ultimate transcendence over his dilemma, it is also clear why Buckler should transform the mountain climb of the story into the hunting sequence.

"Thanks for Listening", the second of the stories sent to Aswell, reappears in the novel as the story which David sets down in his scribbler in Part Six while Toby and Anna go into town.[10] In the short story, so Buckler admits in his letter to Aswell, "the writing is a little overblown and doesn't quite come off even if the intention is honest." In fact the story is sentimental and self-pitying in its portrayal of the point of view of the one who did not go to the war. However, Buckler transforms this defect into a virtue in the novel since this key sample of the way David does write, as opposed to the way he thinks he writes, then becomes part of a planned pattern of irony that will be commented upon again in a moment. As he writes, David is excited by his own creative processes: "He said the phrase out loud. It was true. It was his. He felt like crying. Oh, it was wonderful, to be able to do a thing like this ...."[11] The reader, however, is meant to take a more objective view and be unimpressed by what David actually writes.[12]

The third of the stories sent to Aswell is entitled "Indian Summer", its subject, according to the letter, being "the relation of the man and the woman who are really *in* the war (Anna, here, being the Martha of 'The Trains Go By')." The story later became Chapter XXXVIII in Part Six of the novel, the section in which Toby and Anna climb to the top of the mountain alone and share one moment of consummate perfection which for Anna is describ- ed as "the peak of her whole life." In the novel the function of this section is to underline ironically the fact that David has never achieved a fulfilled relationship with anyone and that, in spite of his desire to climb the mountain throughout the novel, the sym- bolic implications of which have already been mentioned, he has yet to achieve that goal.

In both novel and story, it is Indian Summer, and the treachery of the season is revealed when all turns cold as both characters descend the mountain and the wife intuitively perceives that this will be their last day together and that her husband will be lost at sea. The novel provides a more concise version than the story,[14] though Buckler adds a reference to Toby's and Anna's hav- ing "sloughed off the city way" during their visit, a passage com- paring their silence to that of children in a place of enchantment, a description of Anna's smile, Anna's memories of Christmas with her twin brother when they were children, and an impor- tant paragraph in which the fact that Anna is wearing the clothes of both her husband and brother serves to enforce Buckler's deliberate fusing of the identities of the two men elsewhere,[15] and to reveal the impending near-tragic situation of Anna ("... now these clothes gave their definition to her. She looked small inside them. As a child looks small who has no *other* clothes but the discards, always cruelly too large, of someone else." p. 270).

The three stories sent to Aswell were politely returned by Elizabeth Lawrence in Aswell's absence with the accompanying suggestion that, since war themes are "desperately unpopular with the public at this time," Buckler should broaden the base of his idea "and make the war only an incident in the story of a young man forced to watch life from the sidelines."[16] Whether directly as a result of this suggestion or not, this in effect is what Buckler went on to do. David Canaan is unable to participate in the world into which he has been born on account of his physical incapacities and the alienation he suffers because of his educa- tion and highly developed sensibility. At the same time the op- portunities of city-life are rejected since they appear to deny this innate love and attachment to the land. His inability through physical disability to get enlisted for war service in Part Six is thus merely a minor addition to an already established broader pattern of frustrated alienation.

Part of Buckler's reason for writing to Aswell was to seek some objective judgement as to whether he should risk the financial sacrifice involved in devoting his available writing time to a novel:

> It's something I would like very much to do, but naturally if the idea has all the strikes against it at the start, there would not be much point in attempting it. Particularly when bread and health are such a problem with me that I literally couldn't abdicate the short story market unless there was something definite to hope for in the long run gamble. One must write to sell to live, even if it's only so that one may live to write.

We must be thankful that, in spite of Elizabeth Lawrence's somewhat lukewarm encouragement, Buckler decided to take on the gamble. In the process of broadening the base of his original plan for a war novel, Buckler went back to several of his other stories. One of the most interesting of these is an unpublished work called "The Locket".[17] This portrays the feelings of its narrator (David) who, torn between loyalty to family and desire to experience the world beyond the limited horizons of his rural situation, steals away early one morning to go to sea. His blind grandmother, with whom he has always had a special relationship, hears him and calls him to her. She tells of her hiding of a sailor on the run when she was young and gives David a locket. He recognizes the face in the locket as a kin to his own and realizes that the call to the sea in his blood and his grandmother's sympathetic attitude are due to this concealed part of his family history. Here evidently is an early version of David Canaan's relationship with his grandmother Ellen in *The Mountain and the Valley* and in particular the story of her relationship with a sailor about which she tells Anna in Chapter III. Significantly in the novel the call of the sea and the sound of a train are equated by Ellen,[18] thereby anticipating the climax of David's situation in Part Six when the train passes by bearing Toby to the sea. Similarly, in the novel Anna's future relationship with Toby is also anticipated when she says "I think I'll marry a sailor".[19] The gift of the locket to David occurs much later in the novel, but the crucial self-identification with the sailor is there, as is Ellen's empathy with David, who has just previously attempted to leave home:

This locket had something to do with what had happened today. She'd sensed somehow what had happened.
She'd sensed it because she too knew what it was like
when the moonlight was on the fields when the hay
was first cut and you stepped outside and it was lovely,
but like a mocking ... like everything was somewhere
else.[20]

Another unpublished story exists in three different versions entitled "Children", "Hares and Hounds" and "The Day Before
Never" respectively.[21] It depicts two country children who are
isolated from their peers, the boy because of his cleverness at
school, and the girl because of society's unspoken attitudes
towards her mother who is widely suspected of being sexually
promiscuous. The story develops a theme which Buckler once
described as always being "an insistent one" for him: "The theme
of lonely people who, because their true inner warmth and vitality
is never suspected, come to be cruelly labelled by others as of
one negligible 'type' or another."[22] The cruelty of the girl's situation is revealed in a powerful schoolroom scene in which she is
made victim of ribald smirks when she has to read from the Bible the story of "The Woman Taken in Adultery". The boy's isolation develops into an acute frustration which causes him to smash
his favourite kite. The two children understandably find relief for
their isolation in their friendship.

Clearly these stories anticipate the David/Effie relationship in
the novel though the two incidents mentioned above do not, of
course, occur there. However, the fact that Buckler did conceive
of David and Effie in much the same way as the protagonists of
these earlier stories is clear from some "Notes on David and Effie" which he sent to Doris Mosdell of the CBC in November 1964
in which he states that Effie is " 'set apart' by her consciousness,
no whit less acute because it is not altogether explicit, that her
mother is subtly shunned. And David is somewhat of a stranger
to the others because of his precocity."[23]

The enormity of David's betrayal of Effie in the novel would
have been much greater had Buckler initially made more of the
parallel situations of the two characters. By pruning some of the
material in the stories, he seems, in this instance, to have inadver-
tantly fallen short of his intentions, for the parallels that he
assumes in his "Notes" are in fact hardly apparent.

In another of the early stories, "One Quiet Afternoon", Buckler explored the situation of the prototype for Effie's mother, Bell Delahunt.[24] The story is portrayed through the eyes of a motherless boy (David) who feels a special attachment to the woman (Martha Legros). The insinuations of society cruelly isolate her, and, when her husband begins to accept society's view of her and calls her "a whore", she commits suicide by drowning, a tragic climax parallel to that of her counterpart in *The Mountain and the Valley*.[25] In a letter to Desmond Pacey, Buckler admitted that "One Quiet Afternoon" had been reworked into the novel, and in the same letter a similar admission is made concerning "The First Born Son",[26] which provides an anticipation of the important rock-clearing scene in Chapter XXIV and the ensuing rift between David and his father.[27]

Clearly, as Buckler set out to transform himself from short story writer to novelist, the material of his stories (both published and unpublished) was the first thing he turned to. Already he had the makings of an imaginative world where characters, themes and plot-motifs overlapped from one narrative to another. The choice of a semi-autobiographical protagonist must have followed naturally, for the sensitive, intelligent, isolated country boy, separated from his peers by his precocious learning and desire for something beyond that which rural culture appeared to offer, had already appeared many times in his fiction, sometimes even with the name "David". Equally natural, perhaps, was the decision to make the central focus of the novel the complex development of this protagonist as he passes from childhood to adulthood and gradually emerges as an artist. Two early unpublished sketches among Buckler's manuscripts suggest the growth of this concept. One sketch is entitled "Would you know if you fell over it?" which is a portrait of Karl who, like Buckler, is from the country, is clever and goes to college. Like Buckler and the later David Canaan, he suffers from headaches: "Never resilient physically, the striving to do everything perfectly put a strain on his health he could not stand."[28]

Discovering that he cannot make money, Karl takes up writing as a substitute for competing. Like Buckler he is nearly thirty at the time, and he too returns to the country where he discovers that "Happiness (sic) was where he had left it, snug, unasking, in the country village."[29] Like David Canaan, who never in fact leaves the country at all, he suffers nonetheless from the knowledge that his rural neighbours are "empty, uninhabited by any of the feelings that their secretive masks suggested." More recognizable as an early draft for the novel is a much longer manuscript entitled "Excerpts from a Life" in which the central character is David Redmond (the latter being Buckler's second name). The father is called Martin (the same as David's father in "The First Born Son") and the mother Anna.[30] The prototype for Bess Delahunt is called Ada Legros. Her daughter's name is Effie, and, as in the novel also, the name of the protagonist's grandmother is Ellen.

The two sketches mark successive shifts away from the purely autobiographical towards the fictional world of Entremont and the Canaan family, though, as Buckler later admitted, the principal characters in the book still owe much to his family.[31] In the years following the letter to Aswell there is little in Buckler's correspondence about the novel, but he must have been encouraged following his winning the Maclean's Fiction Prize in 1948 when a number of publishers, including Macmillan and McClelland and Stewart, made enquiries about its progress. In 1950, four years after the Aswell letter, in a letter to Naomi Burton of Curtis-Brown, the publishing agents, Buckler remarks that the structure of the novel is all blocked out and a good bit of the first draft is complete.[32]

More details do not emerge until a year later when Buckler wrote to Dudley H. Cloud of Atlantic Monthly Press who held an option on the novel. The original desire to depict "the frustration of a young man who has to see it all happen to someone else" against a war background has expanded into the complex psychological portrait of the "recurrent dichotomy in David's nature (Country boy or city boy? Naive or sophisticated? Harsh or tender? Over-child or over-adult? Serious or comic? Homebody or alien?).[33] Furthermore, the all-important delineation of the passing of a whole way of life that is so much a feature of the novel and those works that are to follow is now very much to the forefront of Buckler's thoughts as he talks of his concern with "the gradual dispersal of family oneness and (in parallel) in the village itself, as progress(?) laps closer and closer." Of significance also is his comment on Ellen's rug, which, as many critics have remarked, is a major unifying symbol in the novel. According to Buckler this was how the rug was intended for it exists "to show

how the apparently blind and capricious turns of their [the characters'] fortune are the inevitable outcome of circumstance and inheritance."

More is revealed about the composition of the novel in a second letter to Cloud which Buckler wrote after Atlantic Monthly Press had rejected the book.[34] Rather surprisingly, in view of what has here been said, Buckler claims that David's death was "the very first thing I wrote; the foundation for the whole thesis." Originally, he explains, he had planned to begin with David's death, but later he "split the opening chapter and shifted that part to the epilogue." In retrospect we can see that the structural unity resulting from the subsequent "framing" effect of Prologue and Epilogue was a happy stroke in the novel's composition. Not only does it make clear that David's final situation is the sum and substance of his entire past, but, by delaying David's death, Buckler reserves a dramatic climax for the novel that would have been hard to match had we known of David's fate in advance.

What Buckler then says in this letter about his intentions regarding David's death is of such interest that I think it is worth quoting in full:

> It was to be the crowning point of the whole dramatic irony (and, of course, the most overt piece of symbolism in the book), that he should finally exhaust himself climbing the mountain, and, beset by the ultimate clamor of impressions created by his physical condition and his whole history of divided sensitivities, come, at the moment of his death (prepared for, not only by long accounts of the result of his fall, but by the medical officer's advice to him at the time of his enlistment examination; and, more immediately, by the excitement, the panic, the climbing), achieve one final transport of self-deception: that he would be the greatest writer in the whole world.[35]

The objectivity displayed here by Buckler towards his semi-autobiographical protagonist confirms a point Warren Tallman touched upon but never fully developed in his perceptive article on *The Mountain and the Valley*,[36] in which he mentions David's uncritical and over-idealized view of his father. The ironic use of "Thanks for Listening" discussed above suggests that in *The Mountain and the Valley* Buckler indeed intended that the reader share a measure of detachment and perceive that there is a strong vein of irony involved in the portrait of David, an irony, which, as the letter to Cloud shows, is designed to reach a "crowning point" in the final pages. No critic who has discussed the novel has ever suggested an interpretation of the book that matches Buckler's apparent intentions.

This is no place to digress into a consideration of the "Intentional Fallacy" whereby a writer's intentions are mistaken by the critic for the actuality of the finished work of art. Nevertheless, as I hope I have shown, there may well be cause to re-read *The Mountain and the Valley* with some care in the light of Buckler's various statements about the novel. In addition, as I have also tried to show, our understanding of the material he incorporated into it from earlier published and unpublished stories may give one further insight preparatory to a re-reading of the book. If nothing else, the material described here provides an intriguing view of a major Canadian artist at work.

Notes

1   "My First Novel", CBC Radio, Toronto, 2 Dec. 1953. The talk has been published in *Ernest Buckler*, ed. Gregory M. Cook (Toronto: McGraw-Hill Ryerson Ltd.), pp. 22-27.
2   Grateful acknowledgement is given to Ernest Buckler and to the Thomas Fisher Rare Book Library, University of Toronto, for permission to quote from the material in the Ernest Buckler Manuscript Collection, hereafter referred to as "BColl".
3   *Esquire*, Nov. 1937, p. 10.
4   The telegram is quoted by Gregory M. Cook in "Ernest Buckler: His Creed and Craft", M.A. thesis, Acadia University 1967.
5   Letter to Rasco, 1 Dec. 1939. BColl. Box 4.
6   Letter to Edward Aswell, 10 Sept. 1946. BColl. Box 4.
7   The three stories ("Indian Summer", "Thanks for Listening", "The Trains Go By") were never published. They are now in BColl. Box 3.
8   The appropriate sections occur in *The Mountain and the Valley*, New Canadian Library Edition (Toronto: McClelland and Stewart, 1961), Part Six, Chapters XXXV, XXXVI, XXXIX, pp. 245-59, 272-74, 276-78. All subsequent quotations will be from this edition.
9   Cf. *The Mountain and the Valley*, pp. 274 and 276.
10 *Ibid*, pp. 260-63.
11 *Ibid*, p. 261.
12 To his credit David is more clear-sighted in his self-evaluation when Toby later confronts him with the manuscript: "David grabbed the sheet from his hand almost savagely. If Toby read what he'd written, he thought he'd die. The whole thing seemed unutterably shameful. How could he have put down anything so damned sickly and foolish? War was about as much like that as .... He opened the stove and thrust the

papers into the flames" (*The Mountain and the Valley*, pp. 263-64).

13 *Ibid*, p. 269.

14 The most significant cut is the wife's description of a dream she has had. Like many of the dreams later used in the novel, it is foreboding in its implications. It concerns her playing hide and seek with her husband. Whenever he is out of sight, she feels "lost and really like a child" and the dream turns "dark and frightening", the same feelings as she then experiences when they descend the mountain.

15 Cf. *The Mountain and the Valley*, pp. 135, 180, 226, 252, 253.

16 Letter from Elizabeth Lawrence, 1 Oct. 1946. BColl. Box 4.

17 BColl. Box 2.

18 *The Mountain and the Valley*, p. 34.

19 *Ibid*, p. 35. Cf. her anticipation of his early death, p. 52.

20 *Ibid*, p. 172. The importance of David's relationship to Ellen is defined in a note Buckler prepared for the projected T.V. dramatisation of *The Mountain and the Valley* in which Ellen is described as the "source of David's imaginative streak: the one grown-up to whom he can talk and confide in" (BColl. Box 2).

21 BColl. Box 3.

22 Biographical note for *Chatelaine*. Copy in BColl. Box 11.

23 BColl. Box 2.

24 *Esquire*, April 1940, pp. 70, 199-201.

25 *The Mountain and the Valley*, p. 295.

26 *Esquire*, July 1941, pp. 54-55, 114.

27 Letter to Desmond Pacey, 7 June 1961. BColl. Box 6.

28 BColl. Box 2.

29 After completing his B.A. at Dalhousie University and his M.A. at Toronto, Buckler worked for some years in Toronto for the Manufacturers Life Insurance Co. before returning permanently to his Nova Scotia home in the Annapolis Valley in 1936 at the age of 28.

30 BColl. Box 2.

31 "Mona is my youngest sister. (I think I'm giving no secrets away if I say that she is kind of roughly the Anna of the book.) Bob is Robert Simpson, her [navy?] husband. (Not totally unlike Toby and Rex)." Unaddressed fragment of letter from Buckler, 11 Dec. 1969. BColl. Box 11. Buckler also says in this letter that his mother was related to the "Jonathan Swift bunch" (cf. Ch. XII, p. 92, in the novel). His father was the "son of Joseph Buckler and Ellen (Kenny) Buckler. Ellen is, roughly, the Grandmother in the book." The circumstances of her marriage are much as those described in Ch. III of the novel (p. 31).

32 Letter to Naomi Burton, 25 Feb. 1950. BColl. Box 5. He also mentions that the novel is "psychological".

33 Letter to Dudley H. Cloud, 24 Mar. 1951. BColl. Box 15.

34 Letter to Buckler from Atlantic Monthly Press, 4 May 1951. BColl. Box 15. Letter to Dudley H. Cloud, 15 May 1951. BColl. Box 15.

35 This last point ends David's succession of desires to be the greatest general in the world (p. 41), the greatest actor (p. 82), the best doctor (p. 178), the most famous mathematician (p. 209), and the most wonderful dancer (p. 291).

36 "Wolf in the Snow" in *Contexts of Canadian Criticism*, ed. Eli Mandel (Chicago Univ. press, 1971), p. 238.

SHEILA WATSON, TRICKSTER

George Bowering

The prepared reader

In the fall of 1973, Sheila Watson gave her first public reading from *The Double Hook* at Grant MacEwan Community College in Edmonton. She prefaced her reading with a few minutes of talk about the writing and publication of the book that was to become the watershed of contemporary Canadian fiction. Here are the last three sentences of that preface:

> I don't know now, if I rewrote it, whether I would use the Coyote figure. It's a question. However, it begins with a dramatis personae, I suppose, and that is in the mouth of this figure who keeps making utterances all through the course of the novel.[1]

Sheila Watson then uttered the novel's famous first words: "In the folds of the hills under Coyote's eye ...."

Since then, people have been wondering why she might drop Coyote (though they should keep in mind the unlikelihood of a rewriting). On being asked the obvious question, Mrs. Watson said simply that she was responding obliquely to the extensive critical speculations on the function of the Coyote figure.

But Mrs. Watson, as those who have listened to her know, is a wily conversationalist. Return to that oral preface and notice that she said that the dramatis personae is in the mouth of Coyote. It is manifest to the reading eye that the roster is surrounded by white space, indented like verse, and thus that it resembles the poems of Coyote found throughout the text, as on page 115:

> Happy are the dead
> for their eyes see no more.[2]

But the dramatis personae is a different matter, isn't it? It does not sound oracular as the other verses do. It is an enumeration, an introduction of the inhabitants of the creek land. It is, though, because it does not appear the way an unobtrusive realist novel first appears, clearly a voice. It brings attention to its source. And its source is the author. Perhaps when Sheila Watson said "in the mouth of this figure," we should hear a syntactical rime with the reporter's "in the view of this correspondent ...."

As everyone now knows, Mrs. Watson went through a few

years of botheration in trying to see her eccentric book published; and even when McClelland & Stewart published it in 1959,
the publisher presented a text whose introductory design and
punctuation had been tidied by the British printer. Still, the book
appeared as a delicious oddity, a self-conscious departure from
the Canadian norm of eastern realism and western naturalism.
People found it hard to read and delightful to attempt. One reason
for this stir was the syntax and the lyricism: "A stone breathed
in her hand. Then life drained to its centre" (p. 35). Another
reason was Coyote.

Some people thought that *The Double Hook* was an electrifying
or charming oddity, a magic pool beside the Canadian
mainstream. Others, casting an eye less than a year later on the
similarly-designed *Mad Shadows* by Marie-Claire Blais, thought
they sighted a literary revolution. Here were two books that did
not provide windows on the harsh Canadian landscape, but
rather directed the eye and ear to their own pages, their language.
Mrs. Watson was not much interested in a revolution in the Canadian tradition. She has always felt her tradition to be defined by
what she read, and she has always thought of art as opaque, of
writing as writing, not social studies:

> There was nothing particularly revolutionary in Ger-
> trude Stein's theory. At the end of the nineteenth cen-
> tury Konrad Fiedler, one of the German fathers of
> stylistic history, had maintained that "each art expresses
> only itself and the value of its work cannot depend
> upon what an extra-artistic interest reads into it," in
> fact that "the various forms used to express human in-
> tellectual activity express only themselves." Each art
> moreover utters itself in its own form-language ....[3]

Figures in a ground

A typical early response to the book was Elliot Gose's review in
the first number of *Canadian Literature*.[4] He liked the mythical and
symbolic elements, critically assimilable material ever since the
creation of the Romantic novel of the nineteenth century, and seen
in a few Canadian fictions such as *Tay John* (1939), and *Wacousta*
(1832). But, says Gose, the reader will have to decide whether
to approve of "the short bits of poetry Mrs. Watson occasionally
includes in connection with the coyote."

Poetry, or that   poetry   is the ceremony of the word, don't we agree? It is not the signal, but the bringing of transformation. It is creation itself and logos itself. It is, as the first poetry was, naming and counting. (A piece of archness, if I may: if Coyote were Hesiod, Kip would be his wandering and blind Homer.) If poetry appears in a novel especially, it is language drawing attention to its physicality, and hence to the author as invisibly present, just like Coyote.

The Canadian literature of 1959 was presented with these pages given to an unsual amount of whiteness. The action was seen to be, then, within the shape of the page, indicating that the book is a spatial art, unlike film or music with their passive audiences, more like sculpture or architecture. So the reader stays aware of his own movement, aware that he is not at the end of the line, that he is continually looking at the material from his point of view. Mrs. Watson disrupted the 1959 reader's reading habits, so that he was made aware almost of a kind of threat, of at least a laughter beyond the reach of the reading lamp. Many of us are still 1959 readers, at least vestigially. We notice the white space and the short paragraphs, the refusal to describe, the scarcity of furniture, the closure of any distance in narration. The one-to-one relationship of word to world, found in the usual Canadian prose (Rule, Munro), does not hold here. We do not see characters in a setting, but rather what the artist calls "figures in a ground."[5]

"Figure" is a nice word, because it is used in all the arts. It means something fashioned, shaped, and always implies the activity of the author, composer, painter or dancer. In poetry it is another word for the stuff of metaphor. The concept of "character" suggests realist fiction, in which the author tends to convince us that she is less actual than Hagar Shipley. *The Double Hook* resembles *The Waste Land* more than it does *The Grapes of Wrath*.

Margaret Morriss has noticed that "Mrs. Potter is more of a force than a character in the novel.'"[6] But is she really more so than the rest of her family and her neighbours? A fictional character is someone you are convinced you have seen, though she is not there. In that sense the posthumous Ma Potter is more real for Felix and Ara than they are for us. In truth they are all equally figures, made of words. If they live, it is under Coyote's eye. Our reward for reading the book is language, not character development, not edification, not diversion, but language. This language, as anyone exposed to the first page will know, is not at rest and not seeking rest, but challenging us to form a logos out of our own unknowing. Robert Kroetsch sees "the text not as artifact but as enabling act. Not *meaning* but the possibility of meanings." He then goes on to say of

> the artist him/her self:

> in the long run, given the choice of being God or Coyote, will, most mornings, choose to be Coyote:

> He lets in the irrational along with the rational, the pre-moral along with the moral. He is a shape-shifter, at least in the limited way of old lady Potter. He is the charlatan-healer, like Felix Prosper, the low-down Buddha-bellied fiddler midwife (him/her) rather than Joyce's high priest of art. Sometimes he is hogging the show instead of paring his fingernails. Like all tricksters, like Kip, like Traff, he runs the risk of being himself tricked.[7]

Under the eye of the critic

Then who or what is Coyote? The critics of *The Double Hook*, like those figures living in the folds of the hills, have numerous notions. Beverly Mitchell, in a Christian reading, sees Mrs. Watson referring to the Biblical myths and then "displacing" them. Coyote's remarks often resemble those of the fierce God in the Old Testament, and his deeds are equally fierce. He is perhaps the hound of heaven. The people of the creek respond to him with fear, and even create him as an objectification of fear. Beverly Mitchell argues that the various responses of the people demonstrate "the fact that their concept of God is frequently the result of psychological projection."[8] So with their concepts of Coyote, a kind of reversal of the usual process of characterization performed by an author. In this scheme, the birth of baby Felix imitates and introduces the New Testament, in which redemption is offered to the community. Mitchell's allegorical reading, especially in light of her interiorizing of the landscape that seems to her at first damned, a Biblical and otherwise mythical familiarity, would seem one way of finding accord with Mrs. Waton's statement against regionalism.[9]

Margaret Morriss, too, sees Coyote as a symbolic projection, and the fear of him as "the fear of vision, knowledge, and immortality."[10] When he speaks he does so with metaphorical or more properly allegorical language. John Grube says that *The Double Hook* is a symbolic novel, in the mode of *The Old Man and the Sea*. One suspects, especially as Grube's essay is the introduction to the college edition of the novel, that he is trying to find familiar ground for students (he also calls it a parody of Faulkner). So the coyote is something like a marlin or a bear — Grube sees the animal as "fear" turned by Indians into a god, as is death, and describes that fear as "the nameless fear of the unknown." But the Indians, and the figures in the text, seem awfully familiar at least with Coyote's presence.

Nancy Corbett reads Coyote as "detached from the community, uninvolved and therefore merciless as he laughs at what he observes."[11] That would make a fine description of the author of a naturalist comedy; but in this case, I think we have a more coy author, a trickster. J. W. Lennox calls Coyote "the clairvoyant overseer"[12] which would be a pretty good description of an ironic Victorian author. Coyote, he says, comments on what he sees, rather than initiating events. With Ma and Kip he forms a ghostly trinity that keeps appearing as meaning that the rest of the figures would like to do without.

Most critics of the book make only passing mention of Coyote as trickster in the native stories of the Salishan people of the west, and especially here in the British Columbia Interior. Some point out, correctly I think, that Mrs. Watson layers the Coyote story with others, such as the Hebrew and Mediterranean ones, to achieve a universality beyond regionalism. Barbara Godard, for instance, notes that Coyote echoes Jeremiah, and that we get only "fragments" of each story, a hint at the deracination that bedevils the isolated community.[13] Not only does the layering of myths and sources suggest universality, but it also turns attention back upon the people doing the layering — reader and author. I agree that Mrs. Watson rangles Coyote with figures from other myths, that she even invokes the Greek Euros:

> In my mouth is the east wind. Those who cling to the rocks I will bring down I will set my paw on the eagle's nest. (p. 24)

Later we observe Ara's observation of the smoking doorsill of the destroyed Potter house. "The door of the house," she remarks, "had opened to the east wind. Into drought" (p. 114).

But the most interesting aspect of Coyote is his function as trickster, and I think that Mrs. Watson layers him with two other tricksters (three, if you count the author) in the scene wherein James blinds the servant of clairvoyant Coyote. Says James, daring the tricksters of America, Africa and Eurasia: "If you were God Almighty, if you'd as many eyes as a spider I'd get them all." (p. 67)

Leslie Monkman takes more notice of the Indian Coyote than do the other critics, noting especially the contraries in the figure's nature, his aspects of giver and negator, creator and destroyer, duper and duped. He points out that Coyote possesses no moral values, but that he challenges and creates them by his actions. Thus again Coyote, who is invisible though "the whole landscape is presented as embodying his immediacy,"[14] is a projection of various fears and guilts. Over that bridge Monkman also carries the Coyote story into an allegory of Old Testament dialectic. He suggests Coyote as Satan to Nod's Jehovah, and posits a drama occurring under "God's eye vs. Coyote's eye." So his interpretation of Indian myth employs Biblical ideas, seeing "Indian myths which relate that the world was originally created as an Eden until Coyote released from a sack the spirits of fatigue, hunger and disease."

All the readings of Mrs. Watson's Coyote suggest that she has taken the figure from Indian myth in her own mouth and dropped him into her text, where he will always be a reminder of artifice. However I am still unsatisfied. The emphasis on Coyote as projection employs Freudian notions peculiar to Romantic and realist fiction, in which revelation of character is a premier aim. The allegorical readings acknowledge the pleasure and aptness of the literal, but in their next decisions depart from the image of the trickster. Though one must admit that Mrs. Watson connects Coyote more with fear than with fun, one also would like to point out that most of the critics have concentrated almost exclusively on the experiences of the creek people, and hardly at all on the experience of the reader — this despite the constant signals made on the surface of the text. So it was with great pleasure that I found Robert Kroetsch identifying Coyote with a sly author.

The Indians' Coyote
Then who was the Coyote of the Indian people west of the Rockies?

John Berger has pointed out that "what distinguished man from animals was the human capacity for symbolic thought .... Yet the first symbols were animals."[15] In western Indian stories the animals are people, with speech and human foibles. Or put another way: when narrative enters, so does the singular and the humanoid, so that there are coyotes, part of the surround, and there is Coyote, a personality.

There is no scarcity of white men's scholarly treatments of the Coyote stories, but the one I like best is an address by Gary Snyder, who is, happily, both a trained ethnologist and a poet. It is called "The Incredible Survival of Coyote" and accounts for the passage of the Coyote figure into the literature of the white culture that has settled in the North American northwest. The figure he describes seems marvelously apt to *The Double Hook* — both to its narrative and to its composition.

People with European and literary backgrounds are used to gods or spooks with ultimate power over the elements and human lives. Even though the Greek gods symbolized qualities seen in the human psyche, they did not have human personality. It is Coyote's failure, his idiocy, that make him a puzzle to white folk. He has power, but he does not have ultimate power. He is a kind of person, but not one who can be assimilable to the conscious and rational mind. That is why critics can so readily treat him as a projection upon the landscape of the human subconscious. He says, perhaps, you are on your own, but I am always here, watching, and when I get an urge, meddling. That statement might as well be attributed to an author as to a subconscious. An author may meddle whenever she wants to, but in a fiction she does have to deal with materials that readers are accustomed to — such as "dramatis personae".

Gary Snyder points out that Coyote is stupid, bad, indecent, and tricky.[16] He did not make the physical or social world — Earthmaker did. Coyote is Shapeshifter, a meddlesome goof. It is interesting, given the plot of *The Double Hook*, that Coyote taught people how to fish, and that he showed them how to make fire; also that he got them interested in the possibility of death, though that was more from thoughtlessness than from malice. (Comparative mythologists might see him as a foolish rime, then, of Christ, Prometheus and Satan.)

As to Coyote's daily life: he is tricked as often as he tricks (p. 61). He is the funster who is always forgetfully tripping his own booby-traps. He is always travelling, though often wherever you are. Over and over he dies a stupid death and comes back. He can not leave well enough alone, so is always introducing a wonderful new idea into the world (as an author does into a setting). Other animals and people are always trying to deflate his eager busybodiness. Lily Harry, who lives at Dog Creek, where Sheila Watson did, says that Coyote got his yellow colour when Skunk turned around and expressed a popular impatience.[17]

The comic elements of Coyote might seem inappropriate to those readers who see him always associated with fear in *The Double Hook*. But really, isn't that a pretty funny book? Aren't there a lot of fools along the creek and down in the town? Don't we hear at least an echo of Rachel Cameron's escape from "that fool of a fear" as she removes herself from the thralldom of her own Ma and the latter's doctor, whose name was Raven?

Coyote does not represent a clear psychological dualism, then. He is a powerful fool, a smart goof who copes, an anti-hero of his own story, and for the writer who did not want to write a Western,[18] a nice change from the Western's silent hero and rescuer. Remember, though, that Sheila Watson can present not Lily Harry's Coyote, but only her own, only the white person's, only the writer's Coyote. Only, literally, the writing.

Under Coyote's mouth

The word "myth" gets tossed around a lot, by people who may have forgotten for a while that it comes to us from Greek *muthos*, meaning mouth and speech, and is related to Old Slavic *mudh*, meaning to think imaginatively, and even Lithuanian *mausti*, to yearn for, to desire. Myth is not a story about desire (for salvation), but is the expression, the body of desire itself. The desire of the author is in the text itself, and if it is to mean anything, the reader too must experience his own. Roland Barthes has written: "in the text, in a way, I *desire* the author: I need his figure (which is neither his representation nor his projection), as he needs mine ...."[19] (Note that Barthes' translator, Richard Miller, has used some words particular to our concern here.)

As heard in the Edmonton reading, *The Double Hook* emanates from the mouth of "this figure" Sheila Watson; and the desire for more (more novels, please) has been perhaps the most often spoken in the past two decades of Canadian reading. I believe that there is a peculiar reason why our readership has yearned for more of her voice, that it has to do with the revolutionary announcement her novel made. As Gertrude Stein once said, we do not need any more stories about our lives, but we need writing. Of the revolutionary discontinuity in Flaubert's work, Barthes wrote: "there is no longer a language *on the other side* of these figures (which means, in another sense: there is no longer anything but language)."[20]

The figure of Coyote is never "seen" by readers of *The Double Hook*, though his footprints are. Although the novel is structured by the occurrence of seeing, and eyes are the organs by which we know most of its figures, after the first sentence we know Coyote mostly by what our ears hear of his mouth.

From his mouth he breathes cactus into the grassland (p. 22). He boasts that the drought-bringing east wind is in his mouth (p. 24). He announces several times that if one will enter his mouth one will enter darkness and rest.[21] Perhaps somehow by his agency, Ma Potter goes into the darkness when James (whose name means "usurper") speaks from his own mouth. She goes "into the shadow of death. Pushed by James's will. By James's hand. By James's words" (p. 19). Whether that is a sequential order or a climactic one, it is a suggestive one.

When Coyote opens his mouth and uses thunder to call his servant Kip, Ara hears it and loses for the moment her life-giving grace (p. 36). The thunder means nothing to Felix (p. 38), who considers ceremonial words to be God's servants (p. 5l). But at one point even he dreams *a* coyote like a eucharist in his mouth (p. 68). Kip reports that he has seen Coyote carrying Ma in his mouth, as if she like Kip were his pup (p. 57). The voice out of Coyote's mouth is heard when the human component is shifting, at Greta's death and at young Felix's birth. In town, where James first questions his matricidal motivation as if he were a character in a realist text, Coyote's mouth tells him that he was really trying to punish and end himself. It is interesting and appropriate that when the novel goes to town and plays with referential regionalism for a while, Coyote becomes a Freudian fool.

And ambiguous Coyote has the last word ('world"). If one speaks (or cries, as he does) his final lines, one will begin once with high short vowels and end with low long ones, then do it again, with the latter more drawn out this time. Coyotes sounded like that in the hills of my childhood. When we tried to chase one he would easily dash away, then sit and grin at us. But if it was also dark and we could hear one, it was not clear how much of the delicious feeling was neighbourly comfort and how much fear.

The writer writing

There is one critic who has taken wise note of the comic *Double Hook*. Eli Mandel, in *Another Time*, says: "A rough and wicked humour, not unlike that in a mediaeval morality play, cuts deliberately across the high poetic lines, the buzzing energy of the novel."[22] If there is one thing that characterizes Modernist realism, and especially Canadian western naturalism, it is the lack of humour, except for the high-toned cosmic irony. Most fiction in the post-modernist, anti-realist mode is comic (Kroetsch, Hawkes, Calvino) for that reason and others. The "intrusion" of the author is generally, in our time, a matter of wit. In this case, it is the laughter of a coyote.

"Coyote made the land his pastime" (p. 22), we are told, and I cannot think of a quicker way to describe the relationship between author and setting. The realist (regional and otherwise) pretends that he just observes, but that can only happen in books, as they say. Or really, out of them. In a book, which is made of language, one does not have to pretend that some things are real and some illusions. Everything is equally real. A reading from a realist viewpoint says that the people along the creek would only think that there was a creature Coyote, that he is a figment rather than a figure. But realism says that there is no author, too, though there are people inside the book. The opposite, of course, is true.

Everyone notices that the main difficulty in reading *The Double Hook* for the first time is in following the narration, so trained are we to look beyond the sentence toward its referent. The narration is here obtruded upon; or at least we are made to see the foregrounding of syntax, rime and image. So, as Jan Marta has said, "the reader experiences the book as a process, not simply as a product,"[23] and especially not product somehow of environment and character. That is, we observe the writer writing, and we are aware of the reader reading. When John Moss says of the story that "over the whole is an unobtrusive God,"[24] we have to rejoin that in a novel, God is another created figure, equal, nominatively, to all the others.

The calmly presented Coyote was a means by which Sheila Watson could make a non-realist yet non-Romantic text in the 1950s. We needed, perhaps, a reference to "exotic" though indigenous myth in order to swallow the antinomian, the antinominalist. Mrs. Watson's remark that she might not use Coyote in an unlikely rewriting might mean that one does not now need him to declare one's freedom from the orthodoxy of cause-and-effect.

Cause-and-effect is another way of seeing time and motivation, whether the plot is straight or curled with flashbacks. In *The Double Hook*, as in a poem, such as *Four Quartets*, we are led from image to image, back and forth, listening for full truth at all times, not just at the end. If we did the latter we would hear only a coyote's laughing cry.

Downhill to realism

Mandel and Grube have both called *The Double Hook* a parody. I think that Part Four, the account of James's visit to town, is perhaps a parodic departure in mode from the rest of the book, that it trifles with conventional regional mimesis, and that it is then left, rejected by the author in favour of the syncretic writing in the other four parts of the book.

Part Four is characterized by unusual attention to conventional setting, plot, character and theme (what John Hawkes has called the main enemies of fiction), to dialogue that reveals character, to local colour. (I also know that Act IV in a Shakespearian play is crammed with action.) Myth fades in favour of cause-and-effect, and the duality of good and evil. Sex and money, the materials of nineteenth-century realism, are foregrounded. The language becomes less the author's and more an extension of place and character. The book becomes for a while the Western abjured by Watson in her Edmonton talk. Landscape becomes something against which the people are clearly marked. And the "wicked humour" of the earlier writing is replaced by comic visitors from another more common kind of book or movie — a conniving whore, a notorious parrot (ironist instead of trickster), a town schemer whose name is fart sounded backwards.

Yet this is a necessary scene in narrative terms. Not only does the scabrous town full of minor opportunists contrast un-favourably to the *communitas* seen in Part Five; its presentation contrasts to the language of that last part in such a way as to en-sure that we see the last part as authentic. What happens at the end is not totally good, just as what happens in the New Testament is not all flowers, but is true.

The last part is not, however, totally like the first three parts. In the last part, while the figures converge toward community, they seem to decide the course of the narrative a little more, as the author backs away slightly and permits them to handle the language. It is as if they have taken as much mimesis as is proper from the intervening Part Four. It is as if they have joined to take responsibility for their own lives once the book is finished, as if their creator has set their feet on soft ground.

Though the ground is not firm, then, it is not stony either. All readers of the text agree that we have a more-or-less happy ending, a kind of transformation, or resurrection, a new testament. A revelation (I, Coyote, saw this) under the seer's eye. Some readers have gone a little too far in their view of James as redeemer and renewer. He did, after all, murder his mother and blind a young man before returning to the pregnant lass he had abandoned.

But a Modernist, realist book would probably have had James dead in a ditch in the town, his pockets turned out; and a Canadian naturalist novel would have had the weather and objects in nature doing something nasty though unemotional to his corpse. The despair of the Modernists is understandable, given the shocking obliteration of the individual in the twentieth century. But the post-modernists live in a second stage of twentieth-century irony, and they are interested in some kind of reconstruction beyond despair — that is why their fictions are characterized by both laughter and non-realistic treatment. One cannot deny contemporary plagues of war and starvation, but one knows that a further documentation of them is a dead-end street with another blighted youth at the end of it.

Hence the qualified or sometimes demented joy at the end of our contemporary comedies, the unprovable transformations and transcendence of social angsts, the obviously constructed endings of our fictions, the prospects we are left with: not Lieutenant Henry plodding away in the rain, not Duddy Kravitz begging for bus fare. See the fantastic communal uplift at the end of a Jack Hodgins book, or one by Robert Kroetsch, Roch Carrier, or *The Double Hook*.

When James Potter is "freed ... from freedom" (p. 121), so that he must return to the hills, he is freed from the world of the realists. The realist writer says: I put my character into the world and then he takes on a life of his own, and all I can do is observe and record. That is why James' return is so important: he has rather a part to play in the author's writing. He cannot pass into the world any more than his author can create anything other than a design of language.

The language makes allusions, of course; or rather the reader makes associations between words and things. In *The Double Hook* the associations with the dry Interior of British Columbia and with literature are equal — neither has precedence. Coyote is a denizen of both. The author writing was living in both. Her setting was where she was sitting. We do not see the author "in" the book, but the other figures of language there catch glimpses of her, as do the figures of other fictions catch glimpses of "Nabokov", "Joyce", "Vonnegut" and "Calvino". I suppose that we readers catch glimpses of those figures catching glimpses of those figures that we all associate with the authors of the books. In this way we also come under Coyote's eye for a while, and we hear his/her voice. In this situation it is hard to remain or become "objective", isn't it? One is not on this side of this text, receiving meaning. One is in the realm of meaning just as the story is. We cannot "bolt ... out of the present" (p. 91) any more than James could when he tried to escape into plot and setting, to the town where he and we spent most of our time trying to keep track of time and money, till he ran out of both.

The prepared text

The questions remains: why might Sheila Watson not use the Coyote figure if she were to rewrite the novel?

There are many possible answers. As Sheila Watson has said, she is not patient with all the interpretations of Coyote that have been offered over the past two decades, and it is more than likely that the one above will not make her happier. Perhaps she simply feels that the Indian myth figure was a structural imposition on the story of those other figures, something a little too wily, too tricky. Maybe she felt that those human figures are on one hook and the readers on another, and so Coyote incorrectly let off the hook. It might be, too, that the book does not need both Coyote and Watson. If Ma Potter is more a presence, a force, than a "character" and if her disappearance leads to the birth of young Felix and hope for *communitas*, maybe she might represent the controlling author as well as Coyote does. Coyote does appear once as the ghost of the old woman (p. 35). Sheila Watson might even be saying that she has second thoughts about using Coyote because in person and as an author she was a visitor to the land, an outsider from a canned-food environment. She can create only a white Coast author's Coyote.

I lean toward the answer that by 1973 our literature had evolved to such a condition that one could simply write a fiction that was not naturalistic, not regional, not "about" the west or Indians, not thematic; and that one did not any longer have to prepare the audience by suggesting a structure based on indigenous myth instead of sociology.

In any case, Sheila Watson will not rewrite the book, of course. It could not be done, anyway. So the question remains. And why not? The reader who does not in his heart want to bolt out of the present does not so much desire to know what Coyote is but rather what she says.

Notes

1   Sheila Watson, "What I'm Going to Do", *Sheila Watson: A Collection, Open Letter*, Third Series, No. 1 (Winter 1974-75),p. 183.
2   Sheila Watson, *The Double Hook* (Toronto: McClelland and Stewart, 1958; rpt. Toronto: McClelland and Stewart, 1966, introduction by Malcolm Ross). Further page references will appear within parentheses in the text.
3   Sheila Watson, "Gertrude Stein: The Style is the Machine", *Sheila Watson: A Collection*, p. 170.
4   Elliot Gose, "Coyote and Stag", *Canadian Literature*, No. 1 (Summer 1959), p. 80.
5   Sheila Watson, "What I'm Going to Do", p. 183.
6   Margaret Morriss, "The Elements Transcended", *Canadian Literature*, No. 42 (Autumn 1969), p. 63.
7   Robert Kroetsch, "Death is a Happy Ending: A dialogue in thirteen parts", (with Diane Bessai), *Figures in a Ground*, eds. Diane Bessai and David Jackel (Saskatoon: Western Producer Prairie Books, 1978), pp. 208-9.
8   Beverly Mitchell, "Association and Allusion in *The Double Hook*," *Journal of Canadian Fiction*, II, No. 1 (Winter 1973), 68.
9   Sheila Watson, "What I'm Going to Do", p. 182
10   Morriss, *op. cit.*, p. 57.
11   Nancy Corbett, "Closed Circle", *Canadian Literature*, No. 61 (Summer 1974), p. 48.
12   John W. Lennox, "The Past: Themes and Symbols of Confrontation in *The Double Hook* and 'Le Torrent' ", *Journal of Canadian Fiction*, II, No. 1 (Winter 1973), p. 70.
13   Barbara Godard, "Between One Cliche and Another", *Studies in Canadian Literature*, III, No. 2 (Summer 1978), pp. 154-5.
14   Leslie Monkman, "Coyote as Trickster in *The Double Hook*", *Canadian Literature*, No. 52 (Spring 1972), p. 72.

15 John Berger, "Why Look at Animals" in his *About Looking* (New York: Pantheon, 1980), p. 7.
16 Gary Snyder, "The Incredible Survival of the Coyote" in his *The Old Ways* (San Francisco: City Lights, 1977).
17 Lily Harry is the informant for linguist Dwight Gardiner who has been researching the Shuswap language and stories.
18 Sheila Watson, "What I'm Going to Do", p. 182.
19 Roland Barthes, *The Pleasure of the Text*, trans. Richard Miller (New York: Hill and Wang, 1975), p. 27.
20 Barthes, *op. cit.*, p. 9.
21 The tricksters, Coyote, Raven, Spider, are not food.
22 Eli Mandel, *Another Time* (Erin, Ont.: Press Porcepic, 1977), p. 60.
23 Jan Marta, "Poetic Structures in the Prose Fiction of Sheila Watson", *Essays in Canadian Writing*, 17 (Spring 1980), p. 46.
24 John Moss, *Patterns of Isolation* (Toronto: McClelland and Stewart, 1974), p. 166.

W.O. MITCHELL

THE UNIVERSALITY OF W.O. MITCHELL'S *WHO HAS SEEN THE WIND*

Ken Mitchell

When W. O. Mitchell's novel *Who Has Seen The Wind* was publish-ed in 1947, and for some years after, it was generally relegated to the limbo of "regional" writing, with the limitations that label implies. In recent years, the novel has been more carefully re-examined with respect to the use that Mitchell makes of his geographic setting, Southern Saskatchewan, but it seems to me that even those views still treat the setting as incidental when in fact, it is profoundly basic to the rather sophisticated theme developed in *Who Has Seen The Wind*. Such simplistic readings overlook the carefully controlled structure, the subtlety and strength with which the author fuses prairie symbolism with a theme much broader and more significant than a mere account of a boy "growing up" in a small town. For what Mitchell has attempted, in his portrayal of young Brian O'Connal's matura-tion, is to reconcile the conflict between good and evil in the universe, to discover an equation of life and death, creation and destruction. It is only through finding balance for these elements, Mitchell implies, that any human being such as Brian O'Connal can understand the dilemma of human existence.

In this apparently rustic setting of a small Saskatchewan town, clinging to the very edge of the bountiful yet threatening environ-ment of the prairie, the author establishes a microcosm of the universe. It would be far too easy to assume that the prairie, as beautiful and idyllic as it seems from Mitchell's description, is equated with good or righteousness. Nor is the unnamed town which borders on the prairie neatly symbolic of evil, despite the corruption and mendacity which often seem to pervade it. And it is to Brian O'Connal's credit that he avoids such over-simple observations himself as he comes to sense the presence of con-flicts in his world.

It is certainly true that most of Brian's primary observations are made in the "natural" world of the prairie. His most important friendship is with the Young Ben, who personifies the wildness and freedom of habitat; he is always present when Brian makes the discoveries which lead him to later wisdom. He is deliberate-ly portrayed as animal-like, silent and wild as the coyotes that drift across the plains, and the perfect antithesis to the complicated social framework that holds him captive in school. In fact, the Young Ben has withdrawn from human society before it can cast him out. He becomes a spiritual guide to Brian in his search for a divine plan, a combination of priest and disciple. There is "a strengthening bond between them, an extrasensory brothership."[1] Any verbal, or intellectual, communication between them is unnecessary, perhaps even impossible. Yet it is from this vagabond that Brian discovers the essential quality of the prairie.

But Brian learns from the town, too. The other main teacher in his life — more literally — is the school principal, James Digby. He is the Young Ben's thematic opposite, but is at the same time one of the few citizens who show sympathy for the Young Ben. *He* personifies intelligence and rationality (including its weaknesses: consider his failure with Miss Thompson). Unlike his counterpart, Digby depends on thought and formal communication. He likes nothing better than arguing with the minister Hislop and Milt Palmer, the town philosopher. His teaching is as crucial to Brian's development as the Young Ben's is. It is he who articulates — as much as is ever possible — Brian's relationship with God and the universe.

In acquiring his wisdom, his sense of *place* in this puzzling existence, Brian must as Mitchell says, see "the realities of birth, hunger, satiety, eternity, death. They are moments when an inquiring heart seeks finality, and the chain of darkness is broken."[2]

The novel is divided into four major sections, each of which is roughly two years apart and represents a different plateau in Brian's development. One of the motifs that show this development is death, a phenomenon naturally disturbing to a young boy curious about life. It is, after all, that part of the cycle of life which is most difficult to equate with a smiling, bountiful Deity. I think too, that with this motif, Mitchell shows himself in most complete control of his imagery and his theme.

In the first section of the novel, Brian is four years old and ignorant about the forces controlling his life. He is not the lisping innocent that sentimental readers might prefer. His baby brother, Bobby, is ill with fever and in danger of dying, but Brian only resents the attention Bobby is given by the family. In his ignorance, he wishes a cruel and violent death on his grandmother.

He hoped Jake would bring his policeman's knife and

chop her into little pieces and cut her head off, for making him go outside to play. (p. 5)

Brian's first direct involvement with death comes after he fails to get an interview with God at the Presbyterian Church. He discovers a caterpillar inching across the sidewalk.

He squashed it with his foot. Further on he paused at a spider that carried its bead of a body between hurrying thread-legs. Death came for the spider too. (p. 11)

Brian is represented as a careless "killer", who has no more regard for life than the most primitive animal. It is from this level that he progresses. Later in the first section, when Brian's pet pup is taken away, he adopts a baby pigeon as a companion. Through his ignorance and boyish carelessness, he inadvertently causes its death, too. Brian is shocked to tears as a result of his first obvious encounter with a lifeless being, a creature once warm and now gone cold in his hands. Because it touches him personally, he begins to understand the fact of death. He has reached the first plateau of wisdom, and decides to bury the dead pigeon on the open prairie.

"Where the Young Ben is," said Brian. "There is where — not with houses." He was aware of a sudden relief; the sadness over the death of the baby pigeon lifted from him. (pp. 58-9)

As it turns out, Brian has accurately anticipated the Young Ben's presence. He "attends" the burial, crouched behind some bushes, a priest of the prairie ensuring that life returns to the earth to give life.

The first section of the novel ends with Brian's pup returned to him. He is now prepared for its companionship, having learned something of responsibility for life in the incident of the pigeon.

Within himself, Brian felt a soft explosion of feeling. It was one of completion and culmination. (p. 60)

This is the first of many times the "feeling" will come to Brian O'Connal. These experiences seem to be part of what Mitchell calls the "moments of fleeting vision" that come to the boy in his search for the meaning and balance of life.

The second section of Who Has Seen The Wind is an extrapolation of Brian's initial awareness. He learns that death comes to all things, including people, even to those things on which love is focused, like his pet dog. He learns, too, something of the paradox of death, its occasional rightness, its justice, and its inevitability.

We see this most clearly when Brian takes part in a gopher-drowning expedition with his pals. With discomfort, he watches Artie Shaw ripping the gopher's tail off, an act of gratuitous cruelty. Suddenly the Young Ben appears, almost literally rising out of the earth to enforce the natural law of life and death. With "one merciful squeeze" he kills the gopher; in the same movement he attacks and punishes the ignorant Artie Shaw.

> And Brian, quite without any desire to alleviate Art's suffering, shaken by his discovery that the Young Ben was linked in some indefinable way with the magic that visited him often now, was filled with a sense of the justness, the rightness, the completeness of what the Young Ben had done — what he himself would like to have done. (pp. 127-8)

> He senses, without understanding, that the gopher's death is necessary, not merely to "put it out of its misery", but because somehow that is part of the divine plan in nature. Months later, he and Bobby find the corpse on the prairie, "strangely still with the black bits of ants active over it. A cloud of flies lifted from it, dispersed, then came together again ...." (p. 128)

There is an echo in this of Steinbeck's novel *The Red Pony*, in which Jody Tiflin, a boy slightly older than Brian, also learns that life thrives on death. Mitchell's task in handling this theme is much more difficult than Steinbeck's, however, for he must by his own definition account for a Divine Being behind all this. Here is Brian's observation:

> Prairie's awful, thought Brian, and in his mind there loomed vaguely fearful images of a still and brooding spirit, a quiescent power unsmiling from everlasting to everlasting to which the coming and passing of the prairie's creatures was but incidental. He looked out over the spreading land under intensely blue sky. The Young Ben was part of all this. (pp. 128-9)

Not long after, Milt Palmer the shoemaker explains the process to Brian, in his own special idiom:

> "Somebody dies, they're right handy with the Heavenly

Land on High an' a shiny box an' flowers an' a lotta
things ain't got nothin' whatsoever to do with bein'
dead. You know what death is? Rotting — stink — dust
— an' you're back to the prairie again. Take birth —
what's that? Sprinkling with water? Announcement
cards? Seegars? Hospital ward? Hell no! Blood an' water
an' somethin' new for a while — mebbe a shoemaker
that wishes he was a tree." (p. 139)

Brian discovers too that birth and death are never far apart — are,
indeed, inter-related. Forbsie Hoffman's pet rabbits spawn litter
after litter of young; Brian is quite naturally fascinated by the process. But the increase grows alarming as none of the rabbits seems
"to have heard of the Malthusian theory." Food grows short
despite their sheltered, domesticated environment. The natural
elements of population control are missing, and one night Forbsie's desperate father exterminates the lot. Brian is shocked, but
he feels an "uneasiness that recalled to him ... the day on the
prairie when Art had torn the tail from the gopher" (p. 169).

In this section of the novel occurs the first human death, that
of old Wong, owner of the Bluebird Restaurant. The town's
Establishment has callously taken Wong's children away from
him to place them in foster homes, after subjecting the family to
a long history of prejudice and neglect. "Two weeks after his son
and daughter had left, Wong was discovered, still with his red
toque on, swinging from a rafter in the dark kitchen ..." (p. 172).
Wong's suicide springs from the same almost inadvertent
carelessness which resulted in the death of the baby pigeon. This
is not observed by Brian, apparently; but for the reader, the conclusion is inescapable.

The plateau Brian reaches by the end of Part Two is the grievous
loss he feels when his dog Jappy is killed by a passing dray. This
is the first death that strikes right into his heart, and he is not
yet mature or wise enough to accommodate it. He cannot explain
the death to Bobby — just as his father could not earlier explain
the pigeon's death to *him*. Perhaps Mitchell is saying that this
understanding can come only through non-rational, non-verbal
learning, which cannot be communicated to others. All Brian does
know is that "a lifeless thing was under the earth. His dog was
dead" (p. 181).

Once again, the Young Ben materializes for the burial on the
open prairie. He helps Brian cover the grave with rocks, but his

presence does little — this time — to alleviate Brian's loss.

> Somewhere within Brian something was gone; ever
> since the accident it had been leaving him as the sand
> of an hourglass threads away grain by tiny grain. Now
> there was an emptiness that wasn't to be believed. (p.
> 181)

It is his blind self-pity that creates this emptiness.

The third section emphasizes the inevitability of death. Brian's
father falls ill, and the boy is sent to his Uncle Sean's farm, where
he protests the killing of a runt pig. He seems to ignore the lesson
of the gopher, shrieking profanities and refusing to listen to his
uncle. "Killing a thing's no favour!" he shouts. What Brian may
be lacking is the rational maturity that would enable him to con-
nect the gopher and the pig — a quality he later learns through
Digby. At least this is what Ab, the outraged hired man, defines
as Brian's problem: "You don't think," he says (p. 233).

The third level of awareness is reached after the death of his
father, which creates in Brian an unsettling flux of emotions. Standing once again on the prairie, he "did not feel like crying. He
did not feel happy, but he did not feel like crying" (p. 238). This
is not intended to show the developing "manhood" of a boy who
refuses to be reduced to tears. It is the growing recognition that
his father's death is part of the vital process — inevitable and even
necessary to the ultimate survival of life. He thinks:

> People were forever born; people forever died, and
> never were again. Fathers died and sons were born; the
> prairie was forever, with its wind whispering through
> the long, dead grasses, through the long and endless
> silence. Winter came and spring and fall, then summer
> and winter again; the sun rose and set again, and
> everything that was once — was again — forever and
> forever. (pp. 246-7)

Suddenly, inexplicably, Brian does begin to cry — as he goes outside himself and realizes the loneliness his mother must feel. "His
mother! The thought of her filled him with tenderness and yearning. She needed him now. He could feel them sliding slowly
down his cheek; he could taste the salt of them at the corners
of his mouth" (p. 247). His tears are for his mother, a display
of selfless compassion which takes him away from grief and

mourning to a new consideration for life and the living. And Mitchell employs a perfect touch to reinforce the theme of the all-pervading unity of life:

> A meadow lark splintered the stillness.
> The startling notes stayed on in the boy's mind.
> It sang again.
> A sudden breathlessness possessed him; fierce excitement rose in him.
> The meadow lark sang again.
> He turned and started for home, where his mother was.
> (p. 247)

In Part Four, Brian reaches physical maturity and the highest level in his quest. He is twelve, on the brink of puberty, and during this last summer of the novel, from spring to fall, he makes the greatest progress in his spiritual development.

He visits Milt Palmer's shop and overhears an argument between Digby and Palmer about the nature of existence. "Who the hell's me?" asks the shoemaker.

> "Shoes, folks, churches, stores, grain elevators, farms, horses, dogs — all insidea me. You — the kids — this shop, insidea me — me insidea my shop; so that means I got me insidea me. Who the hell's me?"
> Fascinated, Brian stared at the shoemaker; he thought of Saint Sammy; he thought of the feeling. "You got a feeling?" (pp. 291-2)

But Palmer, an adult and an agnostic, does not get "feelings".

> "— I guess that ain't there no-more." He said it, thought Brian, sadly. The shoemaker turned to Digby. "I still don't know who 'me' is." (p. 292)

A little later, Digby ventures an explanation: "You're inside Him, Milt. When I get outside that door, I'm out of you, but I'm still inside Him."

Out of this oblique, Berkleyan discussion, Brian learns enough to decide he's "on the right track" (p. 294). He proves it in the incident of his grandmother's death. In the intervening years since babyhood, Brian has grown much closer to Mrs. MacMurray, listening to her tales of early pioneering days on the prairies. Now as she nears the end of her life, the two have grown particularly close and they spend a great deal of time together. She is bothered by the clock in her room, a "crazy, quivering, enamel box trying to tell all the time in all the world. It had measured out little of her past life, and now it thought it was going to dole out what was left" (p. 289).

Brian senses her hatred for the clock and halts the symbolic progress of time. He "killed it for her; he pulled its plug and turned it around on the dresser" (p. 289). As she increasingly senses the closeness of death, she seems to feel a corresponding need for the presence of the natural world, the prairie. She asks Brian to open the window, that is, to remove the barrier between herself and the outdoors — the wind and the presence of her God. Earlier, she has valued the open window to her room, "teasing her old nostrils with the softness of spring, the richness of summer, or the wild wine of fall" (p. 277). At one point, during a storm, she has kept the window open and "seemed to have drawn new life from the storm" (p. 274). Now, Brian opens it again, against his mother's instructions.

> It slid the full length of his arms, and the warm room was suddenly filled with the mint freshness of the outside. Stray flakes of the winter's first snow floated out of the afternoon and into the room, to melt in mid-air. (p. 290)

(This symbolic association of snow and death is interestingly developed. The slow passage of the old woman's time is described this way: "The eighty-two years of her life had imperceptibly fallen, moment by moment piling upon her their careless weight ....") (p. 277). But Brian's apparently sympathetic gesture has an unexpected effect, because the combination of the open window and her weakened condition causes Mrs. MacMurray's death.

> Feathering lazily, crazily down, loosed from the hazed softness of the sky, the snow came to rest in startling white bulbs on the dead leaves of the poplars, webbing in between the branches. Just outside the grandmother's room, where she lay quite still in her bed, the snow fell soundlessly, flake by flake piling up its careless weight. Now and again a twig would break off suddenly, relieve itself of a white burden of snow, and drop to earth. (p. 294)

The only possible conclusion is that Brian *kills* his grandmother, perhaps sensing her need and desire to return again to the prairie.

Mitchell does not force that conclusion, but intentionally or not, Brian is the agent of his grandmother's death. This would make no sense if it were simply another example of death caused by human neglect and carelessness (even if it is not malicious). The only explanation, in view of Brian's cumulative wisdom, is that he takes an active part in ensuring that the process of creation and destruction goes on — although it is probably an unconscious decision that he makes. At any rate, this atavistic impulse represents his supreme awareness of the function of death

If all of this seems to indicate some macabre predilection of W. O. Mitchell's, it should not. What Brian is faced with learning is an understanding of the universe, the meaning and existence of God. This is the central theme of the novel, and the motif of death makes an especially illuminating contribution. It is a part of nature, and nature — Mitchell asserts — is God. The concept of God is another puzzling subject for Brian's tenacious mind, and here again he proceeds gradually and haltingly to awareness, moving from his naive conception of the Deity as a little elf — "R. W. God" — to something very close to Digby's belief in a universal Presence.

It is here that Mitchell uses his most effective symbol: the wind. The ingenious use of this device unifies the novel and illuminates Brian's search. "Who has seen the wind?" he asks (or states) rhetorically — rhetorically, because of course no one has seen the wind, just as no one (with the possible exception of saints and lunatics) has ever seen God Himself. Despite his innocent childhood pilgrimage to the Presbyterian church, or his vision of God stirring the prairie like a bowl of porridge, Brian can no more visualize God than he can the wind that passes by.

The wind is a common literary device for symbolizing God's presence, but it is especially effective in *Who Has Seen the Wind*. In this prairie setting, it is — like nature (or God) — hostile and benign, creative and destructive. At the outset, even before Brian is introduced, Mitchell outlines this paradox. The prairie lies,

> ... waiting for the unfailing visitation of the wind, gentle at first, barely stroking the long grasses and giving them life; later, a long hot gusting that would lift the black topsoil and pile it in barrow pits along the roads, or in deep banks against the fences. (p. 3)

"Symbolic of Godhood" as Mitchell suggests, the wind brings

both rain and drought to the prairie — holding the power of life and death over the settlers.

On his initial quest to look for God in the church, Brian feels "the wind ruffling his hair" as he knocks on the door. As he awaits an answer, "a fervent whirlwind ... rose suddenly, setting every leaf in violent motion, as though an invisible hand had gripped the trunks and shaken them" (p. 8). The minister's wife gives Brian his first vital information about the God he seeks: " 'It's someone — something you can't hear — or see, or touch' " (p. 9).

With this beginning, it isn't surprising to discover the wind's presence at certain critical points in the novel, those instances when Brian makes a crucial discovery or experiences his "feeling". In the first section, for example, as Bobby lies near death, "the night wind, stirring through the leaves of the poplar just outside [Brian's] room on the third floor, strengthened until it was wild at his screen. He thought again of the strange boy on the prairie and felt, as he did, a stirring of excitement within himself, a feeling of intimacy" (p. 20).

Yet when the incompetent school-teacher, Miss MacDonald, threatens Brian with Divine punishment for a lie in school, the wind turns threatening and harsh, reflecting Brian's perception of the Deity. Vengefully, the wind sweeps "down upon the town ... lifting the loose snow and driving it into the children's faces, stinging their eyes and noses above the scarves tied around their mouths" (p. 94). Terrified of the impending punishment, Brian lies awake, feeling the "gathering Presence in his room as the wind lifted high, and higher still, keening and keening again, to die away and be born once more .... Fearful — avenging — was the gathering wrath about to strike down Brian Sean MacMurray O'Connal ..." (pp. 94-5).

More often, however, the wind blows gently in Brian's presence, usually co-incident with some manifestation of God, or Brian's "feeling". One Sunday, there is a "turning point in Brian O'Connal's spiritual life" (p. 106). At the age of six, he experiences what can only be called a transcendental vision while staring at a few drops of dew nestled among new spirea leaves in the spring.

> As he bent more closely over one, he saw the veins of
> the leaf magnified under the perfect crystal curve of the

drop. The barest breath of a wind stirred at his face,
and its caress was part of the strange enchantment too.

Within him something was opening, releasing shyly
as the petals of a flower open, with such gradualness
that he was hardly aware of it. But it was happening:
an alchemy imperceptible as the morning wind .... (p.
107)

This is really the first time Brian clearly feels and recognizes the
depth of emotion that occurs with his discovery of God in his
world. "He was filled with breathlessness and expectancy, as
though he were going to be given something, as though he were
about to find something" (p. 108). And yet he never does, in an
intellectual sense; he feels vaguely incomplete and unsatisfied.
Moreover, he finds that

... many simple and unrelated things could cause the
same feeling to lift up and up within him till he was
sure that he could not contain it. The wind could do
this to him, when it washed through poplar leaves,
when it set telephone wires humming and twanging ....
Always, he noted, the feeling was most exquisite upon
the prairie or when the wind blew. (pp. 122-3)

The care and precision with which Mitchell develops this symbolic motif is worth examining. It ranges from the look on Art's
face when he is attacked by the Young Ben like that of "a man
whose home has just been levelled by a prairie tornado" (p. 127)
to the "dead and yellowed leaves" Brian sees sliding along the
walk ahead of him "at the bidding of the wind" when his dog
is struck down. As the dog dies, "the wind carried the settling
dust of the street sideways" (p. 179). The darker element of nature
and God is suggested by the "feverish little dust devils" which
whirl through town at certain times, such as when Brian's father
is ill and nearing death.

Mr. O'Connal dies far away, in Rochester, but at the moment
of his death Brian experiences a new intensification of his feeling. Having run away from his Uncle Sean's farm, he is physically
isolated, alone on the prairie during the night.

The night wind had two voices; one that keened along
the pulsing wires, the prairie one that throated long and
deep. Brian could feel its chill reaching for the very centre of him, and he hunched his shoulders as he felt the

wincing of his very core against it. (p. 235)

I take this passage to indicate not only that he is naked and vulnerable to the action of God (as well as to the elements), but also that he experiences the sudden solitude of independence, that cold chill brought on by the loss of a child's dependence on his father.

> As the wind mounted in intensity, so too the feeling of defenselessness rose in him. It was as though he listened to the drearing wind and in the spread darkness of the prairie night was being drained of his very self. He was trying to hold together something within himself, that the wind demanded and was relentlessly leaching from him. (p. 236)

The next day, just before he learns of his father's death, he has "an experience of apartness much more vivid than that of the afternoon before — a singing return of the feeling that had possessed him so many times in the past" (p. 237).

The wind also brings awareness to Brian when he goes out onto the prairie after the funeral to reconcile himself to the loss of his father.

> All around him the wind was in the grass with a million timeless whisperings.
> A forever-and-forever sound it had . ... Forever and forever the prairie had been, before there was a town, before he had been, or *his* father, or *his* father. ... Fathers died and sons were born; the prairie was forever, with its wind whispering through the long, dead grasses, through the long and endless silence. (p. 246)

With this vision of the cyclical pattern of the birth and death of seasons, days, and people — its inevitability and its beauty — he reaches the third plateau. The meadow larks shrill but natural melody expresses his new positive belief: a "fierce excitement rose in him" (p. 247).

The enigmatic quality of the wind is presented most effectively in Mitchell's portrayal of Saint Sammy, "Jehovah's Hired Man", who lives in an abandoned piano box on Magnus Petersen's south eighty. Although this character is often praised — and dismissed — as a colourful portrait done in brilliantly humorous idiom, Sammy's stature in the novel assumes a great

deal more than that of a comic lunatic. In fact, he is the archetypal
figure of the visionary madman. The Lord speaks to Saint Sammy, beginning at the time of his canonization in "the bad hail
year, when Sammy had stood on the edge of his ruined crop,
looking at the countless broken wheat heads lying down their
stalks."

> As he stared, the wind, turning upon itself, had built
> up a black body from the topsoil, had come whirling
> toward him in a smoking funnel that snatched up
> tumbleweeds, lifting them and rolling them over in its
> heart. The voice of the Lord had spoken to him.
> 'Sammy, Sammy, ontuh your fifty-bushel crop have I
> sent hailstones the sizea baseballs. The year before did I
> send the cutworm which creepeth an' before that the
> rust which rusteth.
> 'Be you not downcast, fer I have prepared a place fer
> you. Take with you Miriam an' Immaculate Holstein an'
> also them Clydes. Go you to Magnus Petersen, who is
> even now pumping full his stock trought. He will give
> ontuh you his south eighty fer pasture, an' there you
> will live to the end of your days when I shall take you
> up in the twinkling of an eye.
> 'But I say ontuh you, Sammy, I say this — don't ever
> sell them Clydes, fer without them ye shall not enter
> ....
> 'Hail, Saint Sammy!' the Lord had said. 'Hail,
> Jehovah's Hired Man!' (pp. 264-5)

But the materialistic, machinery-oriented farmer Bent Candy is
coveting Sammy's Clydesdale horses and is threatening Sammy
with eviction unless he sells them. This sacrilege, in Sammy's
mind, both guarantees and justifies the violent vengeance the
Lord will undoubtedly wreak on Bent Candy.

Brian has earlier been fascinated by Sammy's peculiar relationship with God, and at this point goes out to see the recluse.
Together they wait in the strengthening wind for the storm to
strike.

> As far as the two could see, the grasses lay flat to the
> prairie earth, like ears laid along a jack rabbit's back.
> They could feel the wind solid against their chests, solid
> as the push of a hand. (p. 270)

As the Lord speaks to Sammy, His voice "scarcely distinguishable from the throating wind," Brian is "filled again with that ringing awareness of himself."

> "Sammy, Sammy, this is her, and I say ontuh you she is a dandy! ... "In two hours did I cook her up; in two hours will I cook her down! An' when she hath died down, go you ontuh Bent Candy's where he languishes an' you shall hear the gnashing of teeth which are Bent Candy's an' he shall be confounded!" (p. 270)

True to His word and to Sammy's vision, the Lord destroys Candy's new barn as though it had "been put through a threshing machine and exhaled through the blower" (p. 272).

The point of this little parable (which at first reading seems to be a humourously sentimental digression) is not only to reveal to Brian God's capacity for destruction. This is already evident in the ravaging drought of the 1930's, and in the frequency with which he encounters death. The incident suggests that a man like Saint Sammy, mad hermit and an outcast from society, living on the open prairie like one of his own Clydes unbroken and gone wild, is a man much closer to God than, for example, Bent Candy, a deacon of the Baptist Church. And despite his somewhat Old Testament viewpoint, he is much more a Christian man than the Reverend Mr. Powelly, the Presbyterian minister who *seems* to profess Christian virtues but who is a man guided by social, not spiritual laws. Indeed, there are many characters in the novel who claim to be pious, but who are completely ignorant of the natural forces that reveal a Divine Presence. Saint Sammy is a man who *has* seen the wind, and who has come to his vision through suffering and humility.

This contrast between Saint Sammy and Reverend Powelly is a neat example of the central conflict in *Who Has Seen the Wind*. As I said before, one must avoid the tendency to see the conflict as one of rural innocence versus urban corruption. There is corruption on the open range, too. The Old Ben, despite an appealing frankness, is a callously insensitive man. He has all his son's irresponsibility with none of his innocence (and from this, perhaps we can deduce that the Young Ben will become an Old Ben). Bent Candy, too, is anything but a dedicated son of the soil, although he is the most successful farmer in the district. In fact, there seems to be more destruction and desolation in "God's country'' than there is on the streets of the little town. Instead of a contrast between town and country, I believe Mitchell intends a parallel.

The comparison is simply this: that there is a balance maintained between positive and negative (good and evil; creation and destruction) both in the social community and in the natural one. The positive influences on Brian do not come only from the pastoral environment; Digby and Miss Thompson, for example, also have an important effect on Brian's development. There are others, like Hislop, the banished minister, and Milt Palmer, not to mention Brian's parents. The negative element in the community is obviously (one might say, *too* obviously) represented by Reverend Powelly and Mrs. Abercrombie. It is the cruel and meddlesome interference of these two which causes the destruction of Wong's family. Their unswerving dedication to the breaking of the Bens is both impressive and revealing. Through these acts, Brian sees that havoc occurs in the town as well as in the country, possibly for the same reasons, and is therefore inevitable — given the formula of human nature.

Brian, by the end of the novel, is able to fuse his experience of both environments as a result of his special capacity and his insights. It is important to realize that, despite his admiration for the Young Ben, Brian is not at all inclined to run wild on the prairie (or like Huckleberry Finn, to flee from ''sivilization''). What he learns in school and from Digby is ultimately as valuable as what he learns on the prairie from the Young Ben. In his decision to become a ''dirt-doctor'', we see that he is determined to apply the formal ''intellectual'' education he acquires through Digby to the love of land he associates with his Uncle Sean, Saint Sammy and the Young Ben.

This decision of Brian's is one expression of the balance he finally achieves in his new view of the universe, a view that incorporates reason and emotion, hatred and love, creation and destruction — then makes them all one in himself, through an almost mystical process.

Near the end of the novel, he is puzzled by an emotion he recognizes as being long familiar to him. ''It was as though he were recognizing again an experience that his memory had stored for him, but not too well.''

It had something to do with dying; it had something

to do with being born. Loving something and being
hungry were with it too. He knew that much now.
There was the prairie; there was a meadow lark, a baby
pigeon, and a calf with two heads. In some haunting
way the Ben was part of it. So was Mr. Digby. (p. 299)

But he cannot intellectually comprehend this experience,
although he some day hopes to be satisfied. "The thing could
not hide from him forever," he thinks. But Brian is mistaken here.
He can never understand what happens in a rational sense — just
as he will never see God, or the wind. Only madmen like Saint
Sammy can do that. The wind goes on, Mitchell observes in the
final paragraph, oblivious of all, turning "in silent frenzy upon
itself, whirling into a smoking funnel, breathing up topsoil and
tumbleweed skeletons to carry them on its spinning way over the
prairie, out and out to the far line of the sky" (p. 300). Brian's
accomplishment has been to *feel* the wind, to sense the presence
of God in nature. That, Mitchell implies, is all that he or any man
can do — and all that is necessary to advance into maturity.

Notes

[1]   W. O. Mitchell, *Who Has Seen the Wind*, Macmillan of Canada, (Toronto,
       1947), p. 89. Page references are hereafter given in the text.
[2]   Author's epigraph.

THE VANISHING POINT: FROM ALIENATION TO FAITH

Catherine McLay

In his third novel *The Vanishing Point* published in 1973, W. O. Mitchell explores a central truth of modern existence, man's sense of alienation and his need for community to give purpose and meaning to life. In an interview with Donald Cameron, Mitchell comments on the role of fiction:

> To me the only justification for art is that this particular narrative, these particular people, shall articulate some transcending truth .... It's not a new truth or a fresh truth, but it's the first time this truth has been filtered through this particular artist, in this particular part of the world, at this particular point in time. It isn't the truth that's important so much as the illusory journey to that truth, through the artist's illusion bubble.[1]

Mitchell's previous novels *Who has Seen the Wind* (1947) and *The Kite* (1962) have examined the relationship of man both to death and to life, and *The Kite* celebrates the triumph of life in the person of Daddy Sherry, the magnificent old patriarch of one hundred and eleven. In *The Vanishing Point*, the quest for truth is both broader and deeper. For the central character, Carlyle Sinclair, must not only come to terms with death and life; he must also accept man as a social being and attempt to reconcile the division between the individual and his society, the Indian world and the white. Like Thomas Carlyle whose name he bears, he must pass through the "Everlasting No" to come to the "Everlasting Yea". His journey from alienation and doubt to faith in himself, in the Stony peoples, and in society as a whole, is the central theme of the novel. *The Vanishing Point* is Mitchell's most mature work, the clearest statement of his essential humanism, his faith in the human race.

Man's sense of alienation, of separateness and isolation, is one of the central themes of the twentieth century. Like Matthew Arnold, Mitchell sees men as islands, forever yearning yet forever unable to bridge the division between self and self. In a mood of despair, Carlyle Sinclair asks:

> ... wasn't all communication between all humans

hopeless? Out of my skin and into yours I cannot get —
however hard I try — however much I want to! ....
What a weak bridge emotion was for people to walk
across to each other — emotion swinging, unable to
hold the heavy weight of communication .... Just illusion after all, for once the passage was made, the door
was always closed. You stopped at the eyes, and you
had never left the home envelope of self anyway (216).[2]

The roots of *The Vanishing Point* lie in this concept of alienation. In 1953, Mitchell's novel *The Alien* won the MacLeans' Fiction Award and excerpts appeared in *MacLean's Magazine* from
September to January 1953-4. But the novel as a whole was never
published; Mitchell withdrew it and it remained in the back of
his mind for some twelve or thirteen years. Like *The Vanishing
Point*, *The Alien* was based on Mitchell's own experience as a
teacher for some months on the Eden Valley Reserve west of High
River, Alberta. Both novels concern the life of Carlyle Sinclair,
teacher on the Paradise Valley Reserve, and his search to bridge
the gap between Indian and White, man and man. In each, Victoria Rider is central. A student of Carlyle's who has completed
her Senior Matriculation and entered nursing in a city hospital,
she is, as her name suggests, a symbol of Carlyle's success or
failure in adapting the world of the Indians to modern urban
society.

It is largely in the ending that *The Vanishing Point* differs. For
"the alien" in the earlier version is, in a very literal sense, Carlyle
himself; half Indian and half white, he is alienated from both
cultures. Overwhelmed by Victoria's pregnancy and his consequent failure, he refuses to accept less than perfection and, in
one version, commits suicide. *The Vanishing Point* is the work of
an older and more mature writer. Mitchell remarks to Donald
Cameron:

... about fourteen years ago I worked on a novel, very
close to when I thought it was finished, and then I was
unhappy with it. I returned to it several times over a
period of about five years or more — it became a King
Charles' head with me — and then about four years ago
suddenly I realized that what had grown, indeed, said
No. It ended with despair, and while the piece of work
had grown to say No, I myself hadn't; and this is what

had crippled it so terribly for me.[3]

In the middle sixties, Mitchell was attracted to Steinbeck's philosophy, in particular *The Grapes of Wrath*. For Mitchell, the giant turtle, sliding back two steps for every three ahead, becomes a symbol of mankind which not only survives but slowly and surely, despite pain and suffering, progresses towards its destination.[4] The artist, Mitchell claims, "either says Yes to man or he says No to man." *The Alien* said No but in *The Vanishing Point* Mitchell now says Yes.[5]

Carlyle's movement in the novel from death to life, from despair to commitment, is framed by his initial journey into the city, and his final return two weeks later to Paradise. Part One relates the present situation of Carlyle and of Paradise Valley Reserve, and introduces the two complications of the action, the search for the lost Victoria Rider and the approaching death of her grandfather, old Esau.

Part Two regresses to 1950 and traces Carlyle's eight years in Paradise from the beginning to the present. Part Three picks up the thread of events from Part One and moves toward the conclusion, Esau's death and the marriage of Carlyle and Victoria, interweaving events in the present with flashbacks into Carlyle's distant past. Interrelated with these events and memories are the wind-up of Heally Richards' Rally for Jesus, Archie Nicotine's appeal to Heally to save old Esau, and the activities of Norman and Gloria Catface. The tone alternates between comedy, tragedy and black humour, with tragedy predominating until the final pages. Despite certain structural weaknesses and the blurring of view-point at times, the events and characters of the novel are all integrally related to the central theme, Carlyle's search for understanding between man and man, race and race.

In this search all the relationships of Carlyle's past become central and take their place in shaping his thought and character: relationships with his father and Aunt Pearl, with his dead wife and daughter, with his teacher Old Kacky, with Archie Nicotine and the Riders, Powerfaces, Wildmans, Left-hands, and Baseballs of his Reserve days. Gradually he comes to realize the Victoria is not the cause of his search but merely the precipitant:

> The loss of Victoria had shattered something inside him.
> He knew that now. He knew he was not simply trying
> to find her. He knew that he must put back together

>something he had been trying all his life to keep from
>being splintered — broken beyond repair. It was
>something mortally important to him, and it had never
>— ever — been whole for him really; Aunt Pearl and
>Old Kacky had seen to that. And his father.
>Victoria Rider had grown essential; he must find her
>and he must do it to save himself as well. (p. 323)

The ending of the novel, the marriage of Carlyle and Victoria, is not merely a romantic cliché but a comic resolution, a logical outcome of the events and problems of the novel. Carlyle must ultimately choose between life and death. In existential terms, the rejection of suicide is itself an affirmation, an embracing of life over death. In one sense the "vanishing point" of the title is the point of decision, the point of choice between being and not-being. But in another sense, it is the point of understanding, the point at which man imposes meaning and perspective upon the chaos of life, order and form on events and characters seemingly disparate and unrelated. Carlyle's acceptance of this order and meaning is his acceptance of life as symbolized by his marriage and Victoria's coming child.

Carlyle Sinclair's journey in *The Vanishing Point* from death to life is paralleled in the movement of the novel from winter to spring. The opening passages prepare for this movement:

>Spring — actual spring by God! ... Mountain spring ex-
>ploded in his face. Fifteen years and he still wasn't
>emotionally ready for the chinook stirring over his
>cheek and breathing compassion through the inner self
>that had flinched and winced for months from the
>alienating stun of winter. Full reprieve! (pp. 3-4)

But Carlyle is still dominated by winter and death. Spring is his "cup of water on the desert." It accentuates his isolation, his aloneness: he is "starved for the thrust from self to the centre of a loved one" (p. 4). He identifies with the male grouse "drumming life inside, membrane throatbag flushed with blood." But the image of potency is transposed into an image of death in the balloon of dead little Willis which the child Carlyle blew up and released in the play-room: "It died without warning in mid-air, dropped to the floor — a stilled and shrunken scrotum" (p. 5).

The predominance of death and isolation in these early pages symbolizes Carlyle's past. His mother died when he was seven and Aunt Pearl was no substitute, for her life was shaped by her dead husband and her dead son Willis. The death of his father was only the final stage in an already existing estrangement and Carlyle sees their relationship reflected in the hymn "You in your small corner and I in mine" (p. 336). His friend Mate died from diphtheria, contracted from Carlyle. Before coming to Paradise, he lost his wife and unborn daughter.

On the Reserve, the years have been marked by deaths from pneumonia, appendicitis, diabetes, eclampsia, fire: "Each spring death seemed to play a counterpoint to bud and sprout and rising sap and river flow" (p. 224). As he looks back from the vantage point of his ninth year, Carlyle meditates: "All the deaths he died in nine years: Each one leaving him older — sadder — more helpless" (p. 20). The figure of the dying Esau Rider, an almost fleshless skeleton, symbolizes this dominance of death over life. Even the wick of the lamp in Esau's room is described in terms of disease as a "pale, giant tapeworm preserved and floating within the lamp's clear belly' (p. 8). But although the events of the novel move toward the climax of Heally's restoration of Esau and his subsequent death, Carlyle is moving in the opposite direction, towards life as indicated by his recognition: "his own life was just as urgent as poor Esau's death" (p. 9).

The two settings of the novel represent the two worlds in which Carlyle exists and between which he is divided. The city, not specifically identified but recognizably Calgary, is an alienated world from which Carlyle has been absent for many years but from which he is not totally free. Unreal and even, to Carlyle, fantastic, it represents the confused values, the isolation and lack of commitment of modern man. Paradise Valley, the world of the Stonys, is also remote to Carlyle despite eight and a half years there. Between the two lies a suspension bridge which cannot be crossed by cars and which symbolizes the separation of Paradise from the modern world, Indian from white.

Carlyle's journey into the city in Part One is a journey from the past into the present. On the borders live the "periphery people" who "resisted anonymity, clung still to first-name informality" (p. 32), and who raise budgies or operate cottage enterprises. The city proper is impersonal and faceless. Its buildings could be anywhere: the Devonian Tower, the Empress Hotel and Beer Parlour, the Liberty Cafe and in the alley behind, the lair of Norman and Gloria Catface sheltered by orange parachutes, the Bon-

neydoon jail where the Stonys spend much of their city time, the
Foothills Carleton Hotel, the Super-Arcade. Carlyle sees these as
unreal, a pantomime or movie set: "when he left this evening
they would all be taken down" (p. 58). His fantasy of the life of
mannekins in department stores is a reflection not only of his own
isolation but also of the emptiness and superficiality of modern
city life. The flow of traffic becomes for him a ritual dance of negation, a sterile counterpart to the vital Prairie Chicken Dance: the
cars "meet opposite partners; swing and pass each other in opposite direction." And the pedestrians are weighed down with
humanity:

> ... almost all of them carried something. Those who did
> not seemed to; the white-egg burden of their own lives
> perhaps .... all were engaged in a communal pan-
> tomimist illusion of walking up an invisible slope. (pp.
> 57-8)

Anonymous and impersonal, the city is typified by the bus station. It is "not a place where people met people" but an unloading
place where the passengers "looking slightly dazed, as though
they had just stepped bewildered from a car wrecked in a highway
accident" (p. 301). Everywhere Carlyle meets the "lonely ac-
costers" who fix him with an unflinching gaze and spill "precious
intimacy" (p. 63). The old man in the bus station attempts to relive
his whole past; the pathetic man in hospital is convinced his heart-
pacer is linked up backwards; the man in the drug store faces
life alone after the death of his wife; and the man in the Super-
Arcade, when Carlyle turns away from him, reacts sadly "as
though he had just confirmed something again for himself" (p.
97). All these are represented by Luton. As he leans on the car
window, pouring out his whole life with his rancid breath, Carlyle
fantasizes about the "moat which has separated him from all
human contacts" and sees the whole proliferation of plaster
garden ornaments as Luton's reaction to isolation, his choice of
a company which will not show revulsion. While the surface in
all these cases is comic, the comedy is undercut by tragic recognition of man's separateness within the bonds of his own skin.

The city's crowning symbol is the Devonian Tower, a "concrete
erection" with a "May basket balanced on its tip ... [and] a red
oil derrick to spear the last fifty feet" (p. 42). The explicitly sexual symbolism underlines its negation of sex. In its shadow Gloria

and Norman Catface live off the proceeds of prostitution. From it as centre the city reaches out menacingly, threatening to submerge the surrounding countryside with its commericialism and industry. The oil derricks in the outlying areas are "great metal birds tipping and sipping from deep in the earth, releasing the stink of hydrogen sulphide" (p. 28). The city encroaches upon Paradise Reserve where coloured ribbons mark the sites of future wells and its seismic drillings have reduced Beulah Creek far up in Storm and Misty Canyon to a feeble trickle. It even endangers the Arctic, building pipelines across the tundra to transport oil and gas to the urban world and disturbing the ecological balance of caribou and Eskimo.

Its entertainment is cheap. The Shelby rodeo with its parade of chuckwagons, decorated tractors and floats, its merry-go-round, its wheel of fortune and kewpie dolls, is shallow and gaudy. In this setting the Indians become farcical, a travesty of their forebears in buffalo horn headgear, paint, war bonnets, and breechcloths over dyed pink underwear. Its art too is machine-made. Luton's brother and his wife do a vast trade in plastic flowers all over the West while Luton mass-produces sleazy plaster ornaments, rows and rows of identical does and Bambis, bear cubs, geese and flamingoes which represent the true antithesis of art. Carlyle fantasizes that Luton may renounce his ornaments for a Kentucky Fried franchise or a Kiddyland near Banff. But the flamingoes and bambis and bear cubs will not be renounced. Fornicating among themselves, they take control of Luton and in a final nightmare vision Carlyle sees the whole world "up to its arse in fluorescent flamingoes" (p. 41).[6]

In the city the Indians are doomed to fail, unless like Jake Rider they conform fully to white life. Jake's grey business suit, white shirt, Stetson and hand-tooled kangaroo hide boots cost more, Carlyle speculates, than his half-brother's funeral. It is the realization of Victoria's inevitable fate in the city which motivates Carlyle to make such a desperate search for her. And her experience confirms this fear. Her job as waitress in the Liberty Cafe is short-lived when she discovers that "extra services" are required in the evenings. She is "rescued" by Norman and Gloria Catface who live on the proceeds of prostitution and sell her to meet their expenses. Other members of the band too are out of place here. Carlyle habitually visits the city to bail out various members on charges of "drunk and disorderly." For years Archie has dropped by the Express Bar and drunk up the funds he intends to buy rings and a rebuilt carburetor for his car. And he is bailed out by Heally Richards when he is arrested for relieving himself in an alley behind the hotel.

Paradise Valley Reserve is in direct contrast to the city. Although the Stonys may be alienated from modern urban society, they are part of a great oneness, what Mitchell terms the "living whole". But Paradise Valley lies between two modes of life, the city and the present, and the past as represented now only by Storm and Misty Canyon. Carved by the "millennia of wind and frost and water" (p. 109), Storm and Misty is a place of refuge for youth, the hunting-ground for the whole band, and the source of water and food for the Reserve. In it no whites can survive for long. Here Caryle loses his way although even the smallest of his Indian children is at home. And here Archie finds the white hunter, who betrayed the rule of the wilderness, frozen in the snow. Storm and Misty is the centre of old Esau's vision; it is a "shaman place" where he could "purify and prepare, and be absolved from self" (p. 108). But Esau's dream of leading his band back here into the past dies with him. For Stormy and Misty represents what the Stonys have left behind:

> Before white people come to this country Indian had a good livin' — never hungry for himself — for his horse …. We lost all that now; we lost the Indian good life. Those days we had buffalo-hide wigwam that was wind-proof — cold-proof. Now we haven't. The Indian child get sick out of it. There is why my people suffer in their heart. (p. 378)

The new way of life is imposed upon them in part by the church and the government and in part by their own desire to share elements of white society as represented by cars and liquor. In his unconventional but vivid prayer, Ezra Powderface expresses their dilemma:

> We want to live the white way now and put the suffering out of our souls. I know the old people cannot do this …. [But] Thou take the young ones, Heavenly Father — the kids and the like of that …. These are the ones will live the white way and there is why we thank Thee for sendin' us Mr. Sinclair to teach them (p. 126)

But their success in adapting is very partial. They continue to live in summer in airless tents and in winter in cabins which are unrepaired and draughty. Carlyle persuades a few to grow hay for their numerous horses but the day it is ready for cutting they have departed for Shelby's annual rodeo. A few grow gardens but the vegetable diet cramps the bowels used to moose and bannock. Despite the protests of the Reverend G. Bob Dingle and Ezra Powderface, the young couples continue to be united by "blanket marriages", unblessed by the church. Spring is "grabbin'-hold-of-time" in Paradise and the fulfilling of natural urges is immediate and unselfconscious. Both children and adults are embarrassingly uninhibited; not only the boys but also the girls relieve themselves in the open, and Archie is naively innocent of wrong when he urinates in the alley behind the Empress Hotel.

The Stonys are vulnerable to disease and Archie does not speak in jest when he claims that hospitals are places where Indians die. They insist on minor medications such as liniment and castor oil, epsom salts and aspirin, and refuse treatment for tuberculosis, diabetes and pneumonia. As Dr. Sanders remarks bitterly to Carlyle "Your dispensary takes cares of them — when they want me they're moribund" (p. 127).

Their closeness to nature influences their culture. In contrast to the sterile art of the city, Indian art is individual, free and spontaneous. The children draw in coloured chalks on the blackboard: buttercups and tigerlilies, galloping horses, moose and elk. The women embroider on doeskin or bead moccassins. Their dances are ritual and follow the rhythms of animal life, the Rabbit Dance, the Owl Dance or the most popular Prairie Chicken Dance. But this closeness to nature has its negative side, and the beat of the drums, Carlyle feels, is "lobotomy", linking them to animal nature rather than thinking mankind: "right from birth they've got that drum ... with their mother's milk — every week — every month — every year .... It's what we're up against" (p. 204).

A recognition of white attitudes to the Indians is an essential part of Carlyle's education. Much of the white world is hostile, like the Greek owner of the Liberty Cafe who propositions Victoria but later tells Carlyle: "I do draw the line — somewhere — at smoked meat" (p. 280) or the prison officials who express their contempt of Archie in crude humour, or the taxi-driver who patronizingly calls Archie "chief" when he fails to tip him. Even Officer Dan who refers to the lost Victoria on T.V. as "one of our fine young Indian friends" (p. 269) reveals himself when he apprehends Gloria Catface supposedly for soliciting Heally Richards: "You got no licence to sell your Girl Guide Cookies between here and the Devonian Tower" (p. 283). And the Indians retaliate. When Carlyle looks for Victoria at the Indian Friendship Centre, they threaten and punch him, first high on the cheekbone, then in the groin (p. 299).

The dedicated whites, the government officials, teachers and preachers who attempt to bridge the gap between white and Indian, are themselves often patronizing and, even at their most sincere, often as little aware of real Indian needs and desires. Perhaps the most idealistic of these is the Reverend G. Bob Dingle with his blatant health posters and his simplistic religious verses. Dingle sees the Indians as "good people — gentle — happy — just children" (p. 151), and he has a blind faith in their, and man's, perfectability. He lives by illusion, as Carlyle discovers when Dingle insists that the children eat greedily the Minimal Subsistence Biscuit. And the Stony phrase he proudly quotes "No-watch-es-nichuh" means, not "You please very much" as he supposes, but "bull-shit" (pp. 174-5).

Less naive but even less effectual is Sheridan, the agent in charge of Hanley and Paradise Valley. Sheridan shows little interest in Reserve affairs and has little time for Carlyle's plans to upgrade the stock, raise oats, grow vegetables and keep cows and chickens. His life lies in the past and his only real achievement in a lifetime of service has been his development of a baseball team on the Reserve. Dr. Sanders remarks:

> After thirty-five years it doesn't matter whether you lived or died — or retired — all comes to nothing. You could have been added — subtracted — divided — multiplied, and the result would have been exactly the same — except for one thing — those champion Hanley Wolverines. (p. 182)

Another idealist is Fyfe, agent of the federal government and living in Calgary. Even he questions his success. On the verge of retiring he remarks: "Can't help wondering what you've actually accomplished in forty-five years" and admits he only "held the fort" (p. 88). Fyfe is cautious and non-commital. His favourite policy is "wait to see what transpires" and his favourite advice, "don't let yourself get personally involved" (p. 87). His main achievement has been the Fyfe Minimal Subsistence Cookie, an indigestible oatmeal biscuit which the children scatter in parts and wholes over the classroom floor. Responsible, honourable, practical, dedicated, he nevertheless fails to bridge the gap between white and Indian for his whole philosophy has been wrong. He sees the Indians as "terminal cases to be made as comfortable as possible within the terms of the reserve system — the budget and the Indian Act" (p. 91).

The wisest of the whites associated with the Stonys, Dr. Sanders functions in the novel as Carlyle's mentor and guide. Sanders is clear-sighted and sympathetic to the Indian problems:

> They are children, but with adult drives — grown-up hungers — mature weaknesses — envy — love of power — of their own children; they have vanity and — what's very — the key — terrible feeling of inferiority. If you know that — and that they are child-like ... then you won't rant at them because they failed to carry what you piled on them. Don't expect too much of them — don't let them get you angry .... Be a good guardian.
> (pp. 130-1)

And he sees in the paternalism of the Reserve System a slough which has weakened their resistance: "the more you do for them the more you sap their strength" (p. 183). Despite his insight and understanding, however, Sanders is unable to bridge the gap between races, and in Carlyle's eight year he is forced to retire from the scene to win a personal battle against tuberculosis and death.

It is left to Carlyle, then, to act as intermediary between the Indians and modern urban society. He sees the old suspension bridge across the Spray River as a symbol of communicaton between race and race, human and human, to "carry hearts and minds across and into other hearts and minds" (pp. 12-3). But to this point he has failed. He asks himself:

> Had he ever made it across to any of these people? ... How the hell could he ever know! How could he hope to understand what any of them sheltered secret inside themselves. (p. 13-4)

Verbal communication is ineffective. His talk with Esau Rider indicates the circumlocution: "they could go on all morning, circling nose to tail" (p. 8). Conversation with any of them but Archie is almost impossible, "like trying to play catch with someone who wouldn't throw back the ball" (p. 16). And communication without language is even more difficult. They withdraw: "He could not know what went on inside their heads — behind the eyes that refused to hold his" (p. 203). While Carlyle is not a Bob Dingle who teaches Stony children to sing "Bringing in the Sheaves" in Cree or murmers "bull-shit" when he means "You please me very much," he is little more successful than Dingle in bridging the gap, and his insistence on using English indicates the core of the problem: it is Indians who must conform to white standards.

Victoria then becomes central to Carlyle's purpose of communicating with the Stonys. She has been the first and only one to respond to him since the day when at twelve she held his hand on the way to the dentist: "two worlds had merged .... He and she were no longer so vulnerable on this concrete and asphalt planet" (p. 216). But in seeing her as a symbol of his success, he has sacrificed her as an individual, with individual needs and wants. Her growth and maturation have threated his own purposes so that he has chosen to ignore them. He has been in part aware of her sexuality and has seen the budding of her breasts as "poignant as young ferns' tight thrust through earth" (p. 225). But he has disregarded Sanders' warning that at sixteen she is a year older than Martha Bear who disappears up Storm and Misty with Wilfrid Tailfeather. And he has insisted, "She can make it to matriculation. I can get her through" (p. 233).

Victoria completes her Grade Twelve and enters nursing in the city. But it is not in her nature to accept Carlyle's plans for her, and her answer to him, her pregnancy, is the only answer that he will accept. As she says to him: "you are — asking me to turn the mountains upside down ... Stop the spring run-off" (p. 374). Her predominant emotion is not the loss of her career but shame at disappointing him. As Archie remarks, "With white people it's easy for us people to be ashamed in front of them .... You know, Victoria — I come to a conclusion — they want it that way" (p. 296).

Carlyle begins to recognize his blindness as early as the day he learns of her disappearance although he is unable to grasp the significance of his discovery until later. In admiring Fyfe's prize orchids, he favours one with handsome lavender flowers which Fyfe labels a failure. Carlyle objects:

> ... has the orchid been disappointed? Does it consider itself a complete miss? .... You're trying to — for

> something that hasn't anything to do with what the or-
> chid wants ... the orchid's concept — destiny — it takes
> a little longer than the few years you — what it has
> wanted for millions .... (pp. 85-6)

He rejects the scientific breeding which reduces beauty to a
mathematical formula. But he asks himself if he could be equally
"dispassionate about his misses" (p.86). And he comes gradually to realize that he too has interfered with natural growth. He
has tried to impose his standards and his classifications upon Victoria and indeed upon all the Stonys with due consideration for
their inborn needs and desires.

It is only in Part Three that Carlyle is prepared to achieve his
quest. The combined perspectives of the loss of Victoria, the
recognition of the roles of Aunt Pearl and Old Kacky in his past,
and his identification with Heally Richards lead him to see his
own limitations. The memory of Aunt Pearl is significant. The
child Carlyle opposes her desire for ritual and order through
deliberately rearranging the objects on her dressing-table. But her
love of order becomes more, a denial of the natural and spontaneous elements of life, even of the physical body itself, as
Carlyle discovers when Aunt Pearl comes upon him with the
magic lantern, projecting onto the wall the image of his penis,
magnified many times. In his weeks with Aunt Pearl, she imposes
upon him the personality of little dead Willis and his defiance
of her is his reaction to her unnatural rigidity, her life-denying
force.

His memory of Old Kacky too leads to this recognition. Old
Kacky, like Aunt Pearl, imposes order and ritual upon the chaos
of life. And in so doing, he rules out all the natural and
unregenerate areas as represented by Billy Blake's nosebleeds or
Maitland Dean's repertoire of wind-chords (p. 317). Language
becomes grammar; history becomes an account of systematiza-
tion, of governments, laws and constitutions. The parts of the
body are abstracted under scientific Latin names. And art becomes
not an exercise in creativity but a rigid adherence to a set of rules.

The child Carlyle admits that the illusion of perspective works.
But the illusion which he himself has created takes on a power
of its own which to the child is terrifying:

> ... his eyes travelled straight and unerring down the
> great prairie harp of telephone wires ... down the

barbed-wire fence lines on the other side of the
highway. And as the posts and poles marched to the
horizon, they shrank and crowded up to each other,
closer and closer together till they all were finally suck-
ed down into the vanishing point. (p. 318)

Carlyle, in adding a pine-tree and a poplar, is asserting the
freedom of art and the imagination to defy rules and logic and
for this Old Kacky straps him. Carlyle's reaction is not repentance
but fear. This moment marks the beginning of the alienation
which is to possess him for more than twenty years:

Here he stood by himself, and outside the office walls
were all the others properly together and busy all
around his own empty desk. He had vanished from
them. Old Kacky had vanished him from them to
vanishment. And then the really crazy though happened. He was being vanished from himself ... stepping
outside and getting smaller and smaller and smaller ...
dwindling right down to a point. (p. 322)

His immediate physical reaction, the cramping of the bowels and
their release in Old Kacky's drawer, is more than Mitchell's attempt to shock or titillate. It is, like Victoria's pregnancy, the
response of the physical body to an order which refuses to take
account of it. The pervasive imagery of elimination throughout
the novel serves the same purpose; it counters the idealistic and
spiritual in man with a recognition of the primary needs and basic
requirements which make him truly human.

Carlyle's friend Mate insists that the vanishing point is only
an illusion: "the rails don't meet .... C.P.R. couldn't run their
engines if they did" (p. 325). But Carlyle does not wholly escape
from this illusion until he is able to recognize how he himself,
in rejecting Old Kacky and Aunt Pearl, has become another Kacky
himself, another Aunt Pearl. He is not only divided from others,
alienated; he is also separated from himself, schizophrenic. Body
and mind have become rivals; instincts and reason are not part
of a greater whole but distinct. From this point on he is moving
towards the vanishing point of his own life, towards the moment
of choice between being or non-being.

It is Heally Richards and his Rally for Jesus which ultimately
prepares Carlyle to choose between life and death, society and
isolation. The ground has been laid in Part One for Heally

Richards' role in Part Three. Although there is perhaps an overemphasis on Richards and a consequent diversion of interest from Carlyle, the Heally Richards' section is integral to Carlyle's search. Certain elements of Heally's past parallel those of Carlyle and Heally's failure leads to Carlyle's recognition of his own parallel failure.[7]

Unlike Aunt Pearl and Old Kacky, Heally cultivates the dramatic in human life and his religious ritual satisfies the human craving for meaning and significance. He succeeds essentially by what Carlyle calls "primitive oversimplification" (p. 17). His appearance is striking. The pure lard-white of his shoes, socks, suits, tie, hair and eyebrows, contrasted with his tanned face, suggests to Archie the magic of the "backward people" and to the more sophisticated Carlyle a photograph negative. In the Rally he plays on the dramatic elements of redemption and his deployment of Norman and Gloria Catface is brilliant, Gloria in the white doeskin costume of Miss North-West Fish and Game, Norman with the sinister scar cutting across his right cheek, both fresh from their solicitings in the neighbourhood of the Empress hotel. His oratory too is brilliant in subject, rhythm and style.[8] His final address seizes upon a simple incident, the pitch stains on the green wood of the altar steps, and turns it into a striking sermon on man's need for redemption.

The source of Heally's power lies in the needs of his audience. To Archie and the Paradise people he offers something they yearn for, a replacement perhaps for their lost religion, for the tales and legends of Bony spectre and Weesackashack. His appeal is simple and direct and their confidence in his healing powers is absolute. As Archie says "They wouldn't let him onto the radio if he couldn't do it" (p. 18). But he satisfies an even more basic need. Carlyle comes to realize: "he promised to shrive them of their mortality, to lift from them the terrible burden of their humanity, the load of their separateness" (p. 358).

Carlyle comes to realize too the flaw in Heally Richards. His apparent faith, his search for God, is in fact a search for power. Our glimpse into Richards' mind confirms this. The miraculous cures are essential to him for they salvage his flagging self-esteem, assuage the life-long feelings of rejection and inferiority. They cause him to seek for larger and larger audiences, for more and still more conversions and healings. He imagines to himself the building-up of glory through a series of healings to the dramatic

resurrection of Esau Rider before the audience and the cameras
of CSFA-TV:

> Oh, God, please — please choose — through Heally
> Richards — to lift up that old Indian from that stretcher
> before the Mercy Seat! Raise up that feathered buckskin
> Lazarus with Your revivin' pahr! "Esau — Esau — take
> up thy stretcher and walk!" ... Rise up, Esau! And
> Heally Richards too! Right up out of the evangelic bush-
> league — clear to Billy and Gipsy and Aimee and Oral!
> Hallelujah! (p. 348-9)

Esau's sudden restoration and as sudden death in front of the
vast audience and the T.V. cameras is Heally's answer from
above. It is not for man to interfere with life and death, to play
with these for his own selfish ends. So different from Aunt Pearl
in all ways but one, he is yet alike. For, concludes Carlyle, he
is "ordering them into a moral box to suit himself only — not
them" (p. 354).

But Carlyle is not able so easily to see his own failure with Victoria and the Stonys. It is only in the dark hours following his
meeting with Victoria and his discovery of her pregnancy that
he comes to see that he too has placed them in a moral box. He
has fulfilled his own cravings for self-importance at the expense
of theirs. In these hours he descends into the "Everlasting No".
He has tried to be a mirror to Victoria and the Stonys, to show
them to themselves. But they have responded with tricks; for him
they have "capered and postured and made faces" (p. 367). The
mirror tells them they are separate, ashamed. He has failed. And
all have failed with him: Victoria, Fyfe with his Minimal Subsistence Cookie, Heally Richards with his laying-on of hands,
even Esau Rider whose faith has died with him. He becomes
nihilistic: "He hadn't known that it was no use at all — that
nothing could be done at all" (p. 366). And ultimately he despairs
not only of the Stonys but of humanity as a whole: "Victoria is
one knocked-up mess! I am! The Stonys are! Right from the beginning the whole human race has been one God-damned mess!"
(p. 374).

At this point, he must choose between life and death. It is the
beat of the drums in the ritual Prairie Chicken Dance which recalls
him to life. For the pounding rhythms annihilate past and future,
anesthetize from pain and suffering, illness, loss, injustice. They

give the sense of oneness which man has sought in love, in sacrifice, in religious faith, the breaking of the bonds of the self:

> Only the now remained to them — the now so great that only death or love could greaten it. Greater than pain, stronger than hunger or their images paled with future — dimmed with past. Only the now — pulsing and placeless now? Song and dancer and watching band were one, under the bruising drum that shattered time and self and all other things that bound them. (p. 385)

The revelation is sudden. While man is part of nature, of the "living whole", he is also alien to it. And only man can share this sense of alienation; in accepting responsibility for others he enters a new social unity, becomes committed to life: "Man lifted bridges between himself and other men so that he could walk from his own heart and into other hearts" (p. 385). In leaving Victoria on that city street he has destroyed a bridge between himself and the Stonys. His return of faith is essential: he might "try again — for them — for himself — for her!" (p. 385).

The consummation and marriage which ends the novel in the traditional manner of comedy thus becomes an important statement of faith in humanity as a whole. For only through love can man heal the separation between mind and body, between man and man, between race and race. Carlyle's acceptance of Victoria marks his acceptance of his physical self, of the life force. The child to be born of Victoria will share his life, and their future children will help to heal the division between Indian and white. his dedication as a teacher must also be reaffirmed. The little Powderface boy experimenting in the dust before his cabin with a system of ditches and canals will be his next challenge. But this time will be different. He will be aware of the child's needs and desires, of his individuality and his significance as a person, not merely of him as a symbol of his race. For they need each other, he and his pupils; only in working together can they be truly successful and truly human.

The novel closes in the fullness of spring and morning. The trees are in full leaf, the grouse is drumming triumphantly and the pulsing rhythms of the Prairie Chicken Dance are still in the air. Carlyle's revelation, his moment of perfect faith, is marked by two important events on the Reserve: the renascence of Beulah

Creek and the flowing once more of the live-giving waters, and the resurrection of Archie's car signifying the ultimate success of the Indian in adapting to the best elements of white society. Life has triumphed over death, society over alienation. Mitchell has said "Yes" to man.

Notes

1   Donald Cameron, *Conversations with Canadian Novelists* (Toronto: Macmillan, 1973), pp. 51-2.
2   W. O. Mitchell, *The Vanishing Point* (Toronto: Macmillan, 1973). All quotations are from this edition.
3   Cameron, *op. cit.*, pp. 61-2.
4   W. O. Mitchell in discussion with students at the University of Calgary, March 1971.
5   Cameron, *op. cit.*, p. 61.
6   The working title of the novel in 1970 was "The Fluorescent Flamingoes".
7   Mitchell's discussion with students at the University of Calgary.
8   In an interview with William French, Mitchell remarked that he attended many sessions of the Emmanuel Chapel of the Free Assembly of God to capture the rhythm and style of Heally's speeches. See *The Globe and Mail*, Saturday, July 7, 1973.

ABOUT THE CONTRIBUTORS

David Arnason teaches Canadian literature at St. John's College, University of Manitoba. He is a former editor of the *Journal of Canadian Fiction* and is now an editor for Turnstone Press. He has published a number of short stories and a book of poetry, *Marsh Burning*.

Stanley S. Atherton is Professor of English at St. Thomas University, Fredericton. He has contributed articles to scholarly journals and is the author of *Alan Sillitoe: A Critical Assessment*, and co-editor (with Satendra Nandan) of *Creative Writing from Fiji*.

George Bowering's criticism includes books on Al Purdy and *Three Vancouver Writers*, as well as articles on James Reaney, David McFadden, Fred Wah and Margaret Atwood. A collection of essays on Canadian poets is imminent. He also writes poetry and fiction.

Elspeth Cameron is coordinator of the Canadian Literature and Language Programme at New College, University of Toronto. She has published articles on Margaret Atwood, Scott Symons, Marian Engel and others, and books on Robertson Davies and Hugh MacLennan, including the recent critical biography, *Hugh MacLennan: a Writer's Life*.

Wilfred Cude is author of *A Due Sense of Differences*, an evaluative study of four classic Canadian novels. A free-lance writer living in Cape Breton, he is currently working on a critical appraisal of the North American doctorate, and a novel on William Henry Jackson, Ontario secretary to Louis Riel.

John Goddard is a reporter from Peterborough, Ontario, who recently opened a northern bureau of The Canadian Press in Yellowknife. He has worked for C.P. in Toronto, Ottawa and Montreal, and has travelled widely to cover news events abroad, including the release of American hostages from Tehran in 1981.

Henry Makow's Ph.D. dissertation at the University of Toronto was on Frederick Philip Grove's theory of art. His articles on Grove have appeared in *Canadian Literature*, *Dalhousie Review* and the *University of Toronto Quarterly*.

Catherine Mclay teaches Canadian literature at the University of

Calgary. She has edited *Canadian Literature: The Beginnings to 1910*, and has published articles on Shakespeare, Willa Cather, Margaret Atwood, Margaret Laurence and W. O. Mitchell. She is currently working on a critical biography of Mitchell and an anthology of fiction by Canadian women.

Lorraine McMullen teaches Canadian literature at the University of Ottawa. She has published articles on Malcolm Lowry, Leo Kennedy, Frederick Philip Grove, Leo Simpson, Frances Brooke and others; and is the author of *Introduction to the Aesthetic Movement in English Literature* and *Sinclair Ross*.

Ken Mitchell teaches literature at the University of Regina. He has written for radio, television and cinema, and has published novels, poetry and plays. His published works include *Wandering Rafferty*, *The Meadowlark Connection* and the folk-opera *Cruel Tears*.

Donna E. Smyth teaches literature at Acadia University. She has published two plays, *Giant Anna* and *Susanna Moodie*, and a novel, *Quilt*. She has also published short fiction and was a founding editor of *Atlantis: A Women's Studies Journal*. She is currently working on a project on feminist aesthetics.

Lee Briscoe Thompson teaches Canadian literature in the Canadian Studies Programme at the University of Vermont. She has presented and published papers in Canada, the United States and overseas on a variety of Commonwealth and Canadian topics.

George Woodcock was the editor of *Canadian Literature* for almost two decades. His many books include works of philosophy, history, biography and literary criticism: included among them are *Odysseus Ever Returning*, *Canada and the Canadians*, *Rejection of Politics* and *The Crystal Spirit*, for which he won the Governor General's Award.

Alan R. Young is Professor of English at Acadia University. His scholarly interests are divided between Renaissance literature and Canadian literature. His books include *Henry Peacham*, *The English Prodigal Son Plays* and *Ernest Buckler*. He has recently completed a book on Thomas Raddall.

ACKNOWLEDGEMENTS

Grateful Acknowledgement is made to the following:

Lee Briscoe Thompson for "In Search of Order: The Structure of Grove's *Settlers of the Marsh*". This is an altered version of an essay that originally appeared in the *Journal of Canadian Fiction*. Reprinted by Permission.

Henry Makow for "Grove's 'Garbled Extract': The Bibliographical Origins of *Settlers of the Marsh*".

Stanley S. Atherton for "Ostenso Revisited".

Wilfred Cude for "Morley Callaghan's Practical Monsters" Downhill from Where and When?"

John Moss for "Mrs. Bentley and the Bicameral Mind: A Hermeneutical Encounter with *As For Me and My House*".

David Arnason and the *Journal of Canadian Fiction* for "Canadian Nationalism in Search of a Form: Hugh MacLennan's *Barometer Rising*".

Elspeth Cameron for "Of Cabbages and Kings: The Concept of Hero in *The Watch That Ends the Night*".

Lorraine McMullen for "Elizabeth Smart's Lyrical Novel: *By Grand Central Station I Sat Down and Wept*".

John Goddard for "An Appetite for Life: The Life and Love of Elizabeth Smart". This article originally appeared in *Books in Canada*, JuneJuly 1982. Reprinted by Permission.

Donna E. Smyth for "Maggie's Lake: The Vision of Female Power in *Swamp Angel*".

George Woodcock for "Innocence and Solitude: The Fictions of Ethel Wilson".

Alan R. Young and the *Journal of Canadian Fiction* for "The Genesis of Ernest Buckler's *The Mountain and the Valley*". Reprinted by Permission.

George Bowering for "Sheila Watson, Trickster".

Ken Mitchell and the *Lakehead University Review* for "The Universality of W. O. Mitchell's *Who Has Seen the Wind*". Reprinted by Permission.

Catherine McLay for "*The Vanishing Point*: From Alienation to Faith". This essay was originally accepted for publication by the editor in 1976.